Byzantine
and Roman
Architecture

Volume Two

HACKER ART BOOKS, INC. NEW YORK, 1975

BYZANTINE

SIR
THOMAS
GRAHAM
JACKSON

AND
ROMANESQUE
ARCHITECTURE

Second Edition

Volume Two

First edition published 1913.
Second edition published 1920.
Reprinted from the second edition by permission of
Cambridge University Press.

Reissued 1975 by
Hacker Art Books, Inc.
New York.

Library of Congress Catalogue Card Number 75-143353
ISBN 0-87817-073-1

Printed in the United States of America.

BYZANTINE AND ROMANESQUE ARCHITECTURE

by

Sir THOMAS GRAHAM JACKSON, Bart., R.A.
Hon. D.C.L. Oxford, Hon. LL.D. Cambridge
Hon. Fellow of Wadham College, Oxford
Associé de l'Académie Royale
de Belgique

Nunquam vera species ab utilitate dividitur.
QUINTIL. *Or. Inst.* VIII. 3

SECOND EDITION

Cambridge:
at the University Press
1920

IN MEMORIAM
A. M. J.

CONTENTS OF VOL. II

CHAP.		PAGE
XVIII	German Romanesque	1
XIX	French Romanesque. Aquitaine and Poitou	28
XX	French Romanesque. Provence	62
XXI	French Romanesque. Toulouse	82
XXII	French Romanesque. Burgundy	90
XXIII	French Romanesque. Auvergne	127
XXIV	French Romanesque. Normandy	147
XXV	French Romanesque. The Isle of France	159
XXVI	English Romanesque before the Norman conquest	173
XXVII	English Romanesque after the Norman conquest	205
XXVIII	English Romanesque after the Norman conquest (*cont.*)	235
XXIX	Conclusion	257
	Chronological tables of architectural examples	269
	Index	278

CHAPTER XVIII

GERMAN ROMANESQUE

THE history of Romanesque architecture in Germany begins with Charlemagne. We find no buildings in that country older than his time except those which the Romans had left behind them. Charlemagne however was a great builder. Eginhardt his secretary and biographer says he repaired the churches throughout his dominions, but he gives no details. A book *de aedificiis* in the 8th century would have been very interesting, but Eginhardt was no Procopius, nor was Charlemagne a Justinian. Two buildings however, we are modestly told, seem not unworthy of mention, "*the basilica of the most holy mother of God, constructed with wondrous workmanship at Aquisgranum, and a bridge over the Rhine at Moguntiacum*[1]." This bridge at Mainz was only of wood, perhaps of boats, but the basilica at AIX-LA-CHAPELLE was a great work considering its age and situation.

It was destined by Charlemagne to be also his tomb-house, and here he was in fact afterwards buried, seated on his throne, imperially robed, and with his sceptre in his hand and a copy of the gospels on his knee, as he was found when the tomb was opened in 1165. The splendour of this church, says Eginhardt, was the expression of his Christian devotion. He adorned it with

[1] Eginhardt, *Vita Caroli Magni*, cap. xvii.

Aix-la-Chapelle

gold and silver, and lights, and with doors and screens of solid bronze. Hither he would come to the service morning and evening and even by night as long as his health permitted[1].

Imitation of S. Vitale

The building (Fig. 63) was something of an exotic in the kingdom of the Austrasian Franks in the 8th century,

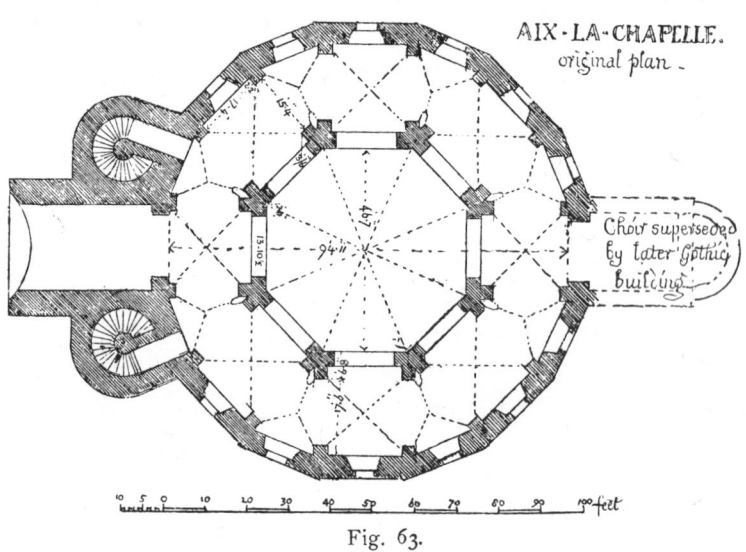

Fig. 63.

and no one who has seen it and also the church at Ravenna from which it is supposed to have been imitated, can doubt its foreign origin. Eginhardt tells us that Charlemagne imported columns and marbles for the work from Ravenna and Rome[2], and he is supposed to have stripped and ruined the splendid palace of Theodoric at the former city which has now practically disappeared. But besides materials there can be little doubt he also

[1] Eginhardt, *Vita Caroli Magni*, cap. xxvi.
[2] Ad cujus structuram, cum columnas et marmora aliunde habere non posset, Roma atque Ravenna devehenda curavit. Eginhardt, cap. xxvi.

AIX-LA-CHAPELLE

imported from Italy his architect and his principal builders. The resemblance to S. Vitale is very strong, and yet there is sufficient difference to show that the builders were men of originality, able to think for themselves, not tied to a simple imitation of their model, and there could have been no such men in Austrasia then. Both churches have a dome over an octagon, a surrounding aisle in two storeys, though a women's gallery was not required by the Latin use, two staircases by which to mount to it at the west end enclosed in circular turrets; and though at Aix there are no exedrae the arches of the upper gallery (Plate LXXXII) have colonnettes in them recalling those at Ravenna, and they have even something like a pulvino on their capitals. Although the diameter of the dome is less than that at S. Vitale by more than ten feet, still a domed building even of these dimensions would be a considerable undertaking at any time, and it is carried out in a very scientific manner. It will be seen from the plan (Fig. 63) that the area of the supports is by no means excessive, and the vaulting of the aisle is very cleverly managed, so as to escape the awkwardness which would have been caused had the outer wall been octagonal like the inner. Instead of that it has 16 sides, so that there is a square bay of simple cross-vaulting in the aisle opposite each side of the octagon, the vault of the intervening triangle being easily managed. This is contrived much better here than at S. Vitale, though there further trouble is caused by the protrusion of the exedrae into the aisle vault.

The gallery above is vaulted differently, by barrel vaults on radiating lines turned from arches thrown across from pier to wall, forming square and triangular bays alternately as below.

Aix-la-Chapelle

Among the capitals some are antique Corinthian, but most of them have been renewed: and of the columns which were carried off by French invaders to Paris not all have come back.

The exterior

The exterior has now a monstrous fluted dome of timber and slate, somewhat grotesque: but probably it had originally a plain pyramidal roof rising from walls carried up as a drum, concealing the dome; and then the two churches at Aix and Ravenna would have been

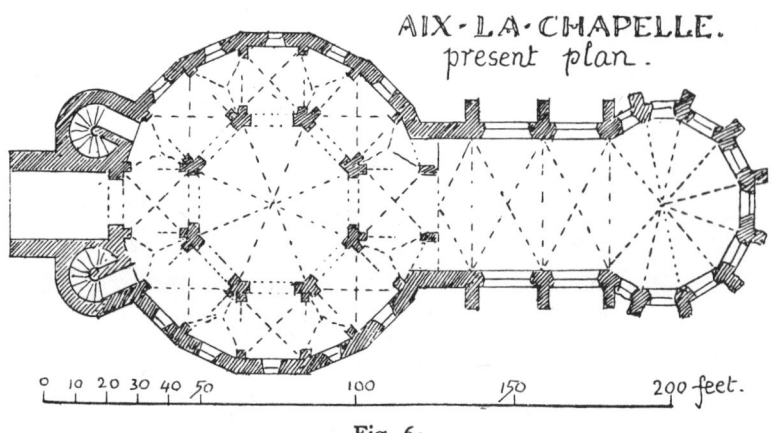

Fig. 64.

much alike outside as well as inside. Further evidence of Italian or Italo-Byzantine workmanship is afforded by the mouldings of the cornices, which are rather clumsy versions of classic detail.

The metal work

The old bronze doors of the west and north entrances still hang on their hinges, and the gallery front has its bronze *cancelli*.

The stunted proportion of the lower order and the absence of bases give the impression that the floor level has been raised.

The original choir was short, like that of S. Vitale, and in 1353 it was replaced by the present long building (Fig. 64), a veritable lantern of late German Gothic. Its expanded circular end is supposed to represent on the same foundations the tomb-house of Otho III who died in 1002 and who was supposed by some to have re-built Charlemagne's church. Fergusson believes the truth to be that he built himself a tomb-house where the choir now ends, which the 14th century architect united by the present choir to the 8th century building. There can be little doubt that we have in the Dom of Aix-la-Chapelle the *basilica, opere mirabili constructa,* of which Eginhardt writes. Aix-la-Chapelle. The choir

Some would have it that Eginhardt himself, who is described as "*operum regalium exactor,*" and "*variarum artium doctor peritissimus,*" was the architect of the building. It is more probable that like Julianus Argentarius at Ravenna he was the administrator of the expenses. Eginhardt

Coeval with Charlemagne's basilica at Aquisgranum, or possibly a little earlier, may be the little chapel at LORSCH, near Worms, which is generally supposed to be part of the monastery dedicated in the presence of Charlemagne in 774 (Plate LXXXIII). It was originally a gatehouse two storeys high, with three open arches in front and three behind. The floor has been removed and the three arches of the back built up in order to convert it into a chapel. The altar stands against the central blocked arch under an additional arch on columns and capitals, which is planted on the wall and encloses the original central arch. Lorsch

This inner, additional arch is in a totally different style from the building, and is decorated with zigzags like

Lorsch   Norman work. The capitals are also of a much later date; certainly not older than the 11th or 12th century.

The building has a high-pitched roof of slate, but the original pitch was low, as may be seen by the starting of a modillion pediment at one end. The details are of a debased classic type. The lower capitals are imitated

Fig. 65.

from composite (Fig. 65), and have no necking; they are well carved, and carry a stringcourse or cornice at the first floor level decorated with a regular Byzantine pattern. The upper storey has a colonnade of little fluted pilasters with queer Ionic capitals (Fig. 66), supporting what in our Anglo-Saxon work we call straight-sided arches. Three of them are pierced with simple round-headed lights, probably insertions. Above at the eaves is a good *Lorsch* plain modillion cornice (Fig. 67), which once was returned on the end walls and ramped into a pediment, though only the starting already mentioned now remains. The walls between the columns are of red stone chequered with white.

It is an extremely curious little building, showing in the execution of the carving a skill and knowledge superior to the local talent of the Germany of those days, and betraying a Byzantine, or Italo-Byzantine hand; but *Betrays Southern influence* the strange design of the upper storey shows no affinity with the art of the Exarchate or the East. Rivoira maintains that it is not a Carlovingian building at all, but the funeral chapel of Lewis III (876–882) who

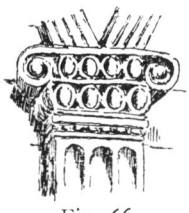
Fig. 66.

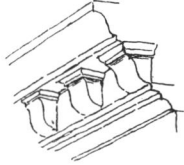
Fig. 67.

according to the *Chronicon Laureshamense* was buried here in the church called "Varia" which he had built[1]. It is impossible however to believe that a building with its long axis north and south, three open arches to the west, and three more to the east that once were open, for they show both inside and out, could have been built for a church. It is recorded that it was consecrated as a chapel in 1053, at which time we may suppose the three eastern arches were closed, the altar placed against the middle one, and the additional arch with its zigzags and Romanesque capitals erected over it for dignity. The

[1] Apud Lauresham, in ecclesia quae dicitur Varia, quam ipse hujus rei gratia construxerat. Cited by Rivoira, vol. II. p. 510. Lasteyrie, *Arch. Relig.* p. 171, thinks the building not older than the fire of 1090. It is remarkable that a capital of the 12th century cloister at Elne illustrated by McGibbon (*Archit. of Provence*, &c.) is precisely like that in Fig. 65.

adjective *varia* is applicable to a polychrome structure, but the vanished abbey of Lorsch may have had many buildings of polychrome masonry besides this one.

<small>Lorsch</small>

<small>Nymeguen</small>

The round church at NYMEGUEN in Brabant, which is illustrated by Fergusson, is obviously a later imitation of Charlemagne's Palatine chapel at Aix, and the interior is closely copied in the trilateral semi-domed apse at Essen[1]. But his building set no general example, and when German Romanesque began to assume the character of a definite style we find the basilican type of church accepted for general use.

<small>German type basilican</small>

Under Charlemagne's weak successors, and in the distracted state of the Empire in the 9th century, there was little room for the cultivation of the arts. In 888 on the deposition of Charles the Fat France was separated from Germany, which remained under elective kings till the Empire was revived by Otho I in 936, who conquered Italy and restored it to Imperial rule, and established a more stable government.

<small>Rise of German free cities</small>

During the reign of the three Othos Germany saw something like the development of free communes which was going on in Italy. Many cities had become important trading communities, especially those on the great water-ways of the Rhine and other navigable rivers. Cologne, Treves, Mainz, Worms, Speyer, Nuremburg, Ulm, Regensburg and Augsburg were already aspiring to municipal freedom. Those of them which depended on the Empire, began to resist the Bishop or Imperial Vicar who was put over them. Henry V (1106–1125) granted them privileges, took away the jurisdiction of Bishops, and made the cities immediately dependent on the Emperor. Those towns on the other hand which were dependent on Dukes and Counts waged incessant wars

---

[1] Illustrated by Rivoira, vol. II. p. 346, who dates it between 1039 and 1056.

Plate LXXXIII

LORSCH

Plate LXXXIV

S. COLUMBA—COLOGNE

with the castles of the nobility. The fall of the House of Hohenstaufen completed their liberty and they were admitted to a place in the Imperial diet, just as the free communes of Italy after the peace of Constance had been recognized as an estate of the Italian kingdom. There was however this difference between the struggle of the cities for municipal freedom in Germany and Italy, that while in Italy the struggle was between the cities and the Emperor the free towns in Germany were the most loyal and obedient subjects of the Empire. The Emperor indeed, says Hallam, was their best friend, as the nobility and the prelates were their natural enemies[1]. *The German Communes*

It is in the great towns on the Rhine which were in readiest communication with Italy, and rapidly grew into important trading communities, that we find the most brilliant examples of early German Romanesque. The great churches of Cologne, Worms, Speyer, and Mainz are inspired by North Italian example. We meet again with the arcaded galleries round the apse, which we knew at Bergamo and Como; with lofty towers (Plate LXXXIV) panelled, and pierced by windows with mid-wall shafts, like those of Milan; and the tall blank arches that break the plainness of the lower walls remind us of Pisa, Lucca, and Toscanella. *The Rhenish cities* *Lombard influence*

The period from Charlemagne's attempted revival of architecture till the end of the 10th century is almost a blank as far as any existing monuments are concerned. At Gernrode there is a church of 968, partly restored however in the 12th century, which affords the earliest instance of the double apse which is one of the peculiarities of German architecture. Various explanations of this feature in German architecture have been *The double apsidal plan*

[1] v. Hallam, *Middle Ages*, chap. v.; Bryce, *Holy Roman Empire*, chap. v.

10   GERMAN ROMANESQUE   [CH. XVIII

The double apsidal plan

attempted. In conventual churches one choir may have been used by the monks, and the other by the townspeople, instead of the English division at the choir-screen. Or as the original churches were not orientated but had the altar at the west end, a second choir and altar may have been added at the east when orientation became the rule. This however fails to explain the churches with an apse of the same date at each end. They are to be found at Hildesheim, Worms, Trier, Mainz, Laach, and may have existed once at Speyer, where the west end has been re-built. They are shown on the curious ground plan of a complete Benedictine

S. Gall

establishment found in the library of S. Gall in Switzerland, which was sent to Gospertus the abbot who re-built that church between 820 and 830, and may possibly have been drawn by Eginhardt himself[1]. It shows a church with nave and side aisles, 200 ft. long and 80 ft. wide with an apse at each end. Below that at the east is a crypt or *confessio*, and in front of it a *chorus cantorum* like those at S. Clemente and S. Maria in Cosmedin at Rome. The entrances for the laity were from a parvise or colonnaded court outside the western apse, with a door to the aisle on each side of it. The eastern apse was to be dedicated to S. Peter, the western to S. Paul. Near the western apse, but detached, were to be two round towers, one on each side with an altar on the top of each, one to S. Michael, one to S. Gabriel, to which the ascent was to be by a spiral inclined plane, if the intention of the draughtsman may be so understood.

Defects of the double apsidal plan

These double apsidal ends of course prevented anything like the façades which are so important a feature of

[1] As the plan is reproduced by Fergusson and most of the histories of Architecture, I think it unnecessary to have it here.

the great churches in Italy, France and England. The cathedral of S. Stephen at VIENNA has a fine Romanesque front with its "giant doorway," but as a rule the entrance to the great German churches is at the side, where there is often a porch of greater or less importance. This involves a considerable sacrifice of effect; the first view of a fine interior from the west end is not lightly to be parted with. Nor does the exterior of the western apse compensate for the loss of such a façade as those which delight us at Lucca and Toscanella, S. Gilles and Poitiers, Wells and Exeter. In the interior also the monotony of two similar apsidal ends is disappointing. Lord Leighton, whose remarks on architecture were always valuable, said in one of his Presidential addresses to the Royal Academy, "externally the effect of this disposition is monotonous and perplexing, but it is in the interior that it chiefly jars on our sense of artistic propriety, and the jar is made more sensible by the fact that the choirs being built over crypts, are, by an arrangement in itself very dignified and impressive, raised to a considerable height above the floor of the nave, from which they are approached either on the sides or in the centre by broad flights of steps. The entrance to these churches is in the majority of cases at the side, and the eye of the spectator, controlled as he enters by no dominant object, is solicited simultaneously and distressingly in two diametrically opposite directions—each individual group of apse and dome suffers by rivalry with the other[1]."

Defects of the double apsidal plan

Lord Leighton's remarks

The typical plan of these double-apsidal churches includes a transept at the west as well as at the east end,

Double transepts and towers

[1] Discourse delivered to the students of the Royal Academy on the distribution of prizes, Dec. 9, 1893, by Sir Frederick Leighton, Bart., P.R.A.

12 GERMAN ROMANESQUE [CH. XVIII

The German six towers   and over the crossing of each of them is an octagonal dome on squinch arches, contained in a tower which is arcaded with an external gallery and has a more or less acutely pointed roof. Right and left of this are two flanking towers, often at the end of the transept so that there are three towers on a line at right angles to the axis of the building at each end of it. In other cases they are given more room by moving the two side towers forward out of line with the central dome-tower. Six towers is the full complement for a Rhenish church of the first

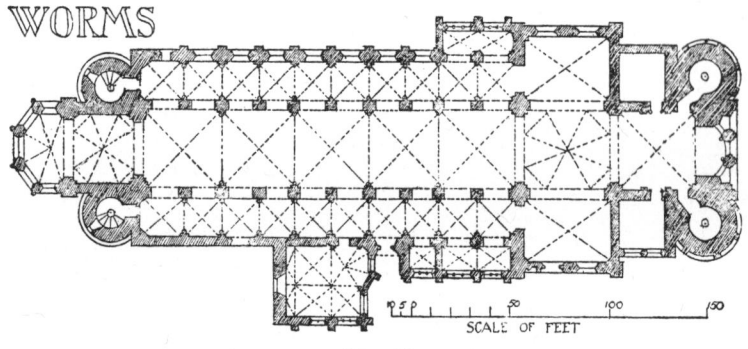

Fig. 68.

rank, and this is the number at Worms, Speyer, Laach and Mainz. All these churches, except Laach which is a little later, date from the first half of the 11th century, though they have been altered to some extent in the 12th century and afterwards.

Worms Cathedral   WORMS is perhaps the most pleasing of the group. It was founded in 1016, but restored and re-dedicated in 1181. It is an immense basilican church, with two apses, but only one transept, which is at the eastern end (Fig. 68). The choir is prolonged beyond the crossing and the apse is masked outside by a straight wall between

Plate LXXXV

WORMS CATHEDRAL. The Western Towers

Plate LXXXVI

WORMS CATHEDRAL

CH. XVIII]   GERMAN ROMANESQUE   13

two round towers with spires. These towers are Worms
Cathedral panelled with pilaster strips connected at each stage by arcaded cornices. They are set in a little, stage by stage, as they rise, which gives a very good outline. The dome-tower has an arcaded gallery round it, and so has the western dome-tower, which is flanked by two other round towers one of which has been re-built in Gothic times. The apse at this end is also later than the Romanesque part, and not so good. There being no transept at this end the flanking towers are brought close up to the central one, which they seem to support. The effect of this group is very noble (Plate LXXXV).

Inside, the nave between the two domed spaces consists of five square bays, cross-vaulted, corresponding to twice that number in the aisle, so that the nave arches are ten on a side (Plate LXXXVI). The piers are all of plain square masonry with only a moulded impost by way of capital. The main piers, corresponding to the divisions of the nave, have attached pilasters and half-columns with cushion capitals running up to take the vaulting. The intermediate piers have a shallow flat pilaster formed by setting back the arch and wall over it, which runs up and carries two blank arches over the round-headed clerestory windows. The vaulting has pointed arches, and is later than the church. But from the plan of the piers and the attached half-columns with their capitals at the proper height to start the transverse rib, and an additional break suitable for a diagonal rib, it seems that vaulting was intended from the first.

The gathering in of the dome should be noticed. It The dome begins with something like a spherical pendentive, which changes suddenly into a squinch arch on which the octagonal dome rests. It looks as if the architect had begun a true pendentive but did not know how to finish it.

Worms, the synagogue

We must not leave Worms without mention of the interesting 12th century Jewish synagogue. It is a rectangular building vaulted from two columns on the central line with good capitals of the Corinthian type, and there are some pretty diaper patterns round the entrance doorway. Three hundred Jewish families are still living at Worms, and from the scale and architectural pretensions of this building the colony would seem to have been still more numerous in the 12th century.

Speyer Cathedral

The great cathedral of SPEYER was dedicated by Bishop Gundecar of Eichstadt (1057–1075), but the upper part was re-built after a fire in 1159. It suffered at the hands of the French in 1689, who expelled the inhabitants, burned the town, and left the church a ruin: only the choir, transept, five arches of the nave, and the narthex escaped, and the upper part of the transept and the cupola of the narthex were destroyed. The French again violated it at the time of the Revolution, and tried to blow it up, but did not succeed. The building was turned into a magazine, and was not restored to use till 1822. The west front with the Imperial Hall, a sort of narthex, dates from 1854–1858.

The ancient crypt (Plate LXXXVII) remains as it was built in 1039. It has plain cross-groining with transverse ribs only, carried by cylindrical columns with cushion capitals.

The church has the full equipment of six towers, and two transepts, but the western one belongs to the new front of 1854. Originally the nave may have ended otherwise. A special feature is the exterior arcaded gallery which runs along the top of the walls above the clerestory

SPEYER CATHEDRAL. The Crypt

Plate LXXXVIII

MAINZ CATHEDRAL. N.E. view

windows. The towers are square, and slender, and are set in each case clear of the transept against its eastern side. They are panelled in the Lombard way.

The splendid cathedral of MAINZ (Plate LXXXVIII) was re-built and re-consecrated between 1037 and 1049 and again restored after a fire between 1056 and 1106. The nave was vaulted with pointed arches by Archbishop Conrad, probably after the fire of 1190. Mainz Cathedral

Though not so badly treated by the French as Speyer, the cathedral during the Napoleonic wars went through many vicissitudes, and was used at one time as a hay magazine, and at another as a slaughter house. It has two apses, two transepts and six towers, that over the western crossing having been re-constructed, according to the guide books, with cast-iron by Moller of Darmstadt, the architect who restored the church after its desecration. The domes are octagonal and rest on squinch arches.

The description of the nave at Worms will apply very well to that of Mainz (Plate LXXXIX). There are the same square piers without capitals, even plainer here than at Worms; but the blank arches springing from the pilaster of the intermediate piers are turned below the clerestory instead of above it. This leaves a space between the two arches, where the triforium, if there had been one, would have been, which is decorated by paintings. The vaulting shafts have cushion caps and carry round wall ribs, and though the other ribs are pointed the springers remain of a former construction with round arches. The quadripartite vault of the nave is very domical.

There is a crypt here like that at Speyer, with tapered columns carrying cushion capitals, and the two storeyed chapel of S. Godehart at the north transept is very curious. The crypt

16   GERMAN ROMANESQUE   [CH. XVIII

Mainz Cathedral

A fine Romanesque doorway at the east end has capitals partly of good Corinthian character, partly of animals; and the bronze knockers here and on the north door are admirable. They date probably from the 12th century; and built into the walls of the south aisle are some very good pieces of Romanesque sculpture dating apparently from the same period (Fig. 69).

Fig. 69.

Laach

The abbey church of LAACH (Fig. 70), near Niedermendig and Andernach, picturesquely placed at the head of a lake and surrounded by wooded hills, dates from the middle of the 12th century having been founded in 1093, but not consecrated till 1156. The church is built chiefly of lava, the product of the volcanic district in which it is situated.

It is much smaller than the preceding churches but has the full complement of two apses, two transepts and six towers, and though the design has been much praised, it seems to me overdone with too many features (Plate XC). The west end is crowned with a square tower over the centre of the transept and has two round towers at the ends of it. Pilaster strips run up them,

Plate LXXXIX

MAINZ CATHEDRAL

Plate XC

LAACH

CH. XVIII] GERMAN ROMANESQUE 17

turned into columns in the top storey carrying arches, Laach
which being wide become distorted on the circular plan;
when seen in profile they undercut the outline with a very
bad effect, making the conical roof seem to overhang
disagreeably. The eastern turrets at Mainz offend
slightly in the same way. The towers of Laach at the
east end are square, and more successful. There is a
certain coarseness about the arcaded cornices under the
eaves, which are much too big.

In the interior some progress has been made towards
the Gothic system of vaulting, which in this case forms

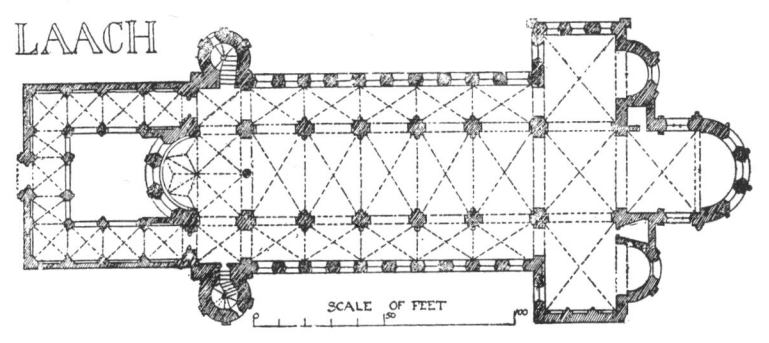

Fig. 70.

part of the original design. The bays of nave and
aisles are equal, instead of there being two in the aisle to
one in the nave, so that the bay of vaulting in the nave is
oblong, the longer dimension being from north to south.
The whole church is cross-vaulted with round arched
transverse ribs but no diagonals. The nave piers are
square, with half-columns towards nave and aisle, and
those towards the nave run up as vaulting shafts with
cushion capitals. The great arches are cut square through
the wall without any moulding, and spring from a small
impost moulding without a capital: there is no triforium,

Laach but a blank wall space, with a single round-headed clerestory window above, and no stringcourse to divide the storeys. The last bay westwards has a gallery which runs back into the apse, forming an upper storey. The lower one contains the tomb of the founder, and is vaulted from a central column. There is no carving, and the whole interior is as plain as possible, but not without dignity.

The severity of the style is relaxed in the pretty little cloister which forms an atrium at the west end (Plate XCI). It has three walks, the ends of those on the north and south side opening by doorways into the nave aisles as in the plan for S. Gall. The western apse protrudes into the cloister-garth. The cloister is vaulted with heavy half-round transverse ribs, and no diagonals, and the walls both outer and inner are pierced with round-arched openings on coupled colonnettes which are tapered and incline a little towards one another like those in the cloister at S. Trophime at Arles. All this is excellent. The capitals are carved in rather a lumpy fashion, the stems of the foliage being worked like strap-work and studded with beads.

Cologne The Romanesque churches at COLOGNE differ from those we have been describing in having no apse at the western end; but though that end was thereby set free for treatment as a façade with a western doorway, no advantage is taken of the opportunity. Three of them, S. Maria in Capitolio, Great S. Martin, and the Apostles church are trilobate, the two transepts being apsidal as well as the choir. S. MARIA (Fig. 71) which was re-built and consecrated in 1047 has an ambulatory aisle round all three, which has a fine effect inside, but imparts an undeniable clumsiness to the outside (Plate XCII). The

Plate XCI

LAACH. The Atrium

S. MARIA IN CAPITOLIO—COLOGNE

CH. XVIII] GERMAN ROMANESQUE 19

details are very plain, there is no carving, there are cushion capitals everywhere; the columns of the apses are cylindrical, and have stilted Attic bases: the nave piers are plain rectangles with an impost moulding instead of a capital: there is no triforium but a blank wall with round-headed clerestory windows above. The nave has later Gothic vaulting on shafts that have been added and are corbelled out above the nave piers.

Cologne. S. Maria in Capitolio

Over the crossing is a dome, which is not circular but rather a square with the corners rounded off so that the

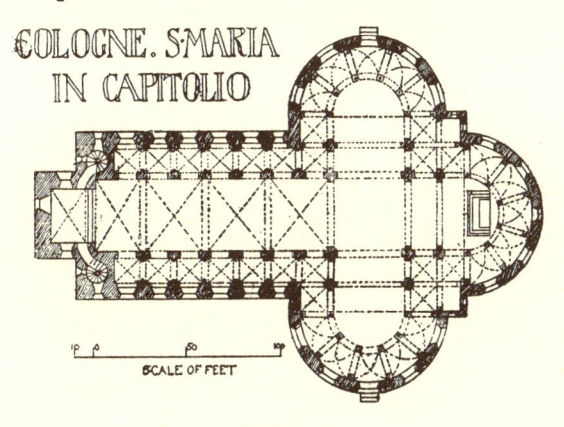

The dome

Fig. 71.

pendentives are small; but otherwise it is a real dome of the Byzantine kind. There is a smaller oblong dome over a narrow bay eastwards before the semi-dome of the eastern apse. The transepts have barrel vaults with transverse ribs, and semi-domes over the apses.

The aisles are cross-vaulted with transverse ribs but no diagonals. At the west end is a narthex or porch as wide as the nave alone, to which it opens with a triple arch, and there is a gallery over it with a triple arch of the same kind.

2—2

Cologne. S. Maria in Capitolio

The crypt extends under both choir and transepts. It has cylindrical tapered columns with cushion capitals, the central column under the apse however is a quatrefoil in plan. The vault is cross-groined with flat transverse ribs and no diagonals, the arris of the diagonal groin being pinched up.

At Great S. Martin (1172) and SS. Aposteln (1193) the triple apses have no aisles, a manifest improvement on S. Maria in Capitolio. The former of these churches with its magnificent central tower and its galleried apses forms a prominent feature in the river front of the town, and has the finest exterior of anything in Cologne. In the interior there is a triforium with pointed arches above a round arched arcade, and except the barrel vault of the transepts and the semi-dome of the apse, the vaults are Gothic.

Andernach

The Romanesque churches of Coblentz and Andernach were built early in the 13th century. ANDERNACH (Plate XCIII) has four towers, two at each end, and no transepts. It has three apses at the east end for choir and aisles, the central one arcaded inside with niched recesses below a range of large round-headed windows. There is a triforium as large as the arcade below, of two lights under an including arch, divided by rather slender coupled shafts. The nave is four bays long to eight of the aisle, the western bay being occupied by a gallery. The nave piers are square with an impost moulding and no capital. The eastern towers have pyramidal roofs;

The German gabled spire

the western, the German gabled spire which is so constant a feature of the style. It is formed by gabling all four sides of the tower, and setting a square spire of timber and slate diagonally on the points of the gables instead of directly on the angles of the tower. The spire is completed

Plate XCIII

ANDERNACH

by continuing the four planes of the triangular inclined spaces till they meet between gable and gable, making the triangle into a diamond. There is an unique example of such a spire in England, at the Saxon Church of Sompting in Sussex.

The fine churches of S. Michael and S. Godehard at HILDESHEIM which date from the middle of the 11th century, with additions in the 12th, are in some respects more highly finished than the great churches on the Rhine, though they cannot compete with them either in scale or in exterior magnificence. There is more carving in the capitals, though they preserve the cubical form of the cushion type, and there is more variety in the nave arcades which are divided by piers between groups of arches on columns. *Hildesheim*

With the eastern part of STRASSBURG Cathedral, which was apparently re-built early in the 13th century, one reaches the last stage of German Romanesque. There is the familiar central tower over the crossing of an eastern transept enclosing a dome on squinches, and at the corners of the choir are two round turrets, but all the arches are pointed, and the turrets are almost reduced to pinnacles. There are evident signs of a coming change, but the Romanesque style lingered long and died hard in Germany, and it was not till the 13th century was well advanced that it finally gave way to the foreign style imported from France, which resulted in the cathedral of Cologne. *Strassburg*

The vast cathedral of TOURNAI, with its five towers, its Romanesque nave and transept, and its 14th century choir, a very lantern of glazed stonework, is one of the most striking in Europe. It lies outside the limits of Germany proper; but its apsidal transepts with their *Tournai in Belgium*

Tournai flanking towers attach it to the style of the great Rhenish churches, and if the Romanesque choir were, as no doubt it was, apsidal too, the plan would have been like that of the three trilobate churches of Cologne. The nave on the other hand has more affinity with the churches of Normandy, so that Tournai serves as a link between the Romanesque styles of northern France and Germany.

The nave The nave (Fig. 72) was dedicated in 1066, but some of the details are hardly consistent with so early a date. It has the large open-arched triforium of the Norman churches, here quite as large as the arcade below. Both of these storeys are vaulted, and above them is a real triforium under the aisle roof with small plain openings under a colonnaded arcade towards the nave.

The nave piers have half-columns on all four sides and between them in reveals are detached octagonal shafts. Each shaft of the group carries its own order in the orthodox style. The capitals are richly carved, those in the lower arcade of a convex form, with interlacing foliage, grotesque animals, knots and twists of various kinds, much elaborated and highly finished. Those of the upper galleries have the concave outline and angle volutes of a more advanced kind than one would expect from so early a date. There are however some like them at the contemporary churches of William the Conqueror at Caen.

The transepts The apsidal transepts are later than the nave and were built about 1146. They have a diameter of 32 ft. and are surrounded by ambulatory aisles parted from them by cylindrical columns 2′ 11″ in diameter carrying round arches of two orders. The semi-dome is supported by converging ribs from the piers between the windows. These transepts are as fine as anything I know in Romanesque architecture.

CH. XVIII] GERMAN ROMANESQUE 23

TOURNAI. CATH:
NAVE. A.D. 1066.

Fig. 72.

Character of German Romanesque

The great early German churches, especially those on the Rhine, have a sort of sublimity about them that is all their own; and though they bear marks of their Lombard parentage they have an individuality which places them in a class by themselves. They are generally on a grand scale, the naves with a span of over 30 ft., and they are very lofty, unlike many early buildings which are low and stunted. Externally they have considerable richness of design, especially when there is the little colonnaded gallery which with its black intervals and well-defined arcades and colonnettes always has a brilliant effect.

Fig. 73.

Their sky line, broken by the numerous towers, gathered together in groups, has a picturesque effect unlike anything to be found in contemporary works in Italy, where even to a later date the exterior, except in certain well-known instances, was less thought of than the interior. At the same time even in the most successful efforts one cannot but feel the presence of a certain clumsiness and want of grace both in general design and in detail which one does not find in the rudest work of the early French and Italian schools. German Romanesque is an honest, sturdy style, which is strong, virile and positive though wanting in the finer graces

CH. XVIII]   GERMAN ROMANESQUE   25

Internally the German churches are plain and severe beyond almost any buildings of the time in other countries. Cushion capitals and plain impost mouldings take the place of carved capitals, and square piers of masonry that of cylindrical or clustered columns. The absence of triforium also increases the bare effect of the walls. No doubt in old days they were painted all over, and would then have had plenty of colour, but in their present bald and bare condition they teach the useful lesson that a building may be made impressive and architectural without ornament. *Severity of German Romanesque*

In the later German work carving comes to the aid of the designer. There are some very beautiful and delicate imposts to the door of the 13th century church at ANDERNACH (Fig. 73), richly carved Byzantinesque borders surround the doorway at BOPPART (Fig. 74), and a frieze of scroll-work runs along the walls over the nave arcades of S. Andrew at Cologne, mingled with other carving which approaches the standard of French work. It is a curious jumble of archaic and progressive art, in which the architecture remains stubbornly Romanesque, but admits decorative features of the new style which had been developed across the frontier in France, and in England. *Carving of later work*

In the earlier churches the aisles were vaulted, but a vault over the nave, though perhaps intended, was not achieved till a later date. They are all vaulted now, and it is remarkable that they stand perfectly well without flying buttresses. The vault of the nave at Laach indeed is tied in with iron from side to side, but I have noticed no sign of weakness elsewhere. France when flying buttresses came into fashion ran riot, and could not make too much of them; and Cologne Cathedral, imitating and *Vaulting without buttresses*

Flying buttresses overdoing the imitation, is smothered in flying buttresses beyond all reasonable limit. In England and Italy they

Fig. 74.

were never fashionable, and when there were any they were if possible hidden under the aisle roofs as they are at Winchester. But many of our great vaulted churches have none. Gloucester has but two on the south side of the nave and they are hidden under the aisle roof: Worcester has some placed irregularly where the construction seems to need support; and there are none at all at Tewkesbury. *Flying buttresses*

It is doubtful whether we should have admired the great German churches in their original paint as much as we do now. Most of those in Cologne have been painted lately or are being painted now, and the result is detestable. Moreover the windows have been filled with coloured glass, thus mixing up two inconsistent modes of decoration. Colour by reflexion in mural painting is killed by the overpowering brilliancy of colour transmitted through stained glass. As a rule you cannot even see it. None of the Byzantine churches which have the finest mosaics in Constantinople, Salonica, Venice, Ravenna, or if I remember in Rome, have any but clear glass in the windows, and consequently the mosaics are well seen and hold their own. Decoration by mural painting or mosaic, and decoration by painted glass, are two perfectly incompatible systems, and the artist must choose between them. To grasp at both and try and use them together is an inartistic blunder. *Mural painting*

Inconsistent with painted glass

CHAPTER XIX

FRANCE

Roman culture in Gaul

IN no province of the Roman Empire was Latin culture more firmly rooted, and in none did it show more vigorous growth than in Gaul, especially in the south, and south-western parts. The schools of Treves, Lyons, Arles, and the Auvergne, and still more those of Toulouse, Narbonne, and Bordeaux were pre-eminent in the empire during the 5th century and are described as the last strongholds of Roman learning in the west of Europe[1]. The native language had given place to that of Italy, and the Latin of Bordeaux was said to have been the purest in Gaul. Provence is still full of splendid remains of Roman architecture, and Italy itself cannot show anything superior to the temples at Nîmes and Vienne, the amphitheatres at Nîmes and Arles, the great theatre at Orange, and the stupendous aqueduct of the Pont du Gard which dwarfs those of the Campagna. The poet Ausonius at Bordeaux and Sidonius Apollinaris at Clermont in the 4th and 5th centuries lived in the midst of a cultivated literary society, of which their writings give a lively picture. The establishment of the Visigothic kingdom, and the settlements of Frank and Burgundian barbarians do not seem at that time to have interrupted the life of the great Roman nobles seriously,

Effect of the barbarian settlements

[1] Dill, p. 407, Guizot Lect.

for we find them still retaining their possessions and living on good terms with the new comers. Sidonius has left an amiable portrait of the Gothic King Theodoric II, with whom he dined and diced.

The remains of early Christian art in this region consist mainly if not entirely in the sarcophagi, of which there are splendid specimens in the museum at Arles, dating probably from the time of Constantine. They have been brought thither from the famous sepulchral avenue of Aliscamps, *Elysii campi*, where one may still walk as Dante did between rows of stone coffins capable of containing heresiarchs. In the delicacy and refinement of the sculpture that adorns them we may trace the effect of Greek tradition, for Arles was an appanage in old times of the Phocaean colony at Marseilles, and the superiority of the art here to that at the neighbouring city of Nîmes is remarkable.

Gallo-Roman sarcophagi

In one sarcophagus, divided into seven compartments by trees which form a beautiful arboreal canopy, are represented six miracles of our Lord, the central panel being occupied by an *orante*, or female figure with hands extended in the attitude of prayer (Plate XCIV). The figure of Christ is repeated in each panel, a youthful beardless Roman, without nimbus, evidently a conventional representation like the Pastor bonus at Ravenna, such as preceded the time when that divine portraiture was attempted which became stereotyped in later religious art. Other sarcophagi have the compartment divided by classic columns or pilasters carrying arches, in one instance round and straight-sided alternately, sometimes with a shell-head, and with figures in all cases of the Roman type, well executed.

If it is safe to assume that these fine sarcophagi which

once furnished the Aliscamps at Arles were carved in provincial Gaul, they show a very flourishing state of art there in the 4th century, at least equal to that of Italy. But of course it is possible that the finer sort may have been brought from Rome, and there is certainly a close resemblance between one of those in the museum at Arles and a sarcophagus in the Lateran Museum.

France in 4th and 5th centuries

For the architecture of the fourth and three following centuries we must trust to description only, for nothing of it remains. At the beginning of that period we find the great nobles of Auvergne and Aquitaine living on their estates in lordly villas with large retinues and households of slaves. Sidonius describes his country house in Auvergne much as Pliny[1] describes his Tusculanum to his friend Apollinaris. Sidonius speaks of dining rooms for winter and for summer, baths with domed roofs on graceful columns, apartments for the ladies, and spinning rooms for the maids, saloons and verandahs.

Primitive churches at Tours and Clermont

Nor was church architecture behindhand. The church built by Bishop Namatius in the 5th century at Clermont-Ferrand is described by Gregory of Tours as measuring 150 ft. by 60, and 50 ft. in height to the roof. It had side aisles, was cruciform and apsidal, with 42 windows, 70 columns and 8 doors. The walls were adorned with mosaic of various kinds of marble[2]. The odour of sanctity was patent to the senses, for the church exhaled "the sweetest scent as of aromas." On a still larger scale was the famous basilica of S. Martin built by Bishop Perpetuus in 472 at Tours, which Gregory the historian and bishop himself re-built after a conflagration.

[1] Plin. *Ep*. v. 6. Sid. Apoll. *Ep*. II. ii.
[2] Parietes ad altarium opere sarsurio ex multo marmorum genere exornatos habet. Greg. Turon. x. 16. He gives a long list of churches built at this time by Bishop Perpetuus and others. sarsurius = musivum opus. Ducange.

Plate XCIV

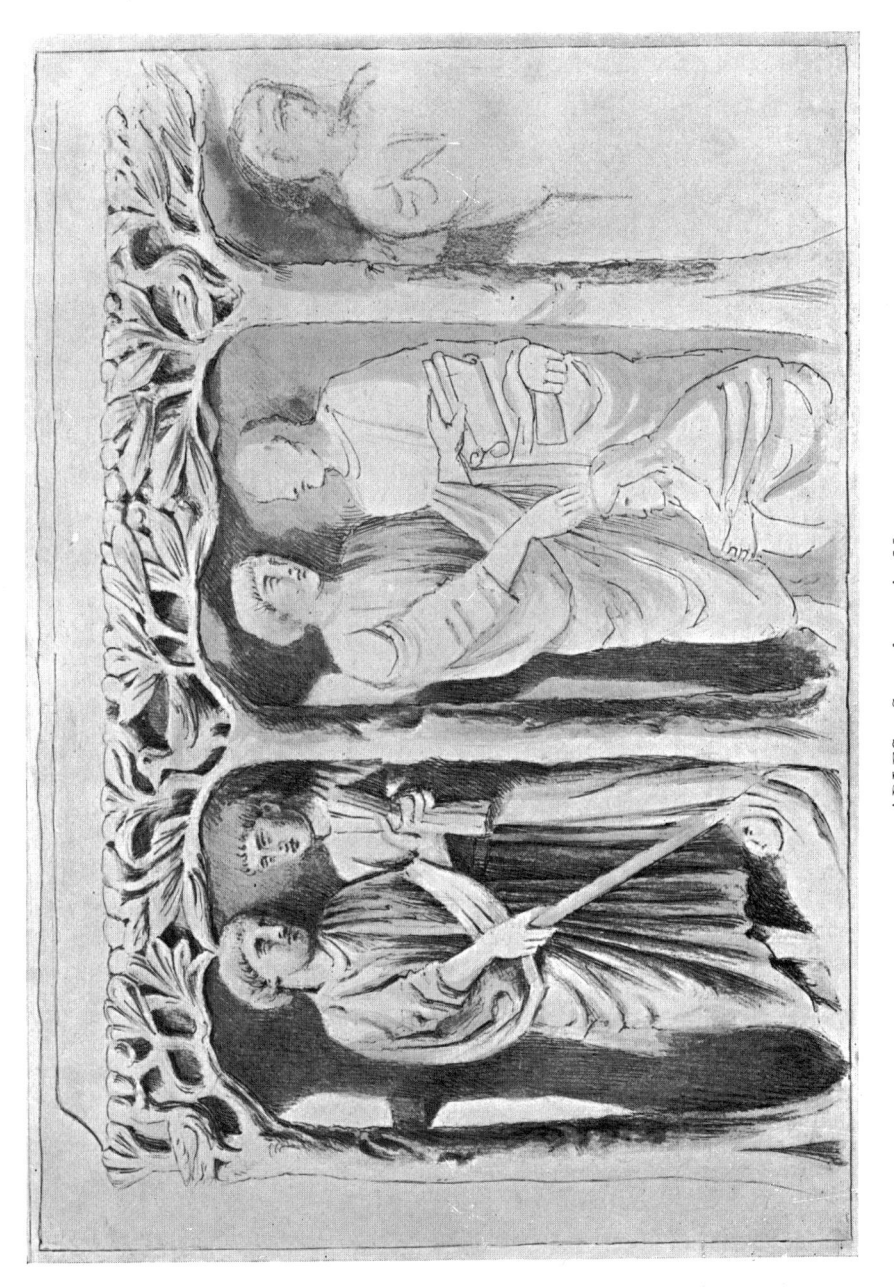

ARLES. Sarcophagus in Museum

It was 10 ft. longer than that at Clermont, though not quite so lofty; it had 52 windows, 120 columns, and 8 doors, and seems to have been preceded by an atrium or cloistered forecourt. Sidonius celebrates this church in an ode of which he sends a copy to Lucontius, ending with a pun on the name of the founder, *Church of S. Martin at Tours*

"Perpetuo durent culmina Perpetui[1]."

He writes to his friend Hesperius[2] an account of the dedication of a church at Lyons built by *Papa Patiens*, pope or bishop of that city, who like himself was a great Gallo-Roman noble, and had used his wealth liberally to help the poor in time of distress. On the walls of the church Sidonius at the bishop's request had inscribed what he calls a *tumultuarium carmen*, of which he sends Hesperius a copy. The church was lofty, and was orientated: the gilded ceiling vied with the sunshine; and though the description is very obscure we can make out that it was lined and paved with various coloured marbles, that the aisles were divided by columns of Aquitanian marble and that the glass of the windows shed a greenish light on the interior. The concluding lines seem to suggest an atrium surrounded by a forest of pillars[3]. *Primitive church at Lyons*

This church at Lyons, of which unhappily no traces remain, probably preceded Justinian's buildings at Constantinople by some 50 years, and was very little later than those of Galla Placidia at Ravenna. Beyond these scanty details and the enumeration of columns, windows

---

[1] Sid. Apoll. *Ep*. IV. xviii.
[2] Sid. Apoll. *Ep*. II. x.
[3] . . . remotiora
 Claudunt atria porticus secundae;
 Et campum medium procul locatas
 Vestit saxea silva per columnas.

and doors,—information just enough to tantalize us,—we have nothing to tell us what the churches of Perpetuus and his contemporaries were like; nothing to show how nearly they approached the standard of Ravenna, or fell short of it.

Decay of Gallo-Roman culture

The letters of Sidonius are the swan-song of Roman culture in Gaul. The polite society that still existed in the 5th century was gradually submerged beneath the flowing tide of barbarism. "Roman society was destroyed in Gaul," says M. Guizot, "not as a valley is ravaged by a torrent, but as the most solid body is disorganized by the continual infiltration of a foreign substance[1]." The arts shared the fate of the general culture and sank with it. In the next century no such church as that of Pope Patiens could have been built at Lyons.

Dearth of primitive church architecture

Viollet-le-Duc[2] remarks that we possess only very vague ideas of the primitive churches on the soil of France, and that it is only from the 10th century downwards that we can form a passably exact conception of what they were like. In each province of France they differed considerably. And when we do meet with anything like a continuous series of examples, we find it impossible

Provincialism of styles in France

to treat of French architecture as a whole. At first Latin influence was paramount, but it affected the architecture of the several provinces in very different ways. During the whole period of Romanesque Art, and indeed for much longer, France was not an united country, but a group of independent, or semi-independent states. Nor was the population homogeneous. In the north and east, which lay more open to colonization by Teutonic invaders,—Goths, Franks, Burgundians and

---

[1] Guizot, *Civilization in France*, Lect. VIII.
[2] Viollet-le-Duc, *Dict. Rais.* vol. V. p. 162.

Normans, all German or Scandinavian tribes,—the people had a stronger infusion of German blood than those in the south, where, though the Goths had overrun the country and reigned in Toulouse, the old Gallo-Roman stock survived in greater purity, as it probably does to this day. "The south of Gaul," says M. Guizot, "was essentially Roman, the north essentially Germanic." In the south moreover there still remained important municipalities of Greek or Roman origin, preserving traditions unknown or obliterated in the north. Consequently architecture fell into very different forms in Aquitaine, in Auvergne, in the Isle of France, in Burgundy, in Normandy and in Provence, and the school of each province has to be studied by itself. *Racial differences*

The Byzantine plan, introduced at Aix-la-Chapelle by Charlemagne, did not establish itself in France. The basilican type was the favourite, and prevailed even in the churches of Aquitaine which borrowed the Byzantine dome. *Byzantine plan not adopted in France*

One curious instance however of Byzantine influence at an early date is afforded by the church of GERMIGNY DES PRES (Loiret), which dates from the beginning of the 9th century. It was built avowedly in imitation of Charlemagne's Capella Palatina at Aix-la-Chapelle, by Theodulph, bishop of Orleans, and like its prototype in Austrasia, to which however, as Viollet-le-Duc points out, its resemblance is very slight, it is an exotic on Neustrian soil. The church was enlarged in 1067 by the addition of a nave which destroyed the west side of the original building. Theodulph's plan was that of a Greek cross inscribed within a square, with a drum cupola on four isolated columns, and the four arms of the cross are raised above the small squares that fill the angles between the arms of the cross, all exactly as in the smaller churches at Constantinople such as *Germigny des Pres*

34 FRANCE [CH. XIX

Germigny des Pres

S. Theodore and the Pantocrator. Here however the four arms end in apses, which are in plan horse-shoes,—more than semi-circular—and some of the interior arches are also of that shape. Further traces of Byzantine or Italo-Byzantine influence are afforded by the mosaics on a gold ground of which there are remains in the apse, and by the stucco modelling round some of the windows, of which Viollet-le-Duc gives an illustration. The mosaic he says is unique on French soil[1].

AQUITAINE

The school of Aquitaine

The territory of the Dukes of Aquitaine in the western and west-central parts of France, included Poitou, the Limousin, most of Guienne, the Angoumois, and latterly Gascony. It was in this district that the influence of Byzantine art was most strongly felt, as is shown by the numerous domed churches to be found there, of which the most remarkable though not the earliest instance is the well-known church of S. FRONT at PÉRIGUEUX. It consists of two parts, of different dates. At the west end there remains part of a basilican church with nave and aisles, which probably finished eastward with three apses. It had transepts which still exist as detached buildings, the original crossing between them and the eastern parts having been destroyed to make way for the second church[2] (Fig. 75). This later building is a five domed cruciform building, so closely modelled on the plan of S. Mark's at Venice that there can be no doubt the architect had seen and measured the Italian church, and did his best to

S. Front, Périgueux

The resemblance to S. Mark's

[1] *Dict. Rais.* I. 38, VIII. 472. This church is illustrated by Rivoira, *Origini*, etc. vol. I. p. 217—220. I have not seen it myself.

[2] Mr Phené Spiers gives a conjectural restoration of the plan of the Latin church. See his article on S. Front in *Architecture East and West*, Batsford, 1905.

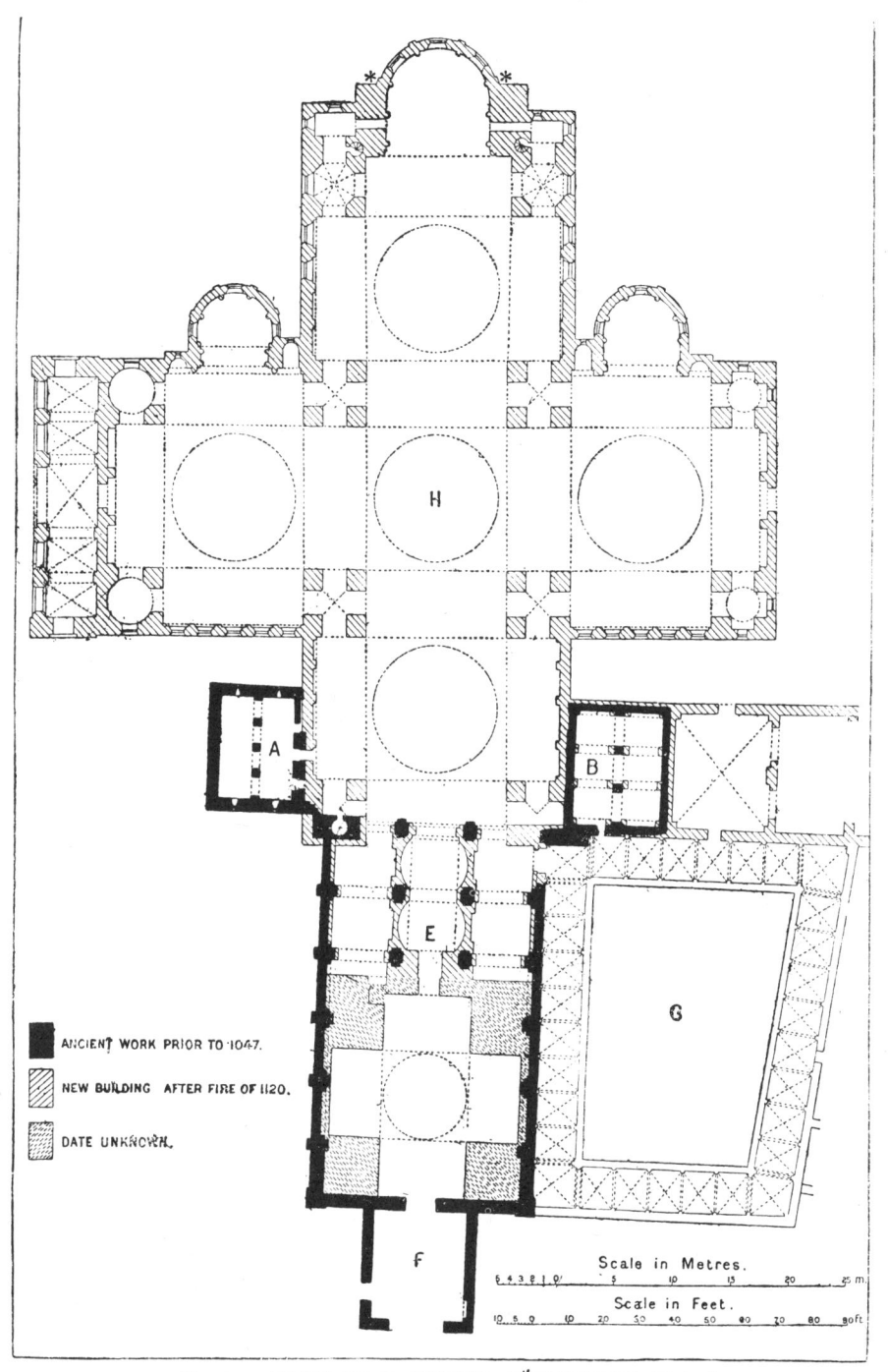

Fig. 75. PLAN OF S. FRONT, PÉRIGUEUX (Spiers)

A, B. Confessionals.
E. Nave of old church.
F. Porch of old church.
G. Cloister.
H. The five domed church of which the apse was taken down in the 14th century.

36   FRANCE—AQUITAINE   [CH. XIX

S. Front, Périgueux

reproduce it on French soil. Not only in plan but in dimensions the two correspond very nearly, and De Verneilh has observed that the differences of measurement are practically such as would arise from the difference between the Italian and French foot. There are certain variations in the construction of the domes and pendentives which seem to show that the architect of S. Front was not a Greek himself though he worked on a Greek model. The domes are not hemispheres but are raised to a point, and the pendentives have a curious winding surface instead of the Byzantine spherical form, and are for the most part built with horizontal beds, instead of with beds radiating from the centre and normal to the curve[1]. The great arches that carry the dome, moreover, are slightly pointed. But in the four great piers at the crossing, with the passages through them at two levels, and in the great arches that spring from them there is a manifest imitation of the construction at Venice (Plate XCV). But as Mr Spiers observes though the architect reproduced the plan of S. Mark's he constructed his domes in the French manner which had been practised for a century before[2].

History of S. Front

The history of the church is this. Bishop Froterius (976–991) began the earlier,—the Latin,—church which was consecrated in 1047. This it is recorded was covered with wood, except the aisles, which seem to have had barrel vaults placed with their axis at right angles to the nave.

[1] Mr Spiers says that the pendentives are struck from the intrados or soffit of the arch, not as usual from the extrados. Consequently the arch forms part of the pendentive, and as it rises the voussoirs incline forwards, *East and West*, p. 181. This is characteristic of the earlier French domes as well as of S. Front. But it is not an original method there for the dome of S. Sophia is struck from the intrados of the arches. The Byzantine pendentives also are often, perhaps generally, formed with horizontal courses. *v.* Van Millingan on *Churches of Constantinople*, pp. 23-24.

[2] *East and West*, p. 193.

Plate XCV

S. FRONT—PERIGUEUX

Plate XCV A

PERIGUEUX.

In 1120 this church was consumed by a terrible fire which even melted the bells in the campanile, the aisles alone escaping, thanks to their stone roofs[1]. It was in consequence of this disaster that the re-building of the church in its present form was begun; the older church at the western end was partly retained, and in the new part the opportunity was taken of building something much grander,—something that might be compared to the great church on the lagoons of which the fame had reached the west (Fig. 51, vol. I. p. 231).

S. Front, Périgueux

It is well known that the south and south-west of France had during the early Middle Ages commercial relations with the Byzantine empire, and especially with Venice where alone in Italy the traditions of Byzantine art lingered, and these countries were then the great mercantile centres of Europe. A colony of Venetian merchants was planted at Limoges about 988–9: their goods were brought to Aigues-mortes on the Gulf of Lyons, whence by mules and wagons they were conveyed to Limoges, and forwarded to the north of France, and from Rochelle to the British Isles. The Venetians had a bourse at Limoges, and their memory was preserved in the names of streets and gates even after they themselves had disappeared[2].

Trading relations with the east

Venetians at Limoges

It cannot be a mere coincidence that it was along this line of commerce with the East that we find a school of architecture in France which deliberately made the dome a principle in church architecture: though S. Front alone has adopted the plan of a Byzantine church as well as the domical covering.

The dome introduced to France

---

[1] Hoc tempore burgus Sancti Frontonis et monasterium cum suis ornamentis repentino incendio, peccatis id promerentibus, conflagravit, atque signa in clocario igne soluta sunt—erat tunc temporis monasterium ligneis tabulis coopertum. *Gallia Christiana*, vol. II.

[2] De Verneilh mentions Rue des Venetiens, Porte de Venise, Eperon de Venise, at Limoges, and says that the ruins of the Venetian houses were to be seen as late as 1638. *L'Architecture Byzantine en France.*

The supposition that the architects and their assistants were Frenchmen and not Italians or Greeks is confirmed by the character of the carving at Périgueux which is much more Romanesque than Byzantine, while that at Venice if not imported from Constantinople was certainly cut by Greek chisels.

Peculiarity of French domes

It is confirmed also by the peculiar use made of the domes in other churches of this district, where they are

Fig. 76.

treated rather as mere vaults, often repeated several times in a row, instead of forming a central dominant feature like the single domes of Salonica and Constantinople round which the church was squarely grouped; nor are they raised on drums or pierced with windows as in the later Byzantine examples, but are often like other vaults covered with wooden roofs, making no show externally. At Souillac, Le Puy, and Angoulême a single cupola emerges as a lantern above the crossing; the rest are concealed by the roof. At Solignac, Cognac, and Fontevrault the domes are all hidden, and the most striking feature of a Byzantine exterior disappears.

S. Front, Périgueux

S. Front however is an exception in this respect, for the domes are treated very architecturally on the outside, constructed of ashlar and crowned with finials[1] (Fig. 76). As Justinian determined when re-building S. Sophia after the fire to have nothing combustible about it, so the builders of S. Front excluded from the construction anything that would burn, and the whole church is roofed in solid stone. At the west end, over the Latin church, is a great tower, dating from the time of the re-building in the 12th century, of which the ornament shows even less Byzantine feeling than that of the rest of the work.

The cathedral of CAHORS is a few years older than S. Front, having been consecrated in 1119, the year before the great fire at Périgueux. It is an aisleless church, consisting of two domes with a diameter of about 60 feet, and an eastern part much altered in the 13th or 14th century (Fig. 77). The domes have regular pendentives and the arches that carry them are slightly pointed. The lateral arches are shallow barrel vaults, carried on piers that project from the side walls to receive them, and sub-arches carry a narrow gallery in front of the windows and through the piers. Painted decoration has been discovered in one of the domes, in which the figures are arranged in the Byzantine manner, and painted ribs converge as at

Cathedral of Cahors

---

[1] De Verneilh shows a pine-cone finial. The pinnacles now crowded on the exterior are due to M. Abadie, by whom the church has been almost re-built and a good deal altered in design. The angles of the arms of the cross were originally finished with pyramids, of which De Verneilh gives illustrations.

S. Sophia on the crown of the dome. The domes are shown externally, but are covered with timber and slate.

Abbey of Solignac

The church of SOLIGNAC near Limoges (Haute Vienne) on the contrary has three domes on pendentives that have

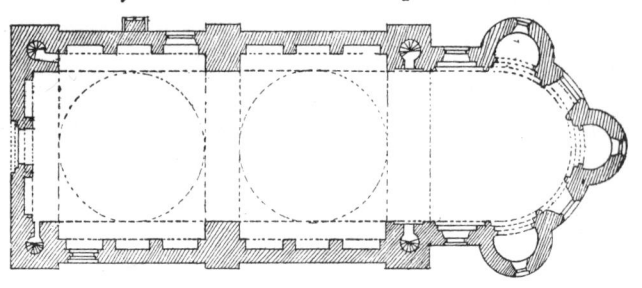

CAHORS

(from De Verneilh)

ANGOULÊME

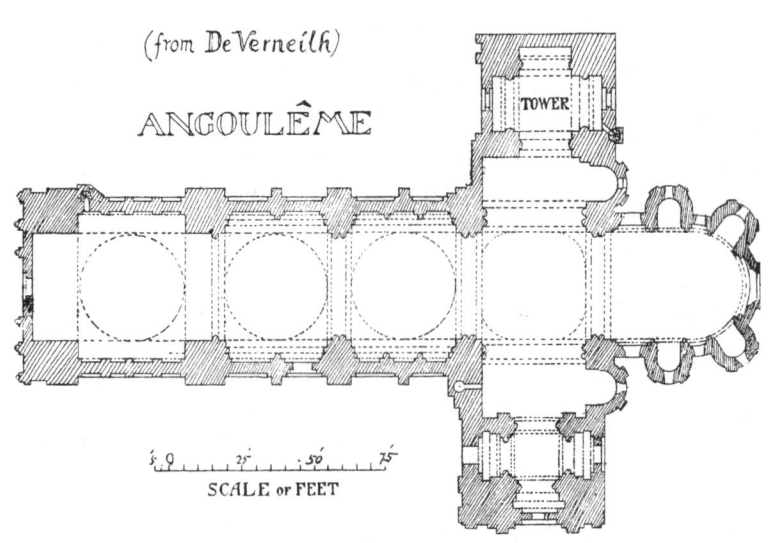

SCALE of FEET

Fig. 77.

always been hidden by the roof. They rest on pointed arches. The apse is round inside and polygonal out, and has chapels opening from it without an ambulatory. The central one is polygonal outside and round inside like the parent apse: the rest including two on the transepts are semi-circular inside and out. The side thrust of the domes is taken as at Cahors by deep side arches with passages through the piers in the same way, on the top of an arcaded set-off (Fig. 78).

Solignac

The cathedral of ANGOULÊME (Fig. 77) was built by Bishop Gerard who occupied the see from 1101–1136.

Angoulême and Fontevrault

Fig. 78.

This church and that of the abbey of Fontevrault, which resembles it so closely in design and dimension that De Verneilh[1] conceives it must have been deliberately copied from it, are aisleless cruciform churches covered with a series of domes on pendentives resting on very slightly pointed arches.

At Fontevrault the pendentives remain but the domes have been destroyed.

[1] De Verneilh, p. 276.

Angoulême

The transepts and choir at Angoulême are covered with barrel vaults. At each end of the transept was originally a lofty tower; that on the south has been destroyed and that on the north re-built. It opens by a lofty arch to the transept, and the interior effect thus produced is superb. The central dome over the crossing is raised on a drum as a lantern. There is a high wall-arcade as at Solignac and Cahors, with two round-headed windows in each bay, and chapels project directly from the great apse without an ambulatory.

Périgueux cathedral

There are many other examples of true cupolas on pendentives in Aquitaine. In PÉRIGUEUX itself the old cathedral of S. ETIENNE which was dedicated in 1047 on the same day as the *Latin* church of S. Front still preserves two of the three domes it once possessed, and De Verneilh reckons that of some thirty domed churches that once existed in the province of Périgord at least fifteen are still standing[1]. The fine church of S. JUNIEN (Plate XCVI) near Limoges has a true dome on pendentives under the western of its two towers. That of S. LEONARD has the same over both transepts, and the lantern tower over the crossing is carried by true pendentives.

S. Junien

S. Leonard

But even when we lose the true construction of the dome on pendentives which comes from Byzantine influence we find the domical idea in various fashions still affecting the design. The cathedral of ANGERS like Angoulême has a single nave without aisles, which is vaulted in large square bays, and though the vaults are constructed with the Gothic ribs and panels, they are raised so high in the middle as almost to have the effect of domes. The same thing happens at the curious church of S. HILAIRE at POITIERS (Plate XCVII) which was re-built after a fire and consecrated in 1059. At first it seems to have

Angers cathedral

S. Hilaire, Poitiers

[1] De Verneilh, p. 276

S. JUNIEN

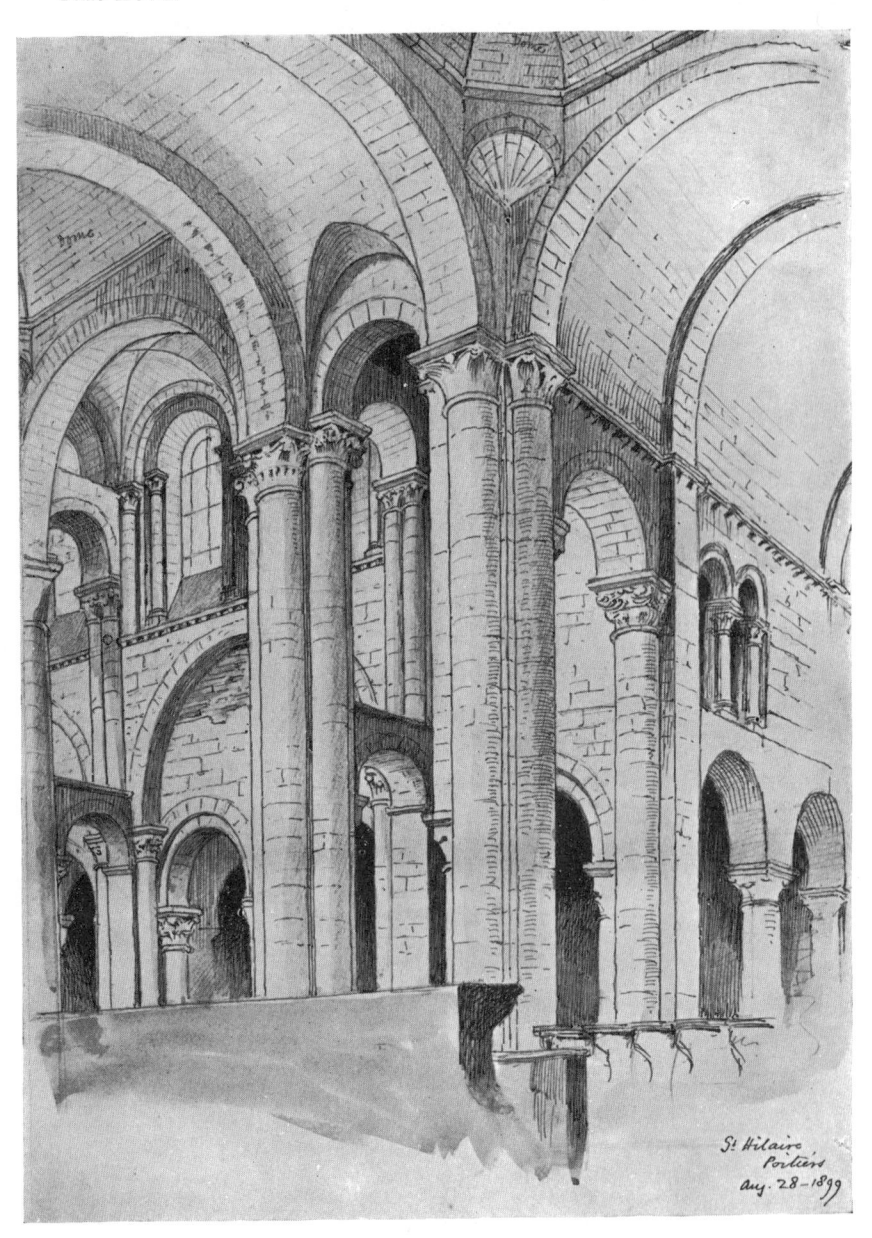

Plate XCVII

S. HILAIRE—POITIERS

been roofed with wood, and when in 1130 it was determined to vault the nave the span was reduced to more practicable dimensions by building an interior arcade on each side which was connected with the older side walls by flying arches and small cross vaults. But the nave was covered with polygonal quasi-domes, irregular octagons, springing not from real pendentives but from "tromps" or squinch-arches thrown across the angles, like those we have seen above in the churches of Syria. These of course are in no sense of the word real domes, but so far as they go they are imitations of the true domes of Périgueux and Cahors.

S. Hilaire, Poitiers

LE PUY-EN-VELAY does not strictly belong to Aquitaine so much as to Auvergne, but there was a strong connexion between the two districts, and the covering of the great cathedral there affords another instance of the influence of the domical idea. This church was built in three instalments. The earliest part is the choir with the transepts, and two bays of the nave, which date possibly from the 10th or early part of the 11th century, but have been much altered in the 12th. The transepts are barrel vaulted and the nave was originally covered in the same manner. The next two bays were added in the 12th century, and have pointed arches instead of semi-circular. This brought the façade to the verge of a sharp descent in the rock, and indeed some way beyond, for the entrance doors were in a storey below the church floor, and the approach to the church was by an ascending flight of steps from the central door, rising through a circular aperture in the floor in the middle of the nave. As an old monkish chronicler has it "one entered the church of Notre Dame by the nostril, and left it by the ears," that is by the side doors of the transepts. The central door of this, the

Le Puy-en-Velay

Le Puy-en-Velay

original façade, has porphyry columns in the jambs, the spoils of some ancient fabric. The original doors of cedar remain, though they are closed, the approaches to church and cloister being now managed differently. They are remarkable works of the time, carved with gospel subjects bearing traces of colour and gilding and explained by rhyming Leonine hexameters. The artist has carved his name on the upright moulding that covers the meeting styles: GAVSFREDVS ME FECIT PETRO SEDENTE. There was a bishop Peter 1159-1191.

The last two bays and the west front were completed in 1180, and are advanced boldly down the steep hillside, giving the façade a splendid elevation. A long flight of steps is carried upwards under them which has a very dignified effect. At the time of this last addition we must suppose that the barrel vaults of the older part of the nave were replaced by the present domical constructions.

The nave (Plate XCVIII) is covered with a succession of octagonal quasi-domes constructed rather in the fashion of S. Hilaire, on squinch arches. On the east and west sides they spring from walls brought up squarely to the plate level, on arches across the nave—a very singular feature. The squinches being raised above the crown of the arch instead of being below it, there is an upright stage—a sort of drum—on which the dome is raised. These domes are concealed under a common roof, their side walls being pierced with windows to form a clerestory, except that over the crossing, which is carried up to form a lantern in a kind of central tower. This however has been entirely re-constructed in the worst taste as regards the interior, and differs widely from the original design.

In 1843 the repair and restoration of the church was

Plate XCVIII

LE PUY

entrusted to M. Mallay, who re-built the south transept, which seems to have been partly destroyed previously, repaired the north transept, re-constructed the central cupola with its piers and the two domes of the nave next to it, and re-built the lower part of the two western bays and the whole of the west front on new foundations, this part of the building having settled and parted from the older part eastward of it. The cloister also was extensively restored by him. The restoration has been much blamed, and certainly there is a good deal of new work that might have been avoided, but he seems entitled to the credit of having saved the building from ruin[1]. No excuse however can be found for M. Mimet, who destroyed the original apse of the choir in 1865, and substituted the present incongruous square chamber. The old semi-circular apse was enclosed in a square exterior construction and did not show outside.

Le Puy-en-Velay

I find no explanation of the disappearance of the 15th century apse of the south choir aisle which I saw and sketched in 1864 (*v.* Plate CXXIII).

The small church at POLIGNAC a few miles from Le Puy has a polygonal quasi-dome on squinches carried by pointed arches, and an apse with a stone semi-dome of a pointed form. Other examples of octagonal domes on squinches in the west of France occur at Notre Dame, Poitiers, and the two churches at Chauvigny.

Polignac

But the most curious outcome of the tradition which inspired the use of this kind of covering is the strange

---

[1] *Manuscrit de l'architecte Mallay*, ed. N. Thiollier, 1904. His editor says "nous ne pourrons pas l'absoudre de toutes les critiques dont il a été l'objet: mais nous ferons dès maintenant remarquer que les reconstructions qu'il a faites, étaient généralement rendues nécessaires par l'état précaire dans lequel se trouvait l'édifice. Cela resulte clairement d'un rapport de Viollet-le-Duc envoyé à Puy à l'époque des travaux," etc.

Loches

church of LOCHES in Touraine, which really consists of nothing but four steeples in a row (Plate XCIX), with the addition of an apse at one end and a porch at the other. The two extreme steeples are carried up like ordinary campaniles, but the other two between them are vast octagonal pyramids, hollow, without windows, dim and mysterious as one looks up from below into their dark cavernous recesses.

Not real domes

All these last mentioned structures are not real domes, having nothing in common with the construction of the Byzantine cupola on pendentives, or with the domes of Périgueux, Cahors, Solignac and Angoulême. In fact the pyramids at Loches according to M. Viollet-le-Duc are built with horizontal beds like the Gothic spire, and consequently have no thrust, being formed by a system of corbelling. But all the same there can be little doubt that they were inspired by Byzantine tradition, for they belong to that side of France in which alone the true dome is found, and in which its appearance can be traced to the commercial connexion which we know existed between those provinces and Venice and the East.

Sculpture in Aquitaine

Sculpture does not play so large a part in the churches of Aquitaine as in those of Provence or Burgundy. The capitals at S. Front are remotely derived from Corinthian as is the case in all early work, but though the church is built on Byzantine lines the carving is singularly free from Greek feeling and is based more on Roman types. Of figure sculpture in this province there is compara-

Poitiers, Notre Dame

tively little during the Romanesque period. At Poitiers (Plate C) the façade of the church of Notre Dame has figure sculpture in the niches and spandrels, and the front of Angoulême is still more elaborately covered with figure

Plate XCIX

LOCHES

Plate C

NOTRE DAME LA GRANDE—POITIERS

CH. XIX] FRANCE—AQUITAINE 47

carving, though not in my judgment so happily. The cathedral of Cahors has some admirable sculpture in the north door. At CIVRAY the church has a remarkable Civray

Fig. 79.

Fig. 80.

façade (Plate CI) with some very beautiful carving, and though a good many of the figures seem not to be in their proper place, and others are sadly mutilated, on the

Civray whole this is one of the most charming façades in western Romanesque. But the west fronts of most of the churches that have been mentioned are singularly plain and unadorned, and in general the sculpture in this district is confined chiefly to the capitals.

These, especially in the apses, are very commonly carved with figures, and gospel subjects, or with fanciful

Fig. 81.

animals, while in the naves they are treated more simply with volutes and leaves descended remotely from the Corinthian type, and sometimes of great excellence. Fig. 79 shows one from the façade of Angoulême, and Fig. 80 another from Poitiers. The shrine of S. Junien in the church at the town that bears his name has an interesting series of niches and figures (Fig. 81).

Plate CI

CIVRAY

S. SAVIN

In many of the capitals of these churches the influence of Byzantine ornament is obvious, derived no doubt from the woven fabrics, and other works of Byzantine art which found their way along the line of Venetian and Eastern commerce. Mixed with this however we find in the 12th century a new influence at work, and the grotesque makes its appearance. This element points to a northern rather than a southern origin, and probably resulted from intercourse with the Normans, Danes, and English. For grotesque is the fun of the north rather than of the south. The interlacing patterns of scrolls and animals biting and intertwining with one another which play so large a part in the Saxon manuscripts are repeated in the carving of wooden churches of Scandinavia, and on the crosses and monuments of the northern settlers in Britain and the north of France. And here in Poitou and Aquitaine this style of ornamentation seems to have encountered the other which came from the east. At Souillac, one of the domed churches belonging to the group which we have been considering, there is a column consisting entirely of birds and beasts and little men, interlaced and gnawing and clawing one another[1], which bespeaks an artistic motive far removed from the sweet severity of Byzantine ornament. Gradually the Byzantine element weakened as French architecture became more national and independent, but it is singular that a capital at Le Puy, which Viollet-le-Duc illustrates[2] as having at last freed itself from Byzantine influence, should be almost identical in construction and design with one in the narthex of the church of the Chora built at Constantinople by the Comneni at the end of the 11th century.

Appearance of the grotesque

Decline of Byzantine influence

[1] See illustration, V.-le-Duc, VIII. p. 196.   [2] *Ibid.* VIII. p. 199.

Aisle-less churches

It remains to notice a few other peculiarities of the Romanesque of western France. Of the 14 churches illustrated in De Verneilh's book not one has aisles. Several of them, like Angoulême, Fontevrault, Souillac, and of later date Angers, are cruciform in plan, but all have simple naves of wide span without side aisles. Eastwards, eight of the fourteen finish with an apse, from which three or more semi-circular chapels project, Fontevrault alone having an ambulatory aisle with chapels starting from it. Five of the number have square ends, including S. Etienne, the old cathedral of Périgueux; and it may be observed that the square end is also found after the Romanesque period in the 13th century cathedral of Poitiers.

Construction of French domes

In all these churches with true domes on pendentives the resistance to the thrust of the cupola is afforded by deep interior buttresses, between which wide arches are turned, the exterior wall of the church being retired to the outside of the buttress piers. This is in fact the Byzantine principle of construction in a modified form. At S. Sophia in Constantinople and at S. Mark's in Venice and S. Front in Périgueux the domes are sustained by arches set four-square having a wide soffit, amounting to barrel vaults. The same principle is applied in these churches of Aquitaine, as for instance at Cahors and Solignac (*v. sup.* Figs. 77, 78), where the buttresses are brought so far inwards that the lateral arches between them amount to narrow barrel vaults sufficient to stay the dome. A shallow pilaster expresses the buttress on the outside of the building. The same construction is adopted at the other domed single-aisled churches throughout the province, and it is not till one comes to the cathedral of Angers in post-Romanesque times, where the domical construction is more apparent than real, and has really been superseded by a form of cross vaulting, that the interior buttresses disappear, and exterior buttresses take their place.

It has been hotly debated whether this singular development of a domical style of architecture in Aquitaine and especially in Périgord, so far from the scene of its original appearance, and without any connecting link in the countries that intervene, is to be put to the credit of native artists or of foreigners from Venice and the East. That it was inspired by the influence of Byzantine art cannot be seriously denied, but whether the artists as well as the art came from the East is less certain. The first suggestion of a better way of covering large interiors than the unstable barrel vaults of native efforts came most likely from Greeks or Venetians who followed the line of commerce through the district. Or perhaps some French architect may have travelled eastward and studied S. Mark's and perhaps S. Sophia, and brought back with him measurements and notes of what he had seen. But in either case the work would have been carried out by the hands of native artisans who while following the general scheme given by the architect, native or foreign as the case might be, would import into the execution much of their native methods of building. We can understand how in this way the style would gradually drift, as it actually did, farther and farther from strict Byzantine example; and how, after beginning with a tolerably close imitation of S. Mark's at Périgueux, it ended in the quasi-domes of Le Puy, Poitiers and Angers, which preserve the idea of the oriental domical covering without its construction.

It would seem that the dome did not make its

Byzantine influence

Modified by local influences

General use of barrel vaults

appearance in Aquitaine till the 12th century. The earlier type of covering was the barrel vault, which still remains in many churches in combination with the dome, or without it. S. Hilaire at Poitiers, and the older or Latin church at Périgueux had originally a wooden roof to the nave, and the aisles alone were vaulted, but before the 12th century most churches of any consequence had stone roofs. Notre Dame at Poitiers has a barrel vault over the nave, and the aisles are cross-groined with a single transverse rib dividing the bays. The church of Montierneuf at Poitiers has vaults of the same kind, though the columns and a great part of the building are modernised. The two churches at Chauvigny have barrel vaults with cross-groined aisles and transverse arches; that at Civray has barrel vaults over the aisles as well as over the nave, and so has that at S. Junien. In all these churches except Montierneuf, which has a high choir of later work, one roof covers both nave and aisles in an unbroken slope, thus forbidding a clerestory. In consequence the upper parts of the nave are very dark. There is no better example of this kind of building

S. Savin

than the fine church of S. SAVIN, which is remarkable for its lofty proportions and its painted decoration (Plate CII).

Temple de S. Jean, Poitiers

This western side of France still possesses one of the few buildings that go back to Merovingian times, which may help us a little to understand the architecture so highly lauded by Sidonius Apollinaris in the 5th, and Gregory of Tours in the 6th century. The TEMPLE DE S. JEAN, as it is called, at POITIERS, is an ancient baptistery, now sunk deep below the level of the modern streets, and bearing manifest signs of antiquity. It is supposed to have been built by Bishop Ansoaldus (682–686) but has evidently undergone repair and alterations.

CH. XIX]   FRANCE—AQUITAINE   53

It is a rectangular building (Fig. 82), gabled north and south, with apses projected from the east and the two sides. On the west it has a narthex of later date. The principal apse, towards the east, is polygonal inside but square without, as the side apses may once have been, though they are now rounded. The arches opening into the apses spring from columns with Corinthianising

POITIERS.
TEMPLE DE ST JEAN.

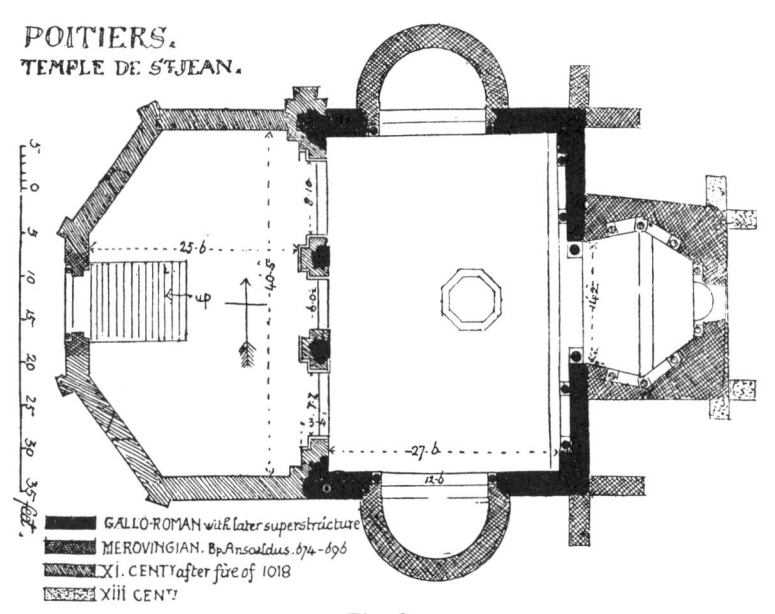

GALLO-ROMAN with later superstructure
MEROVINGIAN. Bp. Ansoaldus. 674–696
XI. CENT? after fire of 1018
XIII CENT?

Fig. 82.

capitals and the walls both in the ground and upper storey are decorated with blank arcading springing from similar colonnettes. Light is given by a clerestory of windows, once round-headed openings, but now formed into circles. The roof is of wood. Sunk in the centre of the floor is the deep baptismal piscina.

The plan is so unusual for a baptistery, which should be round as at S. Leonard near Limoges (Fig. 86), or

S. Jean, Poitiers

octagonal as at Ravenna and elsewhere in Italy, that some explanation seems necessary. It is not improbable, I think, that the rectangular body of the building formed one of a series of halls belonging to some late Roman building, for excavation has disclosed the foundations of a rather extensive range of chambers attached to it, which seem to have no reference to the function of a baptistery. The apses are not of the original date and were added perhaps in Carlovingian times, if not earlier in the time of Bishop Ansoaldus, when we may suppose the building to have been converted into a baptistery and the piscina sunk in the floor, whither all the people of Poitiers brought their children to be christened[1].

The masonry is well wrought, and consists largely of the *petit appareil*, of small stones, often nearly square, which is characteristic of Roman work; but this is not constant throughout the building. The exterior (Fig. 83) is quaintly adorned with fragments of pilasters carrying capitals proportioned to the original full length, but very ill adapted to the curtailed dimensions of the shaft. In the middle a round arch contains a cross within a circle; and right and left are triangular pedimental panels. Similar features appear in the tympanum, which is crowned with a modillion cornice that returns across the base.

Materials used second-hand

The whole is made up of fragments of antique work cut to convenient lengths and arbitrarily adapted. But notwithstanding this barbarous treatment, the general effect is distinctly charming; and it owes much to the inlaid border of red and white that runs up the gable under the cornice, and to the bands of thin Roman

---

[1] Rector autem seu parochus hujus ecclesiae solus olim baptizabat omnes infantes qui Pictavii nascebantur. *Gallia Christiana*, II. p. 1228.

TEMPLE DE ST JEAN.
POITIERS.

Fig. 83.

bricks that are coursed with the stone and formed into simple geometrical figures.

S. Jean, Poitiers

The design of this baptismal church is distinctly influenced by Roman and not by Byzantine example which indeed does not seem to have made itself felt till a later period. The models that were followed in the earlier Merovingian times were the Roman remains of which Gaul contained so many examples: but the art even in the 5th and 6th centuries had no doubt sunk into a very poor resemblance to the models it aspired to imitate. The ancient buildings served not only as models but also as quarries, for the practice of robbing old buildings to furnish new ones was begun long before the Temple de S. Jean. Diocletian's temple at Spalato is decorated with ancient porphyry shafts cut short: Constantine adorned his triumphal arch with reliefs from that of Trajan: and the 70 columns of Bishop Namatius's church at Clermont, and Bishop Perpetuus's 120 at Tours were no doubt rifled from Roman temples and other buildings of Imperial times, and would have been put together with something of the artless simplicity of the Temple de S. Jean though perhaps with a somewhat nearer approach to classic regularity.

Roman and not Byzantine

The influence of S. Front may, I think, be traced as far as Poitiers, where the strange conical pyramids that surmount the two flanking turrets of the west front of the church of Notre Dame, bear a strong resemblance to the domed top of the great campanile at Périgueux, and the resemblance is even stronger in the quasi-cupola of the central tower (Plate C, p. 46). All three are covered with scaled masonry like the domes and tower of S. Front, and are very unlike anything farther east in France. The church itself is barrel-vaulted, with shallow transepts

Ovoid pinnacles and cupolas

Plate CIII

ANGOULÊME

and a lantern tower over the crossing. The west front is richly arcaded, and covered with sculptures which are full of interest, and though it cannot be said that the details show any trace of Byzantine influence there is about the whole design a distinctive character, with a touch of orientalism that seems to mark it off from the Romanesque of the central and eastern provinces. Here however grotesque ornament plays a considerable part, derived from Normandy and the north rather than from the south, as has been already noticed at Souillac and Loches.

S. Front again makes itself felt in the façade of the cathedral of ANGOULÊME (Plate CIII), which is arcaded something like Notre Dame at Poitiers but on a grander scale, and has on its two flanking towers what are half spires and half cupolas, covered with scaling and surrounded by pinnacles which are miniature copies of the steeple at Périgueux. The central cupola is also decorated with scaling like those at Périgueux, and so is the cupola of the Abbaye des Dames at Saintes[1]. On a smaller scale ovoid pinnacles of this kind, covered with similar ornament, occur in the façade at Civray and there is something of the same kind in the quaint and imperfect front at S. Junien (Fig. 84).

Central towers in the form of lanterns over domes either on pendentives or squinches prevail in most of the churches that have been mentioned in this district. But there are several instances of a western tower. S. RADEGONDE at Poitiers has had the nave re-built in the 13th or 14th century, but retains a fine Romanesque tower at the west end, square below, octagonal above, and on the angles where the two parts meet triangular pinnacles like the *Western towers* *Poitiers, S. Radegonde*

[1] Illustrated by V.-le-Duc, *Dict. Rais.* vol. III. p. 305.

Fig. 84.

CH. XIX]   FRANCE—AQUITAINE   59

ears at the corners of a sarcophagus. S. PORCHAIRE in the same city has a fine though incomplete tower at the west end. On the amusing capitals of the doorway the sculptor has represented two animals, which for the benefit of those of us less conversant than himself with such fearful wild-fowl he has considerately told us are lions. On the adjoining capital it is interesting to see the two birds

S. Porchaire

Fig. 85.

probably meant for peacocks drinking from a vase, which is a common Byzantine subject (*v*. Fig. 85). The rest of the church has been re-built.

S. SAVIN has besides its central lantern a Romanesque tower at the west end, surmounted by a splendid Gothic spire, and S. JUNIEN has the same in the centre of its singular west front (Fig. 84), though the upper part is incomplete, and was intended probably to finish like that of S. LEONARD. The latter is a very fine structure indeed, though a little ungraceful in general outline. It stands against the north side of the nave, and the ground storey which serves as a porch to the church consists of open arches on two sides with a clustered pier in the centre.

The tower is square in the lower stages, each of which recedes within that below, and it finishes with an

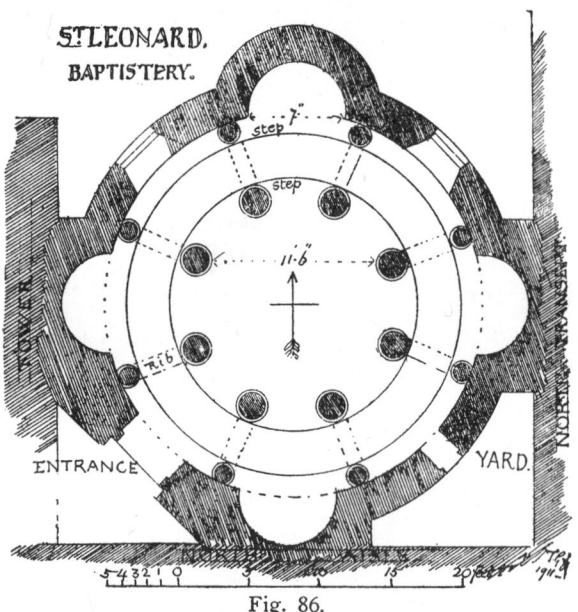

Fig. 86.

octagonal lantern surmounted by a low spire. The octagon is set on the square not in the usual way but obliquely, with an angle instead of a side to the front. This device is peculiar to Limoges, near which town S. Leonard is situated: the cathedral and the churches of S. Pierre and S. Michel aux Lions all have square towers surmounted by lofty octagonal stages set like this obliquely[1].

[1] Illustrated in my *Gothic Architecture in France, England and Italy*, vol. I. S. Leonard, Plate XLVIII, S. Michel, Plate XLIX.

On one side of this tower, filling the space between it and the north transept, and partly built into their walls, is the very remarkable baptistery of an earlier date which has already been alluded to (Fig. 86). Eight columns set in a circle carry a dome, and are surrounded by a circular aisle covered with an annular vault, and with four apses towards the cardinal points. The aisle vault is crossed by transverse ribs from each column to a slenderer shaft against the wall. The capitals are of the very rudest kind and the bases a mere succession of slightly projecting rings. This building has been much over-restored externally, but the interior is less injured, and seems to date from the 10th or 11th century at least.

Baptistery, S. Leonard

CHAPTER XX

PROVENCE

<small>Kingdom of Arles</small>

PROVENCE and Dauphiné had formed part of the kingdom of Arles, which early in the 11th century sank into weakness and dissolution. Dauphiné was bequeathed to the Emperor Conrad II by Rodolph III who died in 1032, the last of the kings of Burgundy, or of Vienne, or Arles, for the title varied from time to time; but it remained practically independent under the Lord or Dauphin of Vienne till Humbert the last of them in 1349 conveyed it with the consent of the Emperor to John, son of Philip of Valois. After being governed by the French Dauphins as a separate principality it was finally united to France in 1457.

<small>Kingdom of Provence</small>

Provence at the dissolution of the kingdom of Arles in the 11th century became an independent kingdom. In 1112 it had passed by marriage to the counts of Barcelona: afterwards to the king of Arragon in 1167, who bequeathed it to his second son. In 1245 Beatrice the sole heiress married Charles of Anjou, the brother of Louis IX and conqueror of the Hohenstaufens. His heirs, direct and adoptive, reigned till Provence was seized by Louis XI, and finally united to France by Charles VIII in 1486[1].

This part of France therefore has a history of its own distinct from the rest, for it had not even that feudal

---

[1] Hallam, *Middle Ages*. Koch, *Révolutions de l'Europe*.

relation to the French crown, which the semi-independent provinces such as Aquitaine and Normandy acknowledged. It is therefore not surprising that the early architecture of post-Roman times in Provence should differ a good deal from that of the rest of France, and constitute a school of its own. It is inspired not so much by Byzantine art as by that of Imperial Rome; and this was natural in a country even now so rich in Roman remains, and probably much richer still from the days of the empire down to the Middle Ages. The dome did not establish itself here for the typical covering, as it did in Aquitaine, but the churches follow the basilican plan of the western empire. The cathedral of AVIGNON, Notre Dame des Doms, however, has a cupola of a kind, or rather a domed lantern, resembling the drum or tower-domes of the later Byzantine churches which have been described already. This church consists of an aisleless nave, six bays long, covered by a pointed barrel roof which is sustained by enormous buttresses, once exterior to the church, but now included within it, the intervals between them having been turned into chapels, and thrown open to the nave. These bays are divided by wide transverse arches, across the nave, and being much longer from north to south than from east to west, they did not readily lend themselves to a cupola, for which a square base is necessary. A square base therefore had to be formed by a succession of arches turned from one of the great transverse ribs to the other, gathering over in a succession of concentric orders towards the centre till the square plan was attained (Fig. 87). Squinch arches reduce this square to an octagon on which the lantern-cupola rests happily. This touch of Byzantine construction however is exceptional in Provence, and the

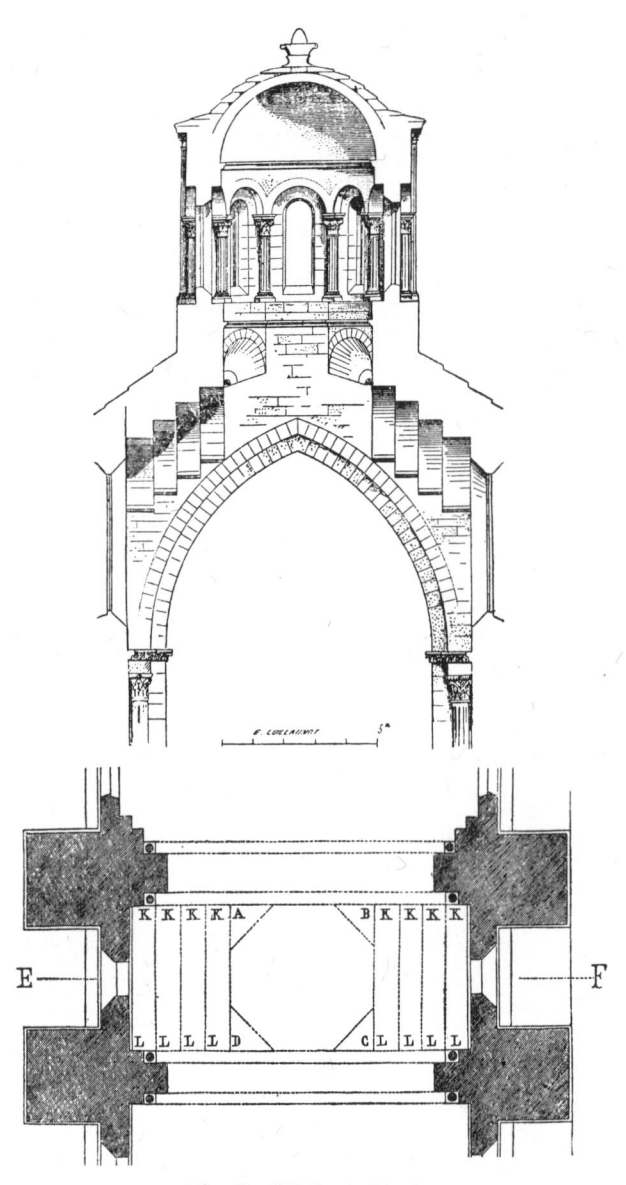

Fig. 87 (Viollet-le-Duc).

western doorway of the porch is distinctly based on Roman example, so much so as to have led the unwary to pronounce it actually Roman work. Though obviously not antique, it is hard to fix its date. Fergusson thinks both the doorway and the whole church were built not long if at all after the age of Charlemagne. He is not daunted by the pointed barrel vault of the nave; for he maintains that "all the churches of Provence, from the age of Charlemagne to that of S. Louis were vaulted, and have their vaults constructed on the principle of the pointed arch[1]"; and that they have been assigned to a later date than the real one, by antiquaries who think the pointed arch came in with Abbot Suger at S. Denis in the middle of the 12th century. He points out that the object of the builders was to cover the barrel vault with solid masonry, instead of the independent timber roof of later times, and that the difficulty of putting a pitched or gabled roof of this kind over a round barrel vault without overloading the crown naturally suggested the pointed section, to which a gabled covering could be fitted more closely and lightly. It is however impossible to attribute the construction of this nave to so early a date as the 9th century, and Viollet-le-Duc is probably nearer the truth in assigning it to the end of the 11th or the 12th. The doorway nevertheless may be earlier than the church, and nearer to Fergusson's date.

Avignon, The porch

Pointed barrel vaults

These solid coverings of masonry,—ceiling, vault, and roof in one,—are of course only applicable to barrel vaults, and became impossible when cross-vaulting came in to raise the side walls to the level of the crown of the vaults, which obliged the roof to be raised with them, and to be made of wood. The Byzantines got over this difficulty

Solid stone roofs

[1] Fergusson, *Hist. of Architecture*, vol. II. p. 45.

Solid stone roofs in a very different way. At S. Sophia, and in the East generally, the outsides of dome and vault were exposed. The ends of the vaults ran out and formed rounded gables, as they still do at S. Mark's at Venice, though they are disguised by the ogee pediments of a later date with their crocketing and finials. At S. Sophia the arched ends of all the vaults show on the face, and all the vaults and domes come to the surface, forming a succession of hillocks and valleys protected by lead and not very easy to clamber over. But in the west this plan never obtained, and the triangular gabled roof, of a pitch more or less acute, is universal. This, when formed with solid masonry over a barrel vault, naturally loaded it very heavily and by increasing its thrust made it more difficult to sustain. The thrust diminished in proportion as the pointed section was made more acute; and except on a large scale, when there was generally trouble, and where buttressing had to be applied to prevent disaster, as was done at Autun and elsewhere, many of these vaults stand perfectly well when the walls are substantial. Most of the old churches in Guernsey and some in south Wales, are roofed in this manner, and stand safely without buttresses.

S. Trophime, Arles The church of S. Trophime at Arles, which it is said was consecrated in 1152, is one of these barrel vaulted buildings, pointed in section, and with a solid roof of masonry above. There are side aisles, ceiled with quadrant waggon vaults, like those of Auvergne, which counterthrust the vault of the nave. The plan is cruciform with a massive tower over the crossing, but a very poor late Gothic choir has replaced unworthily the original Romanesque apse. The style is very simple; there is little ornament in the interior, and the exterior is

Plate CIV

S. TROPHIME—ARLES

Plate CV

S. TROPHIME—ARLES

so hemmed in by other buildings that only the west front, S. Trophand the central tower make any show. The latter is ime, Arles a fine piece of sturdy Romanesque work (Plate CIV) rising with three storeys above the roof, each stage set back considerably within that below, and marked by a cornice of little arches on corbels. The top storey has in the centre of each face a flat pilaster with a Corinthianizing capital, and there is a similar pilaster returned round each angle of the tower. A row of small openings and a corbelled cornice finishes the design at the eaves of a low pyramidal tiled roof, which may not be the covering originally intended, but has a very satisfactory effect.

The west front (Plate CV), otherwise plain, has the Portal of well-known portal which is one of the glories of Provençal S. Trophime Romanesque. It illustrates the advantage this part of France had over the rest in possessing so many monuments of ancient art, for nowhere else does sculpture play so important a part in the design, or attain the same degree of excellence at so early a period. This portal dates from the 12th century, and may perhaps be a little later than the church behind it.

The composition shows the hand of a consummate artist. Splendid as it is, ornament does not run riot over the whole of the design as it does in some later French Gothic portals, but is held well within bounds. Of the three parts into which the front is divided the lower is kept severely plain, and the upper which contains the arch has a great deal of plain wall-space and hardly any sculpture except in the tympanum. On the middle stage the artist has lavished the utmost resources of his art, with the happiest effect, and it forms a magnificent band of decoration from side to side between the two plainer

5—2

S. Troph-
ime, Arles

stages above and below it. In the tympanum our Lord is seated within a vesica, between the four apocalyptic beasts, and angels in pairs fill the flat soffit of the including arch. Below on the lintel are the 12 apostles, forming a frieze which is carried out right and left to the extremity of the portal, and is occupied on the proper right by the happy blessed, and on the left by the damned. The frieze is supported by a colonnade of detached columns between which are full-length statues of saints, and below them are lions rending men and animals and serving as supports for the saints and the columns[1].

The great arch in the upper stage is very slightly pointed and consists of three well-moulded orders, very satisfactory to an English eye, with no sculpture but a leaf round the label, and the angels already mentioned on the inner soffit, which indeed make no show till you stand under the arch. The simplicity of this is masterly, and the bare wall space in which the arch is set contrasts admirably with the splendid stage below. A low pitched pedimental moulding resting on consoles finishes the composition, and produces a distinctly classic impression, which is further emphasized by the colonnaded arrangement, the trabeated design of the freize which rests on it, and the fluted and cabled pilasters of the jamb.

S. Gilles

But this magnificent portal is rivalled if not surpassed by that of the church of S. GILLES (Plate CVI), distant about half-an-hour from Arles by rail. Here there are three doorways in the same style as that of S. Trophime,

---

[1] In this series there is round the corner at the north end the figure of a naked man prostrate and half wrapped up in a bull's hide, of which I should be glad to know the meaning.

but perhaps a trifle older[1], connected by a series of columns carrying a similar frieze. The arches are round without the suspicion of a point like that at Arles, and there is no pediment above. The façade of the church above it was not completed, and there is something wrong with the portal itself. The central arch like that at S. Trophime springs from a frieze of figures, which starts to run right and left over the colonnade, but stops abruptly before reaching the third column at the jamb of the side door. Had it gone farther it would have covered the mouldings of the side arch which springs at the lower bed of the frieze. There are also other signs of disturbance.

A curious projection of two columns on a pedestal at each side of the great doorway (Plate CVI) carries a return of the moulded architrave at right angles to the wall. This must have been intended to support something, and makes one think of the lion and lioness that stand sentry on each side of the great portal at Traü, and project in the same way.

The central tympanum has like that at Arles a figure of our Lord in a vesica, or rather an aureole, between the four apocalyptic beasts. On the lintel-frieze, is a representation of the last supper, and scenes from our Lord's life and passion occupy the continuations over the colonnade, ending with the washing of the disciples' feet on the proper right, and beginning again with the betrayal in the garden and the kiss of Judas on the proper left, in right sequence of event.

---

[1] Mr McGibbon cites the following inscription which is said to be copied from an old one now lost. But it seems imperfect and the date too early for the portal.
    ANNO DOMINI 1116 HOC TEMPLVM SANCTI
    EGIDII ÆDIFICARE CEPIT MENSE
    APRILI FERIA 2ᴬ IN OCTAVA PASCHAE.
               Archit. of Provence, etc. p. 206.

The sculpture at S. Gilles

The sculpture at S. Gilles is very like that at S. Trophime, but it struck me, if anything, as rather superior, especially in the figures, which are admirable. The general design shows the same delicate sense of proportion in the disposition of the ornament. Here too the central stage is the richest; and though the base or podium is ornamented with carved reliefs at the sides of the great door, the relief is with consummate art kept so flat and slight that it observes the necessary subordination to the statuary above it. The ornaments of the mouldings at both churches are based on the Roman antique; in both the guilloche or fret appears, the pilasters are fluted, a feature belonging to the west and not to the east, and the scrolls are purely Latin and have nothing Byzantine about them. The capitals in particular are based on Roman Corinthian, with deeply channelled folds and pipings, and rounded raffling, quite unlike the sharp crisp acanthus, and the flat surface treatment of the Byzantine school. Many of them contain figures of birds and animals admirably posed, and at S. Gilles, along the edge of the architrave that runs under the frieze, is a series of little animals—lions, dogs, and whelps of various kinds—carved with life and spirit that it would be hard to surpass.

The ornaments Roman

The figures Byzantine

In the figures however, with their draperies in straight and deep-cut folds, there appears a character foreign to the classic art of the west. They have nothing about them of the Gallo-Roman style, but breathe instead the spirit of the religious art of the East.

Influence of Byzantine art in the west

Now it has been pointed out in a previous chapter that figure sculpture on a large scale played no part in Byzantine architecture. It is only on a miniature scale that the Greeks employed it; in ivories and triptychs

Plate CVI

S. GILLES

and such-like portable articles, of which a vast quantity found their way along the line of commerce westward. It was therefore from these that the infant schools of France probably derived inspiration. A still more fertile source was found in Byzantine paintings, where figures were introduced without reserve; and in illuminations of manuscripts, and actual pictures, in which the Greeks excelled the westerns as much as they fell behind them in the plastic art. Figures too were largely employed in the embroideries and woven stuffs from Eastern looms; which were rich also in geometrical and floral patterns, that were freely copied in the conventional ornaments of all the western schools, including those of Britain. Lastly the Crusades of the 11th and 12th centuries opened a wider communication between west and east; European principalities were established at Antioch and Edessa and finally at Jerusalem itself, with which constant intercourse would be maintained, and regular commercial relations established; and we have already noticed the normal trade between Venice and the south and west of France which furnished another link with the Eastern world. Byzantine influence

It may be asked why in a country abounding in fine statuary, as Provence and Toulouse undoubtedly did in the 11th and 12th centuries, inspiration should be sought in Byzantine art which repudiated sculpture on a large scale and offered no direct models for imitation, rather than in the classic art near at hand. But imitation of the conventional figures of Byzantine ivories and tissues was much easier than that of the Venus of Arles; and Roman art was regarded as Pagan, and that of Byzantium was religious—hieratic,—and its very stiffness and convention would recommend it to the clergy, regular or secular, in whose hands the arts at that time were Byzantine art hieratic

Contrast between ornament and statuary

exclusively centred. And thus it is that we find in these buildings a singular mixture of motives, the ornament being based on Gallo-Roman example with little or no trace of oriental feeling, while the statuary bears the impress of Byzantium and the East.

While however the artists of the 11th and 12 centuries "went to school," as Viollet-le-Duc well puts it[1], to Byzantine art in order to learn the craft of figure ornament, they soon got beyond mere copying, and introduced their own ideas, and breathed the breath of life into their work. These figures at Arles and S. Gilles are no mere conventional saints, but are beginning to show already that individuality and character which makes them portraits, and this element grew stronger in each successive generation, till it culminated in the intensely living sculpture of the 13th and 14th centuries.

France is perhaps not so rich in cloisters as England, and in the north, at all events, has nothing to show comparable to those of Canterbury or Gloucester. But in the south, especially in Provence, there are fine examples, very unlike ours, but beautiful and interesting.

Cloister, S. Trophime

The best of them is perhaps that of S. Trophime at Arles (Plate CVII), which owing to the declivity of the site stands high above the church floor and is reached by a considerable flight of stairs. The north and east walks are Romanesque, of the 12th century, and the other two sides have been re-built in late Gothic times. But though their arcades are of the 15th and 16th centuries the outer wall even of these sides seems to be of the

---

[1] Les statuaires du XIIe siècle en France commencent par *aller à l'école* des Byzantins. Il faut avant tout apprendre le *métier*...cependant l'artiste occidental ne pouvant s'astreindre à la reproduction hiératique dès qu'il sait son métier, regard autour de lui. *Dict. Rais.* art. "Sculpture." The whole of the article is excellent.

Plate CVII

Cloisters: S. TROPHIME—ARLES

Plate CVIII

Cloisters: S. TROPHIME—ARLES

CH. XX]   FRANCE—PROVENCE   73

earlier date, for it contains doors of 12th century work, Cloister, S. Trophime
and one mortuary tablet if not more of the 13th. There
are many of these tablets let into the wall, which sounds
hollow below them, and, if the guide is to be believed,
which is not necessary, contains the bodies of the persons
commemorated. The oldest of these is in the north wall;
it is to the memory of one PONCIVS DE BASCIO
(? Les Baux) CAPVT SCOLE ET CANONICVS
REGVLARIS $\overline{\text{SCI}}$ TROPHIMI : ANNO DMI
M°C°XL°. This agrees with the apparent date of the
north walk, which is the oldest side of the cloister. The
east walk, though still thoroughly Romanesque, is proved,
according to the *Guide Joanne*, by historical documents
to have been built in 1221. It is evidently later than the
north walk, but even in Provence, where the Romanesque
style held its own longer than elsewhere in France, it is
difficult to place it quite so late. There is one tablet in
its eastern wall, to a Canon and Provost of the church,
which bears the date 1181, and another dated 1183 seems
almost to give the name of the Canon who superintended
its building.

>   VII : $\overline{\text{KL}}$: IANVARII
> ANNO : $\overline{\text{DNI}}$: M : C : LXXXIII : O
> BIIT : PONCIVS : REBOLL : SA
> CERDOS : ET : CANONICVS :
> REGVLARIS : ET : OPERAR$\overline{\text{I}}$
> ECCLESIE : SANCTI : TROP
> HIM : ORATE : PRO : EO :[1]

[1] There is a tablet on the N.W. pier of the cloister to JORDANUS, Dean of S. Trophimus A.D. 1187: one in the north wall records GUILLELMUS CAVALLERIUS A.D. 1203: another on the east wall commemorates DVRANTVS a precentor and canon who died in 1212; there is one on the west wall, to a

Cloister, S. Trophime

The sides of the Romanesque cloister (Plates CIV, CVII, CVIII) are divided by massive piers into three bays each, and the bay is subdivided into four arches, resting on coupled columns, set one behind the other to take the thickness of the wall above.

The shafts are of marble, round or octagonal, tapered, but without an entasis, from $6\frac{3}{4}$ inches at the bottom to $5\frac{5}{8}$ at the top, and they are set with an inclination towards one another, so that they are the same distance apart at top and bottom in spite of their diminution. The great piers dividing the bays, and those at the angles of the cloister are enriched with figure sculpture, and the capitals throughout are delicately carved, either with foliage, mixed in some cases with animals and human heads, or with figure subjects from the Old or New Testament of which the series is continued in the later capitals of the two Gothic sides of the quadrangle. There is the same contrast here as at S. Gilles between the style of the ornamental scrolls and foliage which has no trace of Byzantine feeling, and that of the large figures on the piers, which with the straight columnar folds of their drapery, and their rigid conventional pose, are more Byzantine than Roman. These figures of Old or New Testament worthies serve like the Persians or Caryatides of classic architecture to support the load of the superstructure. The two Romanesque walks are covered with barrel vaults, strengthened by transverse ribs at each of the large piers, and a diagonal one in the corner where the two corridors meet. The vault ramps, so that the consoles and cornice from which it springs on the inner side are considerably

canon VEFRANO, in 1221; and another in the east wall, VILLLMVS . D . MIRAMARS, A.D. 1239. I could not find any others. Miramas is a neighbouring village.

higher than those over the arcading of the side next the cloister garth[1]. This seems intended to accommodate a sloping pent roof, perhaps of solid masonry, which may have been the original arrangement. But when the west and south walks were re-built in later times the front wall was raised and a flat terrace formed all round the court on the top of the cloister. The stone channel to which the original pent-roof descended remains to mark the old level of the eaves. This at least is the explanation given by Viollet-le-Duc, but it must be observed that this stone channel is not level as the eaves must have been were this the true story, but falls quite sharply from west to east along the north side of the cloister. *Cloister, S. Trophime*

All the arcading of the Romanesque part is round-arched, and the piers are strengthened on the outside by buttresses in the form of pilasters with Corinthian capitals. These are fluted, as are also the sides of the piers, another mark of Roman rather than Byzantine influence.

On an insulated rock some three miles from Arles is the abbey of MONTMAJEUR, half convent half fortress, built under the severe Cistercian rule in a much more restrained style than the lovely work at Arles and S. Gilles. Partly cut in the rock, and partly built into the side of it below the mighty tower of the keep is an early chapel enclosing what is known as the rock-hewn hermitage of S. Trophime. The chapel is barrel vaulted, and the shafts from which the vault springs have semi-classical capitals of an interesting kind. The great church on the summit of the rock is very plain; cruciform, and single-aisled, and it has a fine crypt. The most interesting building here is the *Abbey of Montmajeur* *Chapel of S. Trophime*

---

[1] It has been necessary to confine the thrust of the barrel vault by iron ties.

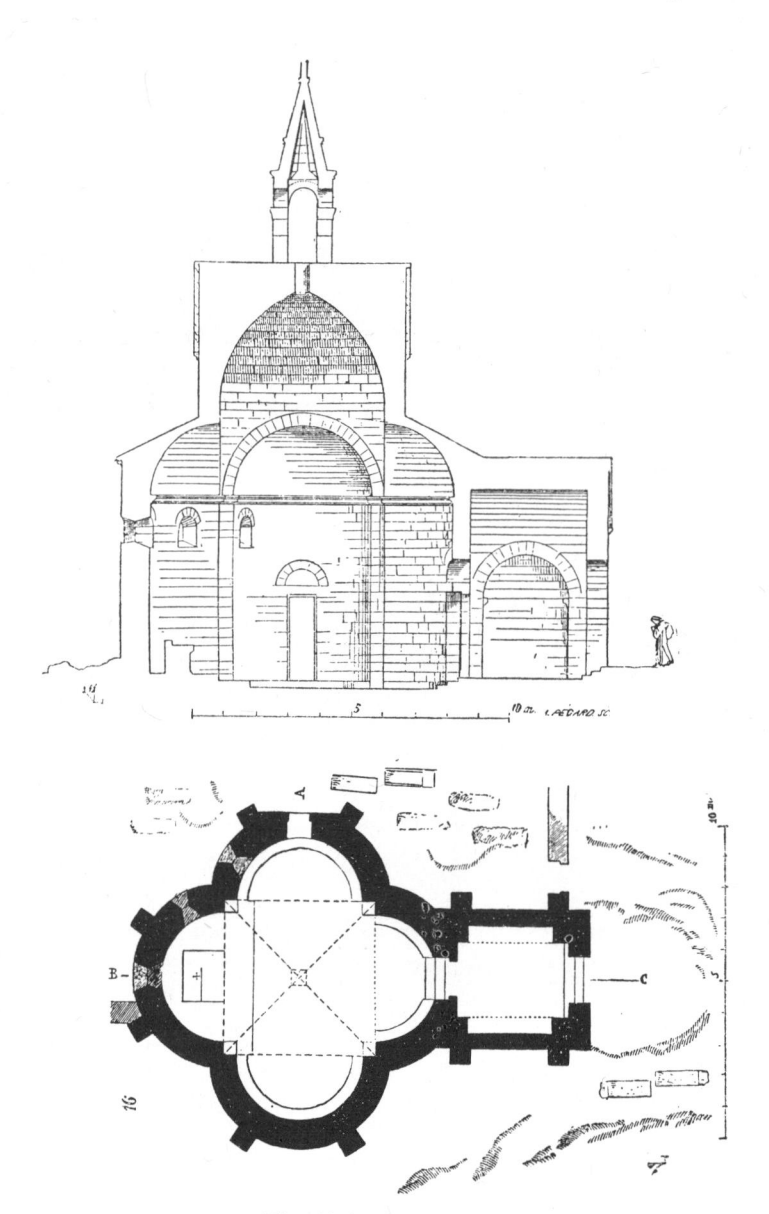

Fig. 88 (Viollet-le-Duc).

CH. XX] FRANCE—PROVENCE 77

cloister, consisting of three bays on a side, each containing Cloister at Mont-majeur
an arcade of three arches on coupled colonnettes with
carved capitals like those at Arles. Each triplet is enclosed
under a single segmental arch, from pier to pier, plain
and unrelieved by a single moulding. The cloister is

Fig. 89 (Viollet-le-Duc).

covered with a pent-roof over a barrel vault, which it is
suggested was the original arrangement at S. Trophime.

A few yards from the abbey buildings stands the Chapel of S. Croix
curious Romanesque chapel of S. CROIX (Figs. 88 and 89),
attributed by a fiction to Charlemagne, but really dedicated

Mont-majeur S. Croix

in 1019. It consists of four apses, forming a quaterfoil preceded by a porch, the central square being carried up as a tower containing a square cupola. The only light is from three little windows close together on one side, and besides the porch door there is another in the side next the windows. It seems to have been the cemetery chapel of the abbey, for hollowed out in the rock all around are shallow graves barely deep enough to contain a body, which if it were ever really placed in them must have been covered merely by a slab level with the ground.

Cloister at Elne

The cloister at ELNE, near Perpignan, which I have not seen myself, is described by Viollet-le-Duc as richer in sculpture than any remaining in that part of France. It does not however appear from his illustrations and those of Mr McGibbon[1] that there is any statuary though small figure subjects are introduced into the capitals[2].

Cloister at Thoronet

At THORONET between Toulon and Cannes is an interesting church with a cloister resembling that at Montmajeur but with an absolutely ascetic refusal of ornament, being built under the Cistercian rule[3]. A similar barrel-vaulted cloister exists on the island of S. Honorat.

Church of S. Trinité

The church of S. TRINITÉ on the same island seems from Mr McGibbon's illustration[4] to be almost a purely Byzantine building.

Pantheon, Riez

But the most remarkable instance of Byzantine work in Provence would seem to be the building at RIEZ near Draguignan known as the Pantheon, which is illustrated by Texier and Pullan, who take it to be a Roman temple afterwards turned into a Christian baptistery (Fig. 90). It is a square building enclosing an octagon

---

[1] V.-le-Duc, III. 433-4. *Architecture of Provence and the Riviera* by David McGibbon, p. 244.

[2] v. *Spring Gardens Sketch book*, vol. VI. pl. X, XI, XII.

[3] It is illustrated by V.-le-Duc, vol. III. p. 422 and McGibbon, p. 279.

[4] McGibbon, pp. 321, 322.

of columns bearing round arches and carried up into a tower with an octagonal dome. The surrounding aisle has an annular barrel vault, being brought into an octagon by semi-circular niches in the angles of the square. The plan is so like those of the Christian buildings in the East that it is impossible to accept the theory of a Roman origin. But for the absence of a projected apse, which is not essential to a baptistery, the plan

Pantheon at Riez

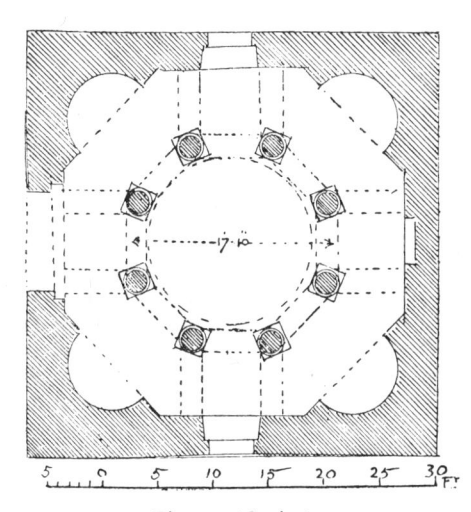

Fig. 90 (Texier).

is that of the Syrian church at Ezra (*v. sup.* vol. I. p. 33, Fig. 6) and belongs to the family of which the church of SS. Sergius and Bacchus at Constantinople is a more advanced member (*v. sup.* vol. I. p. 78, Fig. 19). The octagonal baptistery of the cathedral of Frejus also has four deep niches in the oblique sides, "an attempt," says Mr McGibbon "to make the floor as square as possible," and this again seems to have some analogy with the plan of the Pantheon at Riez.

80   FRANCE—PROVENCE   [CH. XX

Byzantine influence limited in Provence

The impress of Byzantine art however, except in the matter of statuary, is not so marked in Provence as in Aquitaine, where it affected not merely the ornament but the construction of the architecture. In Provence Gallo-Roman tradition ruled so strongly that it seems to have prevented that development of architecture into something further, which took place in the rest of France. Viollet-le-Duc says "Auvergne, but for the cathedral of Clermont, and Provence never adopted Gothic architec-

Gothic not adopted in Provence

ture, and this last province which only became French at the end of the 15th century, passed from Romanesque architecture—degenerated—to the architecture of the Renaissance, having yielded only too late and too imperfectly to the influence of the monuments of the north[1]." He remarks that the Provençal school, however remarkable at its outset, "seemed struck with impotence, and produced nothing but curious mixtures of various imitations which could give birth to nothing fresh; and in the 13th century it sank into decadence." He compares these splendid portals at Arles and S. Gilles disadvantageously with those of Notre Dame at Paris. We may not entirely agree with him there, though no doubt he is justified in drawing a contrast between the progressive character of the northern school, and the semi-Byzantine stationary qualities of that of Provence.

Refinement of the Provençal school

But if about the latter there may be something of the softness and languor of the south, it has also in a marked degree the refinement of the ancient art from which it sprang, the reflexion of an ancient civilization, and the romance of the land of the Troubadours to which it belongs. In Provence we have Romanesque art without its ruggedness. Elsewhere it is tinged with barbarism. At

[1] *Dict. Rais.* vol. I. p. 150.

S. Albans and Winchester, and in the great 12th century churches on the Rhine there is nothing to soften the hard barren outlines of the ponderous construction. At Durham, Waltham, and Norwich the scanty ornamentation of the piers only serves to accentuate their rudeness. But the Romanesque of Provence has all the delicacy of an advanced art bestowed on the simple and strenuous forms of a round-arched style. The buildings we have been considering have a loveliness all their own, and a certain poetical quality that is perhaps wanting in the later triumphs of architecture at Paris or even at Chartres and Amiens.

CHAPTER XXI

TOULOUSE

<small>The county of Toulouse</small>

THE county of Toulouse, including Languedoc, was for a long time unconnected with the French crown, and it was not till 1229, after the desolation wrought by the wars of religion, that the greater part of the territory was added to France. The first king to make any pretension to authority within its limits was Louis VII who had married his sister to the reigning count. But the distance from Paris and royal domain, the differences of language and laws continued to keep the people of this province distinct from those of the north.

<small>Persecution of the Albigenses</small>

They were brought into cruel relation to them however in the 12th century and afterwards, by the crusade preached in 1208 against the Albigenses whose tenets they favoured. "The war was prosecuted with every atrocious barbarity which superstition the mother of crimes could inspire. Languedoc, a country for that age flourishing and civilized, was laid waste, her cities burned, her inhabitants swept away by fire and the sword[1]."

<small>S. Sernin, Toulouse</small>

It is therefore not surprising that the remains of Romanesque architecture in the county of Toulouse are not abundant. The great church of S. SERNIN at TOULOUSE is the most important monument of the style in the

[1] Hallam, *Middle Ages*, chap. i.

CH. XXI] FRANCE—TOULOUSE 83

11th century (Fig. 91). It is an immense cruciform church, with double aisles to the nave, and a single aisle surrounding both the sides and ends of the transepts, and it finishes eastward in an apse surrounded by an ambulatory aisle, with five semi-circular chapels projecting from it. It thus possesses every feature of the complete plan of French ecclesiology.

S. Sernin, Toulouse

The nave is less than 30 ft. wide, and strikes one as narrow for so vast an edifice. Viollet-le-Duc however

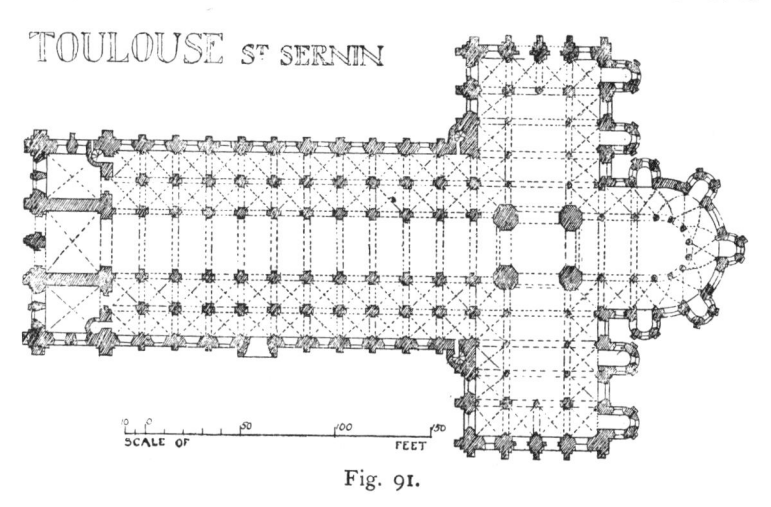

Fig. 91.

takes it as a pattern of good proportion, so pleasing that he was led to study it analytically, and found it was entirely set out on angles of 60° and 45°, the total and intermediate heights being given by isosceles triangles with sides at the angle of 45°, and by equilateral triangles[1]. Over the crossing rises a lofty steeple of octagonal stages set inwards one by one, and finishing with a spire (Plate CIX). To support this, which is a later addition, the four piers at the crossing have had to be enlarged at

[1] *Dict. Rais.* vol. VII. pp. 539–542.

the expense of the interior view of the nave, on which they encroach disagreeably.

The nave has a round barrel vault counterthrust by quadrant vaults over the triforium which of course forbid a clerestory.

On the south side is a porch and doorway with a stilted round arch of two deep moulded orders on jamb shafts, containing in the tympanum a marble relief of the Ascension. In the details classic tradition shows itself, especially in the cornice with sculptured brackets by way of modillions across the base of the gable.

In the apse, with its ambulatory and projecting chapels, we have the French *chevet* completely developed. The earliest Christian churches of course had no chapels. The Greek church to this date only allows a single altar. The earliest cathedrals in France seem to have been without chapels, and indeed without ambulatories. Many of those in the south and west of France still end in plain apses like the cathedral of Angers, or even end square like that of Poitiers and several of the domed churches of Perigord.

Autun, built in the middle of the 12th century, ends directly with three apses for choir and side aisles, and no ambulatory or radiating chapels; and this is the old basilican plan of the Pantocrator at Constantinople, and scores of churches in Italy and Dalmatia. The cathedrals of Sens and Langres, built towards the end of the 12th century, finish with an ambulatory and a single chapel projecting beyond it at the east end. As early however as the 11th century chapels appear in greater number, sometimes attached directly to the wall of the main apse as at Cahors, Souillac and Angoulême (*v. sup.* Fig. 77), sometimes divided from it by an ambulatory aisle as at Vignory,

Plate CIX

S. SERNIN—TOULOUSE

Plate CX

S. BERTRAND DE COMMINGES

Fontevrault, Agen, and the churches of Auvergne. They were more numerous in conventual churches than in cathedrals or parish churches at first, probably because of the jealous exclusion of the laity from the choir which was reserved for the brethren, and this necessitated the provision of other places for the people. But as time went on chapels clustered as thickly round the apses of the cathedrals as round those of the abbeys, and Le Mans has no fewer than thirteen. In England the *chevet* with radiating chapels is found at Westminster, and nowhere else; but Westminster though English in detail is French in plan. Something of the kind is attempted at Pershore, but very ineffectively. At Tewkesbury the attempt is more successful, but even there the resemblance to the French *chevet* is very imperfect, and the architectural effect falls very far short of the foreign model, or indeed of the regular English square termination, with a fine east window.

The French chevet

The chevet in England

At S. BERTRAND DE COMMINGES, on a foot-hill of the Pyrenees where they melt into the plain, is a single aisled abbey church ending in a simple apse. The 12th century cloister attached to it is in a sad state of decay (Plate CX), many of the details being quite unrecognizable. The capitals which are large and disproportioned are carved elaborately with scrolls and figures, and rest on coupled columns, except that in one case the pier is composed of the four evangelists placed back to back against a central shaft, each holding in his arms the apocalyptic beast which is his emblem.

S. Bertrand de Comminges

At the foot of the hill the little church of S. JUST has a fine Romanesque doorway with figures of saints in the jambs serving as supports to the archway.

S. Just

The slopes of the Pyrenees near Luchon are dotted

Pyrenean village churches with little village churches dating from the 12th century with little or no alteration. They have barrel vaults with transverse ribs springing from flat pilasters to divide the bays, and apses with semi-domes. The arcaded cornice is common, and few of the humblest village churches are without it, often very roughly worked. Their towers, when they have any, have mid-wall shafts in the windows,

Fig. 92.

and the apses are covered with semi-domes. The doors often have sculpture, sometimes of marble, executed in a less grotesque fashion than contemporary work in the north. Occasionally as at S. Just, and S. Bertrand the figures are really excellent.

S. Aventin   The church of the mountain village of S. AVENTIN (Fig. 92) is a considerable building, with a central and

Plate CXI

South Portal—MOISSAC

Plate CXII

The Cloister—MOISSAC

also a western tower, both pierced by windows with mid-wall shafts. It is a three-aisled basilican church, the nave barrel-vaulted with transverse ribs, and the aisles cross-groined. The proportion is narrow and lofty, and the building ends eastward with three apses.

The abbey of MOISSAC, north of Toulouse, is a single-aisled apsidal church, of which the nave was re-built in the 15th century. At the west end however it has the original Romanesque tower, to which was added on the south side a magnificent outer portal, and at the same time the tower was turned into a fortress by the addition of a parapet walk round it with crenellation over the entrance. Fortified churches are not uncommon in this district, which suffered severely during the crusades against the Albigenses. The portal is magnificently sculptured. The arch like that at S. Trophime is very slightly pointed and its three orders are divided by a slender reed-like feature that serves for shaft in the jamb and arch in the head, the capital being only marked by a band or knot of carving. This has a later look than 1150, the date assigned to it by Viollet-le-Duc. In the tympanum Christ sits, imperially crowned and enthroned, with the four typical beasts around him, who regard him with an ecstasy which is expressed in a very lively manner. The rest of the space is occupied by the 24 elders who wear crowns and hold musical instruments. Across the lintel is a fine row of rosettes dished round a raised central flower, which has a Byzantine character. The jambs of the doorway (Plate CXI), are curiously scalloped, and the shafts next the opening follow the scalloped outline. The sides of the porch, which projects in front and carries a barrel vault, have two arches on each side containing sculptured figures and a frieze over

Abbey of Moissac

Sculpture at Moissac

88 FRANCE—TOULOUSE [CH. XXI

Moissac them. On one side is represented the parable of Dives and Lazarus: the beggar is lying at the foot of the rich man's table while an angel carries his soul to Abraham, who receives it in his bosom. On the opposite side is the Presentation in the Temple and the flight into Egypt. The central column which divides the doorway and supports the tympanum is composed of animals interlaced like one at Souillac which has been mentioned above, and like the intertwined figures of Saxon manuscripts or Scandinavian carving. Another touch of northern grotesque is the monster at each end of the lintel from whose mouth proceed the ends of the threads which form the border of the rosettes.

The figure carving here, though lively and full of spirit, is very inferior to that of Arles and S. Gilles. The attitudes are forced and extravagant, the figures are attenuated and drawn out beyond all proportion, and the modelling is wanting in breadth and simplicity. It is the work of a very different school, which has little trace of either Roman or Byzantine influence, but in which, with all its imperfections, one seems to see the seeds of growth and of the future Gothic art.

Cloister, Moissac The cloister of Moissac (Plate CXII) is one of the finest in France though it has been a great deal altered since it was first built. Its original date is given by an inscription which with its abbreviations expanded reads as follows:

ANNO AB INCARNATIONE ÆTERNI PRINCIPIS MILLESIMO CENTESIMO FACTVM EST CLAVSTRVM ISTVD TEMPORE DOMINI ANSQVITILII ABBATIS. AMEN

        V · V · V
        M · D · M
        R · R · R
        F · F · F

No explanation has ever been found of these mysterious initials; they have puzzled all the antiquaries. The sculptures and the capitals no doubt belong to the date of the inscription, but the cloister was re-built early in the 12th century, when the abbey adopted the rule of Citeaux, and the old carvings were re-fixed in the new work. The arches of the cloister are now pointed instead of being round and it is not vaulted but has a wooden roof.

CHAPTER XXII

BURGUNDY

The Burgundians

THE Burgundians differed from other barbarian settlers in Gaul, such as the Franks, in that they were Christians before their arrival. The ecclesiastical historian tells naively the story of their conversion. Being ravaged by the Huns "they did not" he says "fly for help to any man in their extremity, but decided to turn to some God. And understanding that the God of the Romans gave powerful succour to those who feared him, they all with common accord came to believe in Christ. And going to a city of Gaul they begged Christian baptism of the bishop." A subsequent victory over a vastly superior host of Huns confirmed their faith, and after that "the nation Christianized fervently[1]." When the Burgundians therefore established themselves in Gaul in the time of Honorius they did so peacefully, not as invaders but as allies of the Romans, and they even turned their swords occasionally in defence of the empire against encroaching Visigoths. Their kingdom lasted till 532 when it was finally conquered by the Franks under the sons of Clovis.

The Burgundians in 5th century

They are described by Sidonius Apollinaris who visited their king Chilperic at Lyons about 474, as not unfriendly neighbours, hairy giants, genial and kindly, but gross in their feeding, and coarse in their habits; and his fastidious

---

[1] διαπύρως ἐχριστιάνισεν. Socrates, *Eccl. Hist.* VIII. 30.

CH. XXII] FRANCE—BURGUNDY 91

taste was offended by their loud voices, their noisy feasts, their rank cookery, their habit of greasing their hair with rancid butter, and the fumes of onions and garlic from their kitchens[1].

It is curious to find that it was among the descendants of this jovial easy-tempered people that monasticism established itself more firmly than in any other part of western Europe. Yet so it was; from the great religious centres of Cluny, Citeaux, and Clairvaux the passion for an ascetic cœnobite life spread far and wide, and thousands of convents obeyed the Cluniac or Cistercian rule in every part of western Christendom.

Burgundy the home of Monasticism

Monasticism is a product of the East, where the rule of S. Basil was established in the 4th century, and at its first introduction into the west it was viewed with disfavour. The funeral at Rome of Blaesilla, a young nun who died it was said from excessive fasting, nearly caused a popular riot in 384. The people, says S. Jerome cried " when will they drive this detestable race of monks from the town? Why do they not stone them? Why do they not throw them into the river[2]." It was not till the first half of the 5th century that monasticism spread, and really established itself in the west; and then it did

Eastern origin of Monasticism

[1]   Quid me . . . .
    Inter crinigeras situm catervas,
    Et Germanica verba sustinentem,
    Laudantem tetrico subinde vultu
    Quod Burgundio cantat esculentus,
    Infundens acido comam butyro.
    * * * * * * *
    Felices oculos tuos et aures,
    Felicemque libet vocare nasum,
    Cui non allia, sordidaque cepae
    Ructant mane novo decem apparatus.
        Carmen XII *ad V. C. Catullinum.*

[2] Guizot, *Civilization in France*, Lecture XIV.

so only sporadically: but at the beginning of the 6th century the system was reduced to order at Monte Cassino in Italy by S. Benedict of Nursia, whose rule was soon obeyed all over western Europe so completely, that Charlemagne caused enquiry to be made throughout his empire whether monks could be found of any other order[1].

Rule of S. Benedict

The Benedictine rule had become lax in Burgundy when the abbey of CLUNY near Macon was founded in 909 by William Duke of Aquitaine. Stricter discipline was restored, and the policy was established of bringing other convents into filial relation with Cluny as their head. The same policy was adopted by the daughter house of CITEAUX, which was founded in 1098, and in 1130 was released from dependence on the parent abbey. The Cistercian rule was obeyed by countless convents in France, Italy, and Germany; and in England it included the great abbeys of Buildwas, Byland, Fountains, Furness, Kirkstall, Netley, Rievaulx, and Tintern, besides other and smaller houses. Each of these two great Burgundian monasteries therefore was the head of a confederation that extended far beyond the limits of the province and even of the kingdom. Over it the abbot ruled like a sovereign; the patronage of the headship of each subordinate house was vested in him, and any monastery that wished to enter the order was obliged to consent to receive his nominee when a vacancy occurred. Subject at first to the bishops, the monks after a long struggle won their independence of episcopal control, and acknowledged no authority but that of Rome. At the latter part of the 11th century the ancient abbeys of Vézelay, S. Gilles, Moissac, Limoges, Poitiers, Figeac, S. Germain l'Auxerrois, Mauzac, and S. Bertin de Lille,

Abbey of Cluny

The Cistercians

Affiliation of convents

---

[1] Guizot, *Civilization in France*, Lecture XIV.

sought and obtained admission to the order of Cluny. In the 11th century three hundred and fourteen monasteries and churches submitted to the rule of Abbot S. Hugh, who reigned like a temporal prince, and struck money in his own mint, like the king of France himself.

It will easily be understood that the existence of these powerful half-independent institutions in Burgundy had its effect on the civilization, and with it on the arts of that province. In those ages of misrule, and disorder, in a land desolated by barbarian invasions and constant wars, where society was sinking into a sort of chaos, it was only in the convents that any security could be found, and that the peaceful arts and agriculture could be carried on without interruption. But more than this:—by the rule of S. Benedict manual labour was actually made a duty, on the same level as self-denial and obedience. This was the great revolution which S. Benedict introduced into the monastic system. "Laziness," he said, "is the enemy of the soul, and consequently the brothers should at certain times occupy themselves in manual labour; at others in holy reading[1]." Round their walls forests were cleared and land was reclaimed; and within them literature dragged on a feeble life, and the manual arts were practised with gradually increasing skill. Nowhere beyond the convent precincts were artizans to be found, or at all events but very rarely, and each establishment had to rely on its own resources to supply its needs. The lay guilds or confraternities of artizans that existed in Italy had not yet appeared in France, and the inmates of the convents had to be their own builders, masons, carpenters, glaziers, and to fulfil every function of the building trade. It must be remembered that they were

Effect of monasteries on art

Manual labour enjoined

Crafts in the cloister

[1] Guizot, *Civilization in France*, Lecture XIV.

Monks mostly laymen

not necessarily ecclesiastics. Many, perhaps most, of the monks were laymen. In the early time they were even discouraged from taking orders, and while the bishops in the 4th and 5th centuries took precautions to limit the ordination of monks, the monks themselves sometimes regarded the priesthood as a snare which interfered with their duty of divine contemplation[1]. Therefore many inmates of the convents were artizans, and according to the rule of S. Benedict they were to continue working at their crafts, though they were not to take any pride in them. In the 12th century, one Bernard of Tiron who founded a religious house near Chartres, gathered into it "craftsmen both of wood and iron, carvers and goldsmiths, painters and stonemasons, vinedressers and husbandmen, and others skilled in all manner of cunning work[2]." The rapid spread of the order gave the craftsmen constant and regular employment. They worked with zeal and enthusiasm, and their efforts resulted as might have been expected in forming a school of architecture in which we find the first seeds of progress and the first signs of growth and development.

The church of Cluny

In 1089 Abbot Hugh began to re-build the church at CLUNY, the number of monks having outgrown the existing building. No great church was built in those days without a miracle, and S. Peter is said to have given the plan in a dream to the monk Gauzon who laid the foundations. The great church was finished by another Clunist, Hezelon, a Fleming, from Liege. It was the vastest church in the west of Europe. The nave was covered with a barrel vault like the churches already described; there were double aisles; two transepts with

---

[1] Guizot, *Civilization in France*, Lecture XIV.
[2] Ordericus Vitalis, cited Baldwin Brown, *Early Art in England*.

apsidal chapels on their eastern side; a *chevet* with ambulatory and five semi-circular chapels; a large narthex or ante-church five bays long, quite a church by itself; and at the extreme west end two towers. It was not dedicated till 1131, and the narthex was only finished in 1220[1]. The church of Cluny

The conventual buildings were all in proportion, the refectory being 100 ft. in length by 60 ft. in width which would require, one would think, a row of pillars down the middle. The side walls were decorated with paintings of biblical subjects, and portraits of founders and benefactors, and on the end wall was represented the Last Judgment. Over each of the two crossings of the church was a tower, and two more towers rose over the ends of the western transept. The domestic buildings

Cluny stood unaltered till the Revolution, but beyond a few walls nothing now remains except part of the southern great transept with the tower upon it. The arches are pointed, and the tower is brought into an octagonal lantern and has rather a German look. The flat pilasters are fluted and have capitals of a Corinthianizing character, mixed with others of animals and grotesques. In this we see the effect of Roman example which can be traced throughout the Burgundian buildings, though its influence was not strong enough to impede the further development of the style as it did in Provence.

Cluny had been founded by the reforming party in the Benedictine order who tried to bring it back to its original unworldliness and voluntary poverty. But as has been the case in all similar attempts human nature was Luxury of Cluniacs

---

[1] V.-le-Duc, *Dict. Rais.* vol. I. p. 258. He says elsewhere that this was the only instance in France of a double transept. It occurs however also at S. Quentin.

Cluny

too strong for the reformers; as Cluny grew in power and wealth it fell into ways of luxury and ostentation, and the new abbey church was made as stately and ornate as the art of the day allowed.

Foundation of Citeaux 1098

This departure from the original principles of the Benedictine rule offended the stricter members of the order, and led to a second reformation. The abbey of CITEAUX was founded in 1098 by one-and-twenty Benedictines from Cluny, who were shocked at the growing luxury and splendour of the parent house, and retired to a desert place and extreme simplicity of life. The fame of the order grew rapidly, especially after S. Bernard joined its ranks, and in twenty-five years the Cistercians had spread over Europe and numbered 60,000. The constitution of the order, which was drawn up in 1119,

Severity of Cistercian architecture

laid down strict rules for the buildings. The monastery Close was to contain all necessary workshops, a mill, and a garden, so that the monks need not go abroad. The church was to be of great simplicity; there were to be no paintings or sculptures; the glass was to be white without cross or ornament, and the bell-tower was to be low and unostentatious.

S. Bernard

In the year 1091 S. Bernard was born of a knightly family near Dijon. He entered the convent of Citeaux at the age of 22, and before he was 24 he was elected first abbot of the daughter house of CLAIRVAUX. His new abbey was built strictly according to the severe Cistercian rules, and the Emperor Lothaire who visited it with his suite was struck with its modest simplicity. In a letter to William, Abbot of S. Theoderic (Thierry), S. Bernard inveighs against the luxuriousness of the Cluniacs. He condemns the splendid dress of the monks: "a King, or an Emperor," he says, "might wear our garments if they were cut to his fashion." He exposes the parade of the bishops and abbots, who carry all their furniture and plate about with them when they travel. "Could you not use the same vessel for sprinkling your hands, and drinking your wine? Could you not have a candle without carrying about your own candlestick, and that of gold or silver? Could not the same servant be both groom and bedmaker, and also wait at table?" Alluding no doubt to the great church then building at Cluny, he speaks of the immense heights of the oratories, their immoderate lengths, their great empty widths, their sumptuous finish, their curious paintings, which attract the eyes of the worshippers and hinder their devotions, and seem to represent mainly the ancient rite of the Jews. "What fruit," he continues, "do we expect from all this,—the admiration of fools, or the offerings of the simple?" *S. Bernard on luxury*

Condemns fine architecture

"Even on the floor are images of saints, which we tread upon. Men spit in the face of an angel, and trample on the features of saints."

Then he turns to the cloisters and their carving. "Why these unclean apes? Why these savage lions? Why these monstrous centaurs? Why the half-men? Why the spotted tigers? Why the trumpeting huntsmen? You may see many bodies with one head, and again many heads on one body; quadrupeds with the tail of a serpent, fish with the head of a quadruped, beasts, in front a horse, dragging half a goat behind. Here a horned animal carries a horse behind. In short there appears so great and strange a variety of divers forms that you may if you please read in marble instead of books, and spend the whole day in looking at these things one by one rather than in meditating on the law *Condemns grotesques* of God. Good God! if you are not ashamed of such silly things, why do you not grudge the expense[1]?"

<small>Influence of Cistercian rule on design</small>

These Puritan principles, however, did little to check the artistic ardour of the 11th and 12th centuries. Art was alive; in those days it ran in the blood of both Burgundian, Frank and Provençal. The utmost the Cistercian rule did was to direct the character of architectural design, not to hinder it. The early Cistercian buildings are plain and unadorned with sculpture, but they are not the less beautifully designed, and they illustrate the great truth, so often forgotten, that architecture does not depend on ornament, and may, if required, do without it. Just as the Moslem managed to build beautifully and romantically though his religion debarred him from the resources of sculpture, so the Cistercians, while obeying the severe restrictions of their rule in the matter of decoration, have managed to leave us some of the loveliest buildings of the Middle Ages.

<small>Ruin of Cluny, &c.</small>

Of Cluny, as we have seen, little enough remains. What is left of Citeaux and Clairvaux—chiefly modern—has been turned in one case into a penitentiary, in the other into a prison. The great church of S. Bernard, where he was buried, was pulled down not by the revolutionaries, but by the restored Bourbon king. We can only conjecture their vanished splendours by the analogy of contemporary Burgundian buildings, of which the province fortunately possesses many fine examples[2].

<small>Abbey of Vézelay</small>

The abbey church of VÉZELAY was begun in 1089, at the same time as the new church at Cluny, but at Vézelay the art took a great step forward. While

---

[1] Sancti Bernardi *op.* ed. Mabillon, vol. I. *Apologia ad Guillelmum Sancti Theoderici Abbatem,* cap. X. XI. XII.

[2] M. V.-le-Duc says that the church at Citeaux had a square east end. Cluny and Clairvaux were apsidal. *Dict. Rais.* vol. I. p. 270—2.

at Cluny, as also at Autun and other churches which were built 60 or 70 years later, the nave was covered with a barrel vault, at Vézelay for the first time the attempt was made to apply to the great nave vault the principle of cross-vaulting which had till then only been employed in the lesser vaults of the aisles. This was a great step in advance, and paved the way for the further development of vaulting into the Gothic construction of rib and panel. It got rid at once of a constructional difficulty and a practical inconvenience. *Vézelay*

The difficulty of constructing a barrel vaulted nave lay in the necessary buttressing, for its thrust was continuous along the whole length of the wall. Consequently in the churches of the Auvergne, and at S. Sernin, Toulouse, and many others the side aisles were vaulted with quadrant vaults, half semi-circular, starting from a stout outside wall, and abutting on the nave wall against the springing of the main central vault. The inconvenience of this is that no clerestory windows are possible, and the nave, lit only from the ends, is very dark. To remedy this the next step was to raise the nave and to form a clerestory. But in doing this the nave vault was deprived of the support of the aisle vaults, and disaster followed. At Autun an improvement was made by making the nave barrel vault pointed instead of round, which diminished the thrust, but not effectually, and before long flying buttresses had to be applied to resist it[1]. At the best this plan only allowed very small clerestory windows, low down in the wall, below the springing of the barrel vault. The obvious way of *Inconveniences of barrel vaults* *Pointed barrel vaults at Autun*

[1] The fine church at Saulieu is vaulted with a pointed barrel vault in the same manner, and the walls have given way in consequence. When I saw it in 1908 its condition seemed very perilous.

Difficulties of cross-vaulting the nave

getting large clerestory windows was to cross-vault the nave, but this presented difficulties of another kind. The aisles had long been cross-vaulted after the Roman fashion. Their bays were generally square in plan, and the intersection of two equal cylinders presented no difficulty. But the nave being perhaps twice as wide as the aisles, the bay of vaulting would not be square but oblong; and consequently the transverse arch and cross section would be so much wider than the wall arch and the longitudinal section that the two cylinders would not intersect agreeably. This difficulty was got over at S. Ambrogio in Milan by making each bay of the nave vault as long as two bays of the aisle which brought it to a square plan, and made the intersection regular (*v. sup.* vol. I. p. 262, Fig. 58). This, however, is not the way followed at Vézelay, where the nave vault corresponds bay by bay with that of the aisle (Fig. 93). No attempt was made to raise the side arches to the level of the transverse, but they were high enough to give plenty of room for a good clerestory, and their cross vault was ramped upwards intersecting with the main longitudinal vault as best it could. In this way a good light was acquired for the nave, and the difficulty of the continuous thrust of a barrel vault was avoided.

Resultant thrust of the cross vault

For the effect of cross-vaulting is to concentrate all the thrust on isolated points, that is on the piers that divide bay from bay. But the system was not complete, for the builders of Vézelay did not understand at first the need of strengthening these points sufficiently to take this concentrated thrust: and to their surprise the vaults began to push the walls out, the arches became distorted, and at the end of the 12th century flying buttresses had to be applied at the points where resistance was required.

Fig. 93 (V.-le-Duc).

Vézelay, the vault

Still the step first taken at Vézelay was a great advance on previous construction, and led on naturally to the further development of vaulting on more scientific principles.

The choir and transepts of Vézelay were re-built in the 13th century, between 1198 and 1206[1], in a vigorous early pointed style, of which they afford one of the finest examples. But the Romanesque nave which was dedicated about 1102 remains, and the narthex which was dedicated in 1132. In the latter, benefiting by their experience of the nave, the builders adopted a more secure way of supporting the main vault. The narthex, like that at Cluny is a church by itself (Plate CXIII), with a nave and aisles, three bays long and two storeys in height. The aisles are cross vaulted in the lower storey, while the upper, which is a **triforium** or gallery, has a ramping vault that gives effectual abutment to the vault of the central nave. In the narthex the pointed arch makes its appearance in the constructive features for the first time. All the nave arches are round.

Vézelay, narthex

Vézelay, nave

The nave and aisles are in a sombre round-arched style; and the stringcourses and labels are heavy, and decorated with rosettes, a favourite Burgundian ornament. The piers are compound, with attached shafts; and the arches, as well as the transverse ribs of the vault are built with alternate voussoirs of white and dark brown stone, one of the few instances of polychrome masonry in France. There is no triforium, and the clerestory windows are plain semi-circular headed openings, splayed all round both inside and out. A characteristic feature

---

[1] V.-le-Duc, vol. I. p. 232. He says the Abbot Hugh was deposed in the last year for having run the monastery into debt to the amount of 2220 silver livres or £45,600 of our money.

in the design is a wavy—heralds would call it nebuly—ornament that runs round the wall arches, and the small outer order, or one might almost call it the label of the transverse arches of the nave vault.

The great west doorway leading from the narthex to the nave (Plate CXIII) is perhaps the finest product of Burgundian Romanesque. It is round arched, and has the usual central pillar dividing the opening and supporting a horizontal lintel. In the middle of the semicircular tympanum is a figure of Christ in a Vesica, bestowing the gift of the Holy Spirit on His disciples, typified by rays emanating from His fingers, and directed to them severally. Round them is a semi-circle of figure subjects in square panels, which is interrupted by the top of the Vesica. There are two orders in the including arch: the inner is filled with small figure-subjects in 29 little circles, representing the signs of the Zodiac, and the occupations of threshing, reaping, putting corn into a sack, and so on. The outer order has a series of conventional bosses.

Vézelay, portal

The smaller figures on the lintel and in the compartments of the arch have defied interpretation. It is difficult to see the meaning of the men and women with dog's heads or pig's snouts, or of the dwarf about to mount on horseback with the aid of a ladder. The larger figures in their convoluted draperies show the influence of Byzantine art, but the sculpture is far removed from the style of that at Arles and S. Gilles. All trace of classic grace is gone, and the design is rather barbarous. The figures are attenuated, and disproportioned, and thrown into attitudes that are forced and extravagant. And yet in spite of its barbarism, the work has not only an undeniable life and spirit but also a

Figure sculpture at Vézelay

Vézelay

kind of primitive refinement. A certain delicacy is given by its peculiar method of execution. The figures are carved as it were in low relief on a flat surface which is then sunk all round them to some depth. This same treatment may be observed in the beautiful Byzantinesque scrolls on the lintels of the north and south doorways at Bourges where the leaves and flowers are carved with a very flat treatment, and much undercut, which gives them a very precious and delicate effect and apparently almost the frailty of paper. There is the same treatment on the rather rude classic frieze of the Roman arch at Susa.

Much of the effect of this grand doorway is owing to the central pier, with its double tier of shafts below and figures above, spreading out to great width as it rises; the upper part immediately below the lintel being occupied by a figure of the Baptist, holding a large disc with a mutilated figure of the mystic lamb, for which the disc formed a nimbus. The same division into two tiers is observed in the jambs.

Vézelay, Chapter House

In many parts of the church, both Romanesque and later, the influence of Roman art is observable, but it is even more remarkably displayed in the Chapter House which dates from about 1150[1]. The great consoles or brackets from which the vaulting ribs spring have the volutes, the foliage, the hollow abacus and the rosette of

Sculpture Roman not Byzantine

the Corinthian capital (Plate CXIV). There is no trace of Byzantine feeling in the leaves, which have the deep channelled folds, the piping and the rounded raffling of the Roman type, as distinct from that of the East. The same influence is observable in the vestibule or cloister to which the Chapter House opens, with its square fluted

[1] V.-le-Duc, VIII. p. 211.

Plate CXIII

The Narthex and West Door—VEZELAY

Plate CXIV

VEZELAY

CH. XXII] FRANCE—BURGUNDY 105

piers and arches (Fig. 94). It has left its mark also on Vézelay
the later choir, which dates from the last year of the
12th century and is in a thoroughly developed pointed Roman
style. The great columns of the apse are monoliths, in the
tapered and with an entasis: one wonders whether they Gothic
may not be real antiques used at secondhand; and in the choir

Fig. 94.

triforium of the apse and that of the north transept square
fluted shafts occur among the ordinary round ones.

The same broad Roman treatment characterizes the Avallon
nave capitals in the fine Romanesque church at AVALLON
and the details of its famous western portals. This
church is basilican in plan, with nave and side aisles
each ending in an apse, and owing to the slope of the
site the floor descends from west to east instead of

Avallon — ascending in the usual manner. The effect of this is not otherwise than agreeable, and the plan might be adopted with advantage in modern churches where similar difficulties of level present themselves. The nave is cross-vaulted, with transverse ribs only, and the aisles also, but they are so narrow that their vaults are longer than they are wide, and as the transverse arches are not much stilted, they have the effect of arched surfaces from one transverse rib to another, and the groins almost disappear. The old system of the barrel vault has gone, and that of the cross vault is being tentatively applied. All the main arches are pointed.

The great portals, which consist of a large doorway to the nave and a lesser one to the south aisle, are full of elaborate but unequal detail. The jambs have columns divided by a particularly beautiful upright acanthus leaf border. Some of the columns are plain, some smooth spirals; others are polygonal and twisted, and one is spiral and carved like chain mail which looks as if it ought to collapse. In the arch of the smaller doorway the scroll-work has a ropy look which is not happy, and the great rosettes on one order are coarse and out of scale with the delicate ornament of the jambs. The same ropy scrolls, and coarse rosettes appear in the south aisle doorway at Vézelay. A band of the Guilloche or Greek fret runs round the lesser arch, carved in that perspective manner which occurs also at S. Gilles, and in many ancient mosaic pavements.

Stages of Burgundian sculpture — In the ornamental sculpture at Vézelay and Avallon we seem to see the early Burgundian school in three successive stages. In the nave at Vézelay the capitals abound in grotesques and figure stories, many of them of religious significance, but some of the type on which

S. Bernard pours his sarcasm. In the narthex, the foliaged capital begins to take the place of these storied compositions, though some of them occur too. But in the Chapter House at Vézelay and at Avallon the purer Corinthian type prevails, so that one wonders whether S. Bernard's diatribes had their effect. It is interesting to see how, while in so short a period as that covered by these buildings the Burgundian carvers made a great advance in technique, they clung with determination to the model supplied by classic art, so that their later work is often nearer to Roman example than their earlier.

Burgundian capitals

Fig. 95.

The Cistercian abbey church of PONTIGNY about 10 miles from Auxerre contrasts strongly with the splendour of the Cluniac buildings. It was built in the latter part of the 12th century with a severity of design that would have satisfied S. Bernard himself. The only tower is a piquant little turret and spire on one side of the façade which is treated with much simplicity; and the great doorway leading to the nave has a plain cross in the tympanum instead of the sculptures of Vézelay, or Moissac. Some of the capitals in the nave are little

Abbey of Pontigny

Pontigny more than geometrical blocks, as abstract as the Moslem capitals in the forecourts of mosques at Constantinople (Fig. 95). But with all its severity the church is beautiful. Let S. Bernard do his best with his spiritual fork, the artistic Burgundian nature nevertheless "usque recurrit." It shows itself in the delicate proportions, in the chaste virginal restraint of the general effect, in the few concessions made to sculptor's art in the matter of simply foliaged capitals, which with all their severity are admirable in their way, and in the glazing of the windows, where though painted glass was forbidden by the strict Cistercian rule, the glazier has revelled in fancy patterns of lead-work.

Autun cathedral The cathedral at AUTUN is later than Vézelay, but the nave retains the pointed barrel roof on transverse arches of the early constructive method, although in the arcades the round arch has given way to the pointed (Fig. 96). Flat pilasters, fluted, carry the nave arches and form the sides of the piers; flat fluted pilasters in front of them rise through triforium and clerestory to carry the transverse ribs of the vaults. Smaller pilasters, flat and fluted like the others divide the round-headed arches of the triforium. A heavy stringcourse carved with simple rosettes like those at Vézelay and Avallon, runs below the triforium, and a smaller one above it is studded with round pellets. Of the capitals some are composed of foliage, twisted, reverted and tied, but many are storied with figure subjects. The bases are Attic in section and tolerably correct.

The aisles are cross-groined with transverse ribs but no diagonals. The nave barrel vault springs so low down that there is only room for very small clerestory windows, as has been explained already (*v.* p. 99), and the church is consequently very dark. There is no

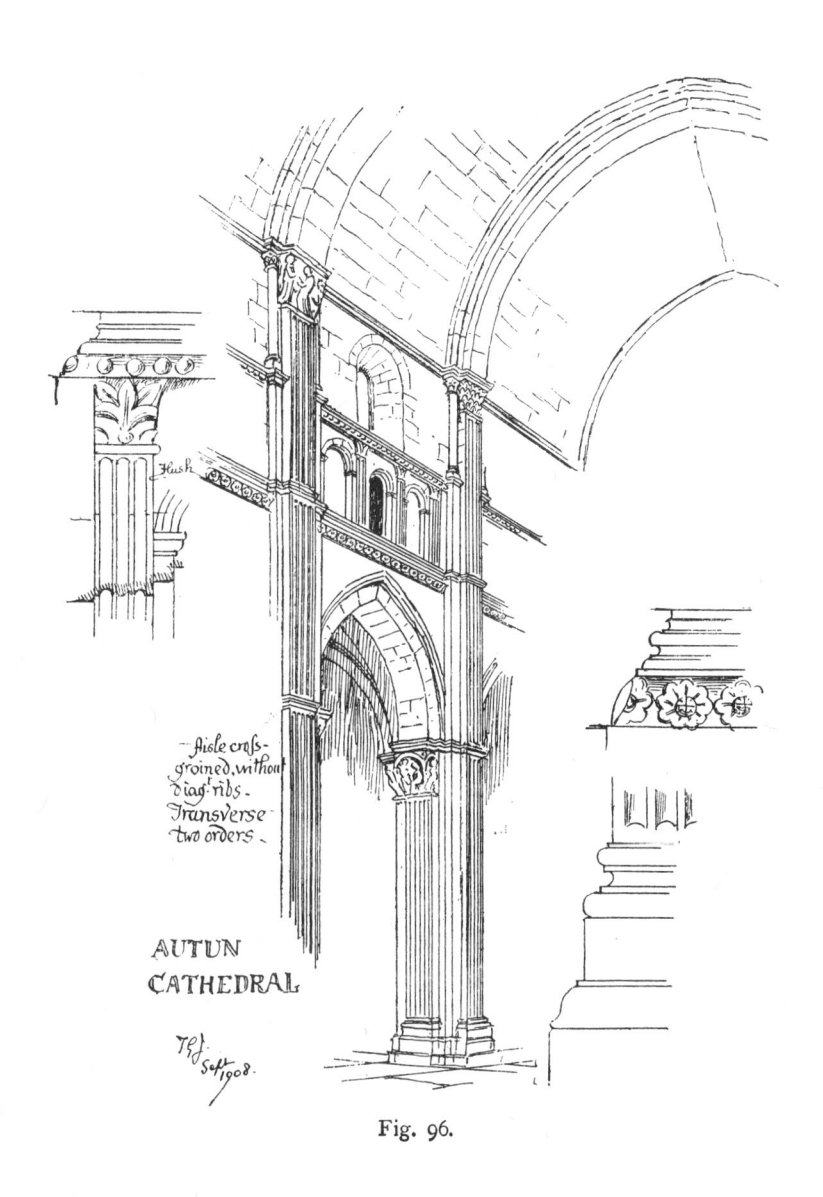

Aisle cross-
groined, without
diag. ribs.
Transverse
two orders.

AUTUN
CATHEDRAL

Fig. 96.

Autun

ambulatory, or *chevet* of chapels, but the church finishes like a basilica with three simple apses at the ends of the choir and its aisles. There are shallow transepts and a central tower over the crossing.

Portal and porch

At the west end is one of the fine porches (Fig. 97) characteristic of Burgundy, but instead of being enclosed like the narthex at Cluny and that still existing at Vézelay the front stands open with arches to the street, a difference which expresses that between Cluny and Vézelay which were regular establishments, and Autun which was a cathedral and secular. The narthex has a central nave and an aisle on each side like the others; all are vaulted, the nave with a semi-circular barrel vault on transverse ribs that spring from attached columns. Under this porch or narthex a magnificent flight of steps reaching from side to side rises with dignity to the portals of the church[1]. The central doorway resembles the great portal of Vézelay. The tympanum contains a figure of our Lord in a vesica which is held up rather ungracefully by two angels at the foot, and two more flying upside down at the head. The scene is the resurrection; angels are blowing the last trump; other angels are receiving the blessed spirits; Michael weighs them in a balance, and devils are carrying off the damned, and thrusting them into the mouth of hell. A similar division of the good and the bad is going on below in a string of little figures along the lintel. A series of texts in Leonine Hexameters on the upper margin of the lintel is interrupted in the middle by the words:—

GISLEBERTVS hOC FECT

[1] Mr Hamerton says the steps are modern, and that before they were made the ascent was by a slope of bare earth.

Fig. 97.

Autun

Of the including orders in the arch, one has a scroll, and the other little circles as at Vézelay with signs of the Zodiac and other figures in them. The columns in the jambs are diapered and scaled, and carry "storied" capitals, and the central pier, like that at Vézelay, has columns and capitals below, and figures above, in this case a bishop supported by two angels.

The sculpture

The sculpture at Autun does not appear to be by the same hand as that at Vézelay, and Gislebert, or Gilbert seems to have reverted somewhat more closely to the Byzantine style in his finely folded and convoluted draperies. The figures at Autun are even more attenuated and drawn out than those at Vézelay, some of the angels being between 10 and 11 heads high. The bishop on the central pillar is in a more advanced style, but the whole of this pier seems modern, and though it no doubt preserves generally the original design one cannot base any argument on its technique.

S. Jean, Autun

The interesting church of S. JEAN at AUTUN observes the Roman tradition in its fluted pilasters, and Corinthianizing capitals, but it has taken a step in advance of the cathedral in its vault, which is cross-groined, so as to allow of large side windows. The church is cruciform, and has no aisles. There are strong transverse ribs carried curiously by short colonnettes bracketed out from the wall pier (Fig. 98), which consequently projects considerably into the church, and helps the abutment. There are no diagonal ribs, and the bay being much shorter from E. to W. than from N. to S. the cross vault has to ramp up like those at Vézelay. The apse is vaulted with radiating ribs between which the panels are arched.

Valence cathedral

At VALENCE the construction of the cathedral is different (Fig. 99). The nave has a barrel vault with strong

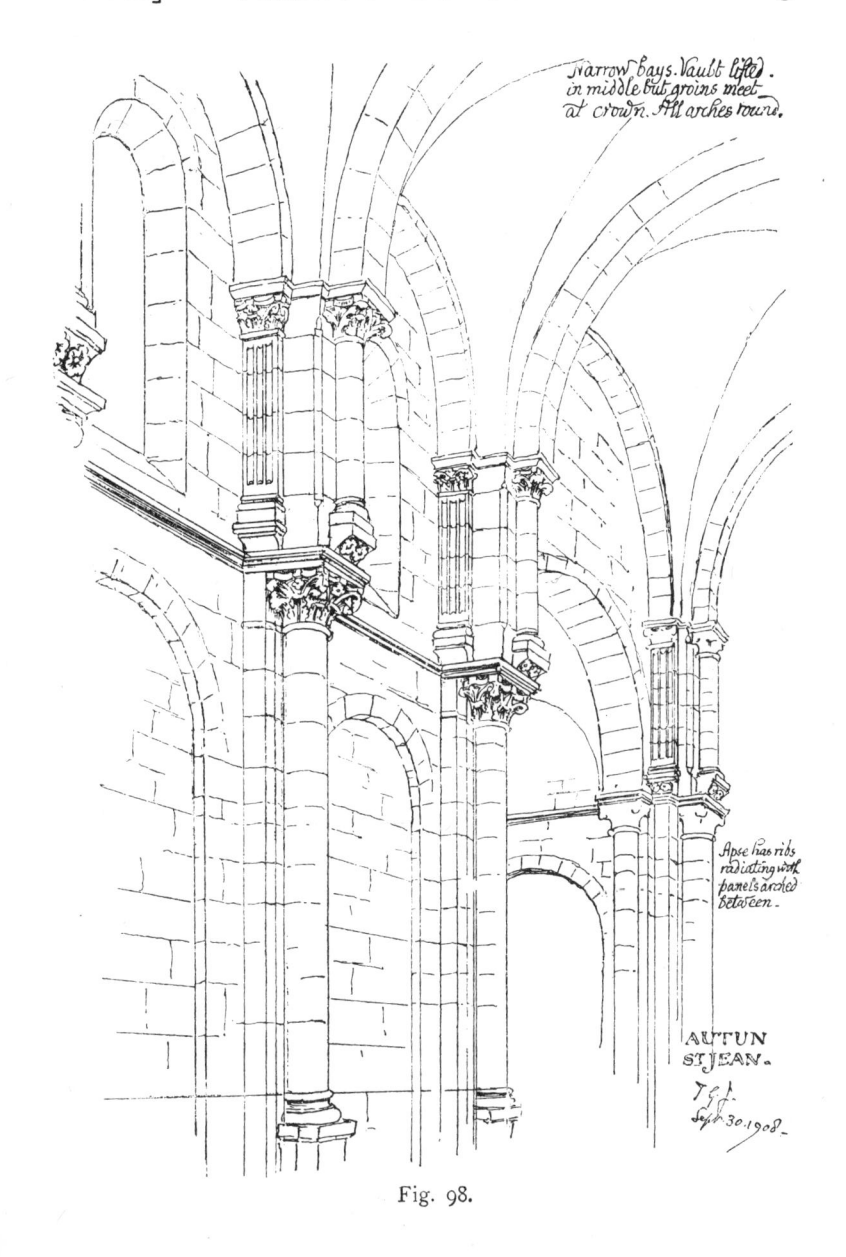

Narrow bays. Vault lifted
in middle but groins meet
at crown. All arches round.

Apse has ribs
radiating with
panels arched
between.

AUTUN
ST JEAN.
T.G.
Sept 30.1908

Fig. 98.

Valence cathedral — transverse ribs springing from semi-circular shafts attached to the front of a square pier. Similar half columns are attached to the other three sides and carry the round arches of the nave and that across the aisle. There is neither triforium nor clerestory; for the aisles, which are cross-groined, are nearly as high as the nave, the vault of which springs from the level of the crown of the aisle arch. Consequently the great vault of the nave is well abutted by those of the aisles. The light is given by large round-headed windows in the upper part of the aisle walls, with jamb shafts in reveals at the sides.

The construction has a certain resemblance to that of some churches in distant Aquitaine, such as that of S. Savin (*v. sup.* Plate CII).

The church is cruciform, with unusually long transepts, and in this district one is surprised to find over the crossing a flattish dome on regular pendentives, another Aquitanian feature. The span of the nave is 28 ft. from centre to centre of the columns, that of the aisles 14; and there are eight bays west of the crossing, which gives the usual basilican proportion, the nave being twice as wide as the aisles, and four times as long as it is wide.

The apse has a semi-dome and is surrounded by a cross-groined ambulatory with four projecting semi-circular chapels. These are buttressed outside by square piers with Corinthianizing capitals like those of the nave pillars. All the windows are round-arched, some with coloured voussoirs, and in the blank arcades occurs the horseshoe trefoil of Auvergne and Le Puy. Throughout this interesting church Roman tradition runs strongly.

Vienne cathedral — It is apparent also in the fluted pilasters and other features of the cathedral of S. MAURICE at VIENNE, a town rich in Roman remains. The desecrated church of

VALENCE CATH^l
Sept 18.1909

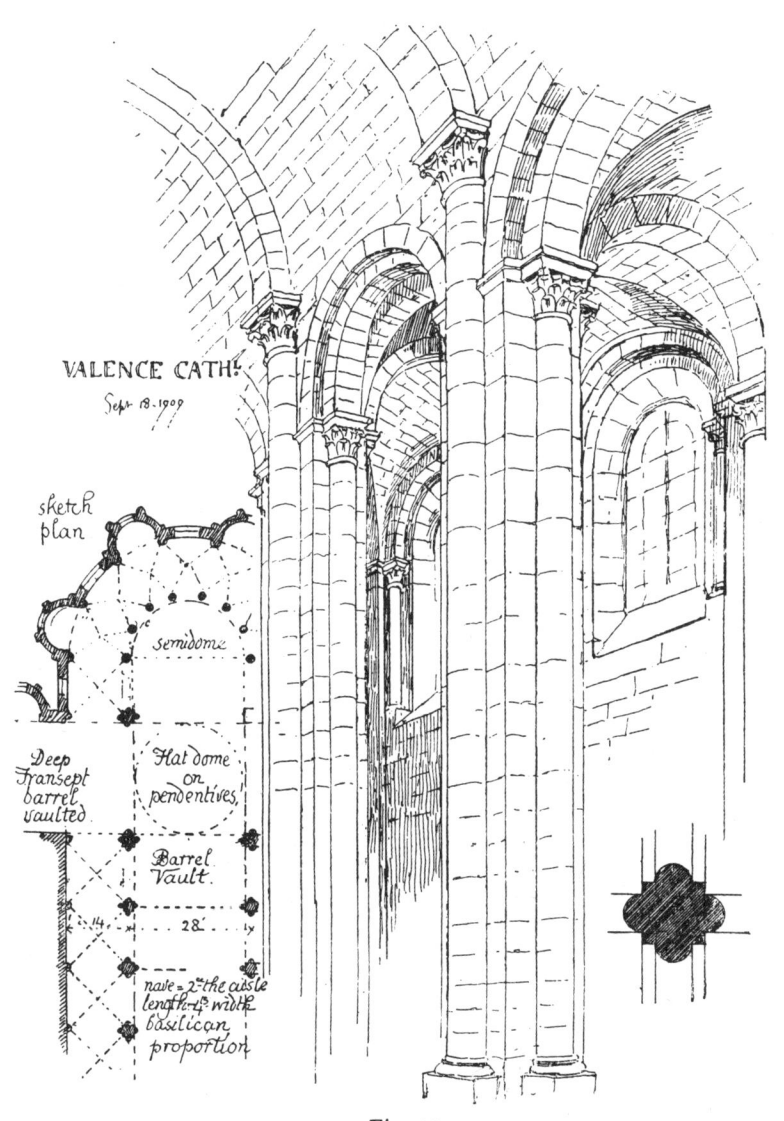

sketch plan

semidome

Deep Transept barrel vaulted

Flat dome on pendentives

Barrel Vault

14. 28.

nave = 2× the aisle length = 4× width basilican proportion

Fig. 99.

<small>S. Pierre, Vienne</small> S. PIERRE, now the museum, was once a Roman hall which was divided into nave and aisles by two walls pierced with arches on plain square piers. At the end, built against the Roman wall and pediment, is a fine Romanesque tower (Plate CXV), once preceded by further buildings now nearly obliterated. The tower is oblong, having three windows in front and two at the sides. Over those of the top stage but one are the horse-shoe trefoiled arches that have been noticed at Valence and will be noticed at Le Puy and in the churches of Auvergne. A plain tiled roof now forms the covering, and the termination originally intended is a matter for conjecture. Among other Burgundian towers there is a good one at Vézelay attached to the south transept, and of the two that originally flanked the west front, one still retains its original upper part, though it has been a good deal spoiled by modern work. At SAULIEU is a fine though imperfect tower, rather later, and with pointed arches.

<small>Abbey of Ainay, Lyons</small> At LYONS, the centre of the old Burgundian kingdom, though the church of Bishop Patiens, which Sidonius Apollinaris celebrated in an ode, cannot now be traced, there remains in the church of the abbey of AINAY (Fig. 100) a building of considerable interest, dating from the 10th and 11th centuries but much altered in subsequent ages. The plan is basilican and cruciform, with barrel-vaulted nave and aisles under the same roof. The columns are cylindrical with capitals of a rude Corinthianizing character. At the east end are three apses corresponding to the nave and aisles and covered with semi-domes.

There are two towers, one over the crossing, low and square, carried on four great granite columns which are

Plate CXV

S. PIERRE—VIENNE

CH. XXII] FRANCE—BURGUNDY 117

antiques cut short, and covering an octagonal dome Abbey of Ainay, resting on squinches with round-arched arcading like Lyons those at Le Puy. The top stage has round arched openings with coupled colonnettes, and finishes with a corbel table and cornice.

The other tower is at the west end and has a low pyramidal spire, and at the angles, by way of pinnacles, four curious "antefixae" or horns, consisting of the fourth part of a pyramid or cone, like those at the angles of a Roman sarcophagus, which probably suggested their

Fig. 100.

form. This seems to be a Burgundian feature, occurring also at Guebviller and in a more elaborate form at Itomes, two churches illustrated by Viollet-le-Duc[1] and I found it in the mountain valleys of Dauphiné at Monestier and in other village churches in the passes leading to Italy. The four granite columns in the interior may perhaps be some of the *Fulmenta Aquitanica superba* of which Sidonius sings (*v. sup.* p. 31).

There is a western gallery over the porch, opening

[1] V.-le-Duc, III. 315, 317; IV. 453.

Chapel of S. Blandina, Lyons

to the nave. The transepts are shallow and do not project beyond the aisles. Outside the south wall of that on the south side is the chapel of S. Blandina which dates probably from the end of the 10th century, but has

Fig. 101.

CAPITALS in CHAPEL of St BLANDINA. LYONS

been so much restored as to have lost its authenticity in a great measure. It consists of a barrel-vaulted nave ending in an apse, raised on four steps, with a crypt below, covered with a cross-groined vault and perfectly plain. The apse is square but has a semi-dome, the corners of the square being curiously cut off by curved arches carried on small columns. The capitals of these columns have escaped restoration and are very typical of their period (Fig. 101).

The cathedral of S. BENIGNE at DIJON still retains the crypt or lower storey of a curious round chapel originally attached to the east end of a basilica which preceded the present Gothic building. All the upper part of the rotunda was destroyed in 1792, but plans, sections, and elevations of the complete building have fortunately been preserved in Plancher's *Histoire générale et particulière de Bourgogne*, published in 1739, when the edifice was intact. At the extreme east end still remains a very early building of the 6th century with a crypt and two storeys over it. The church of the same date to which this adjoined was re-built at the opening of the 11th century by Abbot William of Volpiano in Lombardy, and dedicated in 1018. His building was a basilica ending with three apses, and between these apses and the 6th century chapel he constructed the round church which has been mentioned, to contain the tomb of S. Benigne, of which the crypt alone remains (Fig. 102). It consists of two concentric aisles surrounding a central space, the diameters of the three circles being approximately 20, 40, and 60 ft. respectively[1]. Over the circumambient aisles were two other storeys like them, the lower at the floor level of the church, the upper at that of the triforium. Eight columns surround the middle area, carrying round arches and forming an octagon, and sixteen carry the outer arcade between the aisles. The

[1] The dimensions are given as 5·90 m., 12·10 m., 18·30 m. Rivoira, vol. II. p. 6.

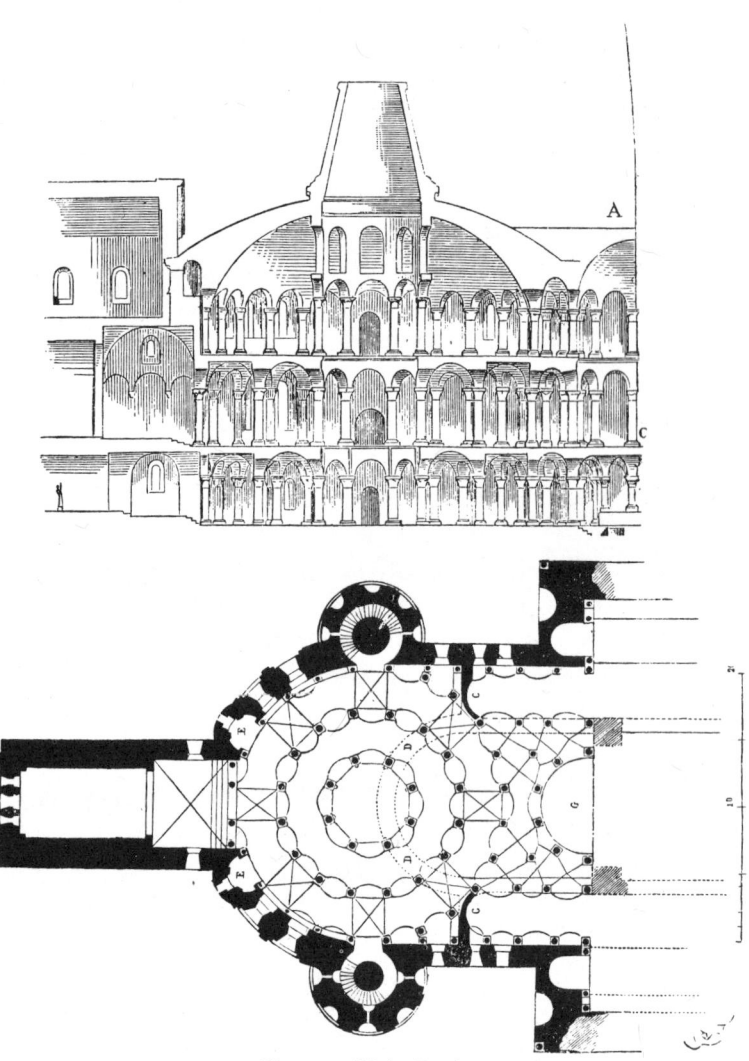

Fig. 102 (V.-le-Duc).

central space was originally open to the sky; a barrel vault covered the next ring, and a vault part barrel and part cross-groined the outer one. In the upper storey the outer ring of columns was omitted, but that round the central area ran up as an octagonal tower, against which an annular quadrant vault springing from the outer wall abutted. In later times a lantern seems to have been placed over the central opening. Two massive round towers projecting from the north and south sides contained winding staircases communicating with all three storeys. Dijon, S. Benigne

It is curious that Abbot William's rotunda seems to have been imitated at Canterbury. About 30 years after the dedication of S. Augustine's Abbot Wilfric returned from France, where he may have seen the church at Dijon, and at the end of his basilica connecting it with an existing Lady Chapel, he too built a round chapel of which the foundations were laid bare in 1915. The monks however found it inconvenient, and though the county of Kent rejoiced in its beauty it was pulled down in 1080[1].

The design of Abbot William's work is rude in the extreme. The arches are cut square through the wall without any moulding, and the capitals of the monocylindrical pillars are mere cubes of stone with the four angles chamfered from square above to octagon below. The few faint attempts at sculpture are barbarous and infantile. Towards the west, where re-construction took place after the central tower of the basilica fell in 1096, causing considerable damage to the adjacent parts, the sculptor has attempted something more ambitious but with lamentable results. The architectural design how- Rudeness of the work

---

[1] Letabatur novo opere Cantia quamquam monastice habitationi incongruum fecisset artificum imperitia. See account and plans in *Archaeologia*, vol. LXVI.

William of Volpiano

ever is far ahead of the decorative work, and displays great originality. When perfect, this rotunda, in spite of its barbarous detail, must have been a very striking and interesting monument, and its construction which lasted for nearly eight centuries was daring and successful. Its architect Abbot William was an Italian of Swabian descent on his father's side, but his mother was of a noble Italian family. He entered the abbey of Cluny under Abbot Maiolus, and was made Abbot of S. Benigne about 990. Two lives of him, which have been preserved[1], bear witness to his activity in opening schools for poor clerks, seeing that not only in Burgundy but throughout all France they were deficient in knowledge of chanting and reading. His energy in building was not less than his zeal for education. Finding the church of S. Benigne past repair he took that as a divine call to re-build it. Bishop Bruno of Langres found the means, and collected columns of marble and stone from all about, probably despoiling older structures, and Abbot William brought master craftsmen, and himself directed the work[2]. Scholars, craftsmen of various trades, and skilled husbandmen flocked to him in great numbers from his native Italy[3] by whose art and genius we are told the place profited much. He died at Fécamp in Normandy, in which connexion we shall hear of him again.

Round churches

It is generally said that these round churches, whether built over a tomb, like this one at Dijon over the tomb of S. Benigne, or over a cenotaph like that at Neuvy

---

[1] Mabillon, *Acta Sanctorum ordinis Sancti Benedicti*, vol. VI. part I. p. 286.

[2] Reverendus abbas magistros conducendo et ipsum opus dictando. *Cronaca S. Benigni Divionensis*, D'Achery, *Spicilegium*, II. p. 381.

[3] Item :—Coeperunt denique ex sua patria, hoc est Italia, multi ad eum convenire : aliqui literis bene eruditi, alii diversorum operum magisterio docti, alii agriculturae scientia praediti. Quorum ars et ingenium huic loco profuit plurimum. *Ibid.*

S. Sepulchre which enclosed a model of the tomb at Jerusalem, or like the Templars' churches with an obvious reference to the object of their order, were imitated from the Church of the Holy Sepulchre. The rotunda there was originally open to the sky in the centre, and was surrounded like that at S. Benigne with concentric aisles, and Viollet-le-Duc points out the resemblance between the two which suggests imitation[1]. Sigr. Rivoira on the other hand who writes with the object of minimising the influence of the East on the architecture of the West during the Romanesque period, thinks the suggestion came rather from the domed mausolea of Roman work such as that of the Princess Constantia which was built between 326 and 329, and that of the Empress Helena. Neither of these however had an open eye in the centre of the dome, though S. Costanza has the annular vaulted aisle which occurs at Dijon. He says that the fashion of rotundas with cupolas and annular vaults was imported from Rome to the East, and not as some suppose from the East to the West[2]. However this may be it would not follow that the rotunda at Jerusalem was not taken as the model for S. Benigne and other round churches in the west of Europe in the 11th century because it was itself based upon western examples of the 4th. Of Neuvy S. Sepulchre it is expressly recorded that it was built "*ad formam S. Sepulchri Jerosolimitani*[3]."

Round churches

Church of the Holy Sepulchre

It was from the workshops of Cluny that architecture made a fresh start in France. But independently of the shelter afforded by the cloister to the peaceful arts the Burgundians themselves seem to have had a natural turn for the manual crafts. The Byzantine historian of the

The Cluniac school

[1] V.-le-Duc, VIII. 283.
[2] Rivoira, *Origini*, etc. vol. II. p. 32.
[3] *Archives des monuments historiques*, cited V.-le-Duc, VIII. 283.

5th century says of them that "they lead an easy life all their time. For they are nearly all of them craftsmen, and subsist on the wages they get thereby[1]." Under the protection of the Church their native bent for the arts found full scope for its efforts, and a school of architecture was founded of which the influence spread far and wide wherever the Cluniac order extended itself. At the end of the 12th century architecture ceased to be in the hands of the clergy and passed into those of laymen in France, as it had done long before in Italy, but till then the Cloister was the centre of all progress in the civil arts and in the spread of knowledge. Hallam, while condemning superstition and other evils that attached to the monastic system, says[2], "we can hardly regret in reflecting on the desolating violence which prevailed that there should have been some green spots in the wilderness where the feeble and the persecuted could find refuge. How must this right have enhanced the veneration for religious institutions! How gladly must the victims of internal warfare have turned their eyes from the baronial castle, the dread and scourge of the neighbourhood, to those venerable walls within which not even the clamour of arms could be heard to disturb the chant of holy men and the sacred service of the altar!" The regular clergy conducted schools in which were taught letters, philosophy, theology, such science as the age possessed, and the arts. From this centre masters of the various crafts issued forth to carry them into other places. In 1009, before the great church of Cluny was built, Abbot Hugh the

The cloister the refuge of the arts

Foreign influence of Cluny

---

[1] ἔθνος ἐστὶ βάρβαρον πέραν τοῦ ποταμοῦ ʽΡήνου ἔχον τὴν οἴκησιν, Βουργουνζίωνες καλοῦνται. Οὗτοι βίον ἀπράγμονα ζῶσιν ἀεί· τέκτονες γὰρ σχεδὸν πάντες εἰσίν, καὶ ἐκ ταύτης μισθὸν λαμβάνοντες ἀποτρέφονται. Socr. *Hist. Eccl.* VII. c. 30.

[2] *Middle Ages*, chap. IX. part I.

Venerable sent out a disciple Jean de Farfa with instructions and a specification for the buildings of the monastery in his native place. "The church was to be 140 feet long with 160 windows, glazed; to have two towers at the entrance, forming a parvise for the laity; the dormitory was to be 140 feet long, 34 high[1], with 92 glazed windows each over 6 feet high by $2\frac{1}{2}$ wide; the refectory was to by 90 feet long and 23 high, the almonry 60 feet long, the workshops of the glaziers, jewellers, and goldsmiths 125 feet long by 25 wide; the stables for the monastery and for guests 280 feet long by 25[2]."

The ample provision made for workshops shows how vital a part of the conventual system the crafts were considered in the 11th and 12th centuries, and how they were practised and developed within the protection of the cloister side by side with the literary labours which have given us the splendidly written manuscripts and illuminations of those centuries. Convent workshops

The Cistercians were not behind the Cluniacs in the matter of architecture, though one can always recognize one of their churches by its severity and restraint of ornament. In subduing the decoration they followed, at all events at first, the rigid rule of S. Bernard; and this had the effect of retarding the progress of Romanesque architecture during the latter part of its course, so long as its practice was confined to clerical hands. Monastic architecture as time went on lost the life and freshness of its earlier stages, and tended to become stereotyped. Long after in lay hands the art had begun to develop new forms, and to employ novel principles of construction the monastic buildings bore a conservative character, and lagged behind The Cistercians Stagnation of monastic architecture

---

[1] This must have included in the height a ground storey below.
[2] L'Abbé Cucherat, *Cluny au XI siècle*, cited V.-le-Duc, l. 125.

those that were being raised by the new schools that arose outside the Cloister.

<small>Material in Burgundy</small>   Burgundy, besides the natural capacity of its people for the arts, and the powerful influence of the great regular establishments which fostered their efforts, possessed also great advantages in the splendid stone that was quarried there. Nowhere perhaps did the crafts of masonry reach higher perfection than there and in the bordering province of Champagne, during the succeeding <small>S. Urbain of Troyes</small> period of the Gothic style. In the church of S. URBAIN at TROYES we have a miracle of masonry. Every part of the construction shows complete knowledge of the strength of the material and exact appreciation of the task imposed upon it. The supports are reduced to a minimum, and seem scarcely equal to their work. To an artist's eye the work looks thin and wiry: it seems as if science were getting ahead of art, and the design savours more of engineering than of architecture. Wonderful as it is, fuller satisfaction may I think be got out of the massive work of the Burgundian Romanesque where there is a more generous allowance of material and more obvious sufficiency of support, even if it be often superfluous. And in the quaint imaginings of the storied capitals, amid which the fancy of the carver ran riot, and in the strange stiff sculptures of the tympana to which archaicism seems to lend a mystery, one finds something more interesting and even more sympathetic than in the brisk caps *à crochet*, and the more facile sculptures of the later Gothic at the end of the 13th and in the 14th centuries, by the side of which the earlier sculptures betray, it must be admitted, a spice of barbarism.

CHAPTER XXIII

AUVERGNE

THE county of Auvergne, with Clermont for its capital, till the middle of the 10th century recognized the Duchy of Aquitaine as its feudal superior, and after that the Counts of Toulouse got possession of it. In the early part of the 12th century however the Counts of Auvergne again did homage to Guienne[1]. The political connexion with these different powers at different times explains to some extent the architecture of the province, which at Le Puy seems influenced by the domes of Aquitaine, and in the decorations of Notre Dame du Port at Clermont, and the group of buildings belonging to the same class, appears to be affected by the traditions of the south.

The architecture of the province however has a strong individuality, and the churches of Auvergne may be said to have a style of their own. The best known examples are those of Notre Dame du Port at Clermont-Ferrand, Issoire, S. Nectaire, and Brioude, all of which except the last named, which is rather later, date from the beginning of the 12th century. *The Auvergnat style*

The plan is cruciform, but the management of the crossing is singular, and very beautifully contrived. The ground plan (Figs. 104, 105) does not suggest the peculiarity of the upper part, for the deep transepts instead of

---

[1] Hallam, *Middle Ages*, chap. I.

128 FRANCE—AUVERGNE [CH. XXIII

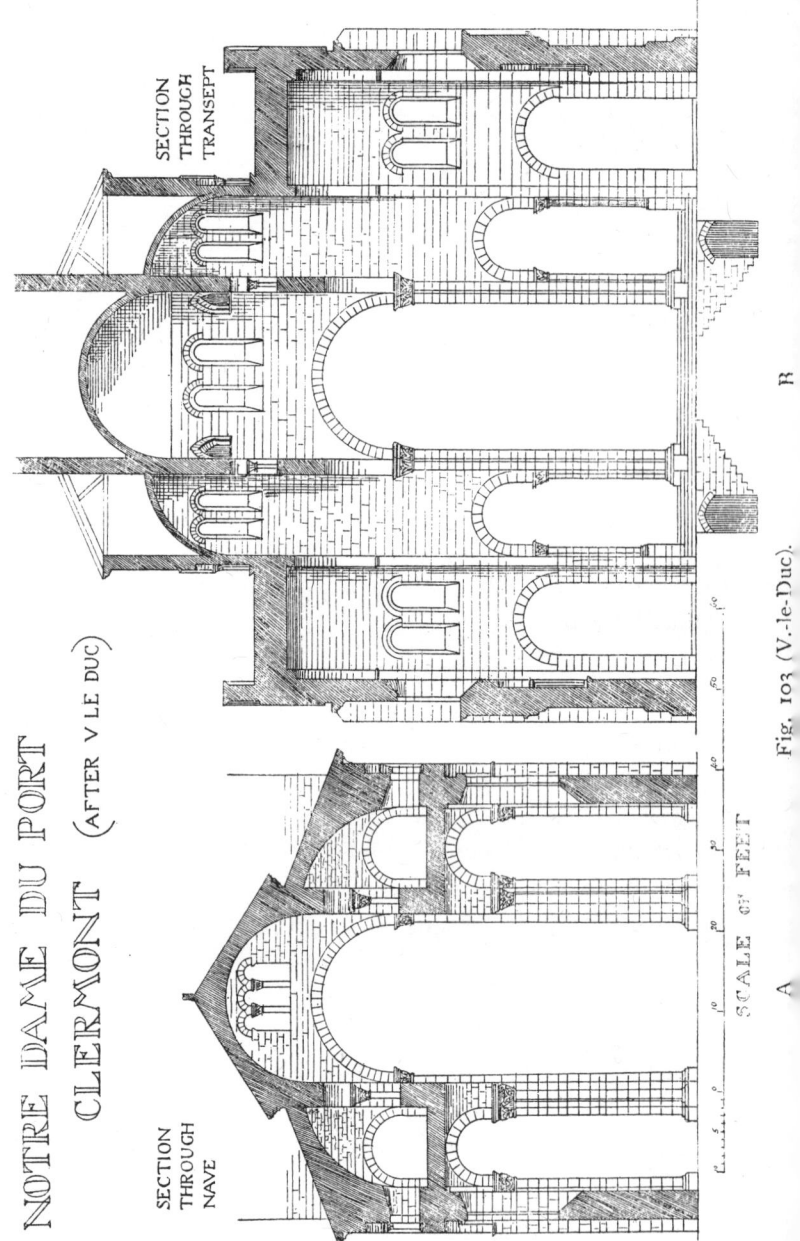

NOTRE DAME DU PORT CLERMONT (AFTER V LE DUC)

SECTION THROUGH TRANSEPT

SECTION THROUGH NAVE

SCALE OF FEET

Fig. 103 (V.-le-Duc).

rising in the usual way for their whole extent to the same height as the nave and choir, have only their inner part, corresponding to the nave aisles, carried up, while so much of the transept as projects beyond the aisles is kept lower (Fig. 103 B). All four arms of the building are covered with barrel vaults which are stopped at the central crossing by a tower and cupola. This is not constructed as a true dome, but an octagon is formed by squinch arches, and carried up as an octagonal tower to a considerable height, where it finishes with a pyramidal roof.

<small>The Auvergnat transept</small>

This break in the height of the transept is an admirable contrivance for setting off the central tower and spire to the best advantage. It escapes the fault of appearing to bury the tower between converging roofs, and also that of seeming to carry the tower on the roof itself. Instead of this the short high transept, not much wider than the tower, seems to afford it a good broad base to stand upon, and to form a sort of shoulder to support it, which it does with a very dignified effect. At the same time the floor space is not affected or diminished by the unequal height of the transept roof, and an opportunity is afforded for windows to light the central part of the church.

The central tower is supported on four great arches which are steadied by the barrel vaults of the nave and choir on two sides, and on the other two by half-barrel vaults over the raised parts of the transept, which pitch against it (Fig. 103 B). These half-barrels in their turn have their thrust resisted by barrel vaults running crossways to them over the lower part of the transept.

The barrel vault of the nave is supported by a continuous half-barrel vault over the triforium of the aisles (Fig. 103 A), the aisle below being cross-vaulted.

<small>Construction of roof</small>

The strength of this construction consequently depends entirely on the stability of the outer walls, which are very slightly buttressed, but are very massive, and as they have proved effective the construction may be pronounced to be in perfect equilibrium.

The Auvergnat construction

On these vaults the roof is laid directly, without any timber construction such as was required when the art of cross-vaulting with rib and panel was perfected. The barrel vault, especially when pointed as it was in later examples, could easily be covered with a gabled roof. In Constantinople and the East the curved back of the vault would have been allowed to show itself, as it does in the smaller temple of Diocletian's palace at Spalato, and the lead or tiling would have been laid on the back of the arch, but this fashion never obtained in western Europe, where the gabled roof is universal.

Its defects

The drawback to this mode of construction is that the half-barrel vaults over the triforium, in order to abut the great central one over the nave, had to pitch against it at such a height as to make a clerestory impossible; and the only light the church could receive was by the lower windows in the aisles, those at the east and west ends, and what little stole in through small windows at the back of the triforium.

Polychrome masonry

Another striking feature of these Auvergnat churches is the polychrome masonry with which they are decorated (Plate CXVI). Situated as they are among the extinct volcanoes of the Puy de Dome, the black basaltic rock of the district is used as a freestone in their construction; and advantage is taken of this to mix it with yellowish white stone in mosaic patterns on the exterior walls. Not only are the arches made with black and white voussoirs alternately, but the gables, and the spandrils of

Plate CXVI

BRIOUDE

Plate CXVII

NOTRE DAME DU PORT—CLERMONT-FERRAND

the arches are faced with mosaic in geometrical figures, not unlike those at the Byzantine palace of Constantine Porphyrogenitus (Plate XXIII, vol. I. p. 140), and a fine wide frieze of it is carried round the main apse below the cornice. In the little chapel of S. Michel, which crowns so picturesquely its needle of rock at Le Puy, little bits of white marble are introduced with good effect among the patterns of black and yellow. This form of decoration seems to suggest an oriental origin, for mosaic was distinctly a Byzantine art to begin with. As the fashion for polychrome masonry did not spread in France, nor indeed did it continue even in this district, one may imagine it the result of some fortunate visit to the Auvergne of a Greek or Venetian, to whom the sight of mosaic was familiar, and who, struck with the possibilities of so unusual a material as the black basalt, conceived the happy idea of contrasting it in patterns with lighter stone. The Auvergnats did not persevere in the kind of design so happily begun, and the later cathedral at Clermont is built entirely of basalt without any relief, and with a dismal effect of colour. Except to a certain extent at Vézelay I know no other instance of polychrome masonry in France, and in that respect English architecture is perhaps richer than French. *[S. Michel de l'Aiguille; Polychrome masonry abandoned]*

There is a strong classic feeling in the cornices of the exterior of these churches, which have a considerable projection and are carried on regular modillions. These, at Notre Dame du Port, are queerly fashioned as if they had been of wood, and the carpenter had begun to sink the sides, leaving a bracket in the middle, but had left off before cutting out the curled shavings resulting from the operation of his chisel. Some such incident of the workshop probably suggested the design. This fancy *[Classic feeling in Auvergne]* however is not peculiar to Auvergne. Corbels with these curious curled sides occur in the cornice of the church of S. Radegond in the outskirts of Tours, and in that of the ancient baptistery of S. Leonard near Limoges.

Notre Dame du Port, Clermont

The church of NOTRE DAME DU PORT, at CLERMONT-FERRAND, is the best known example of these Auvergnat buildings, and exhibits all the local peculiarities that have been mentioned. It is cruciform, and the transepts are broken in height to form the shoulder or base for the tower over the crossing[1], which contains an octagonal dome on squinches (Fig. 104). The nave

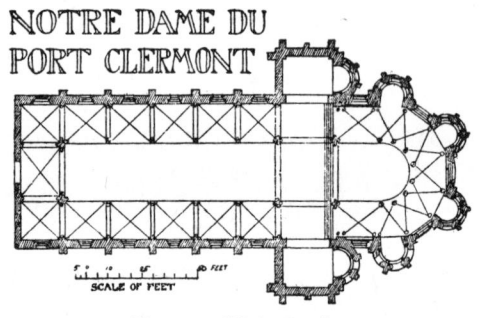

Fig. 104 (V.-le-Duc).

has a barrel vault; the arches are plain and square in section without mouldings, and the piers are square with an attached shaft on all four sides, of which that towards the nave runs up as if to carry a transverse arch which however is wanting. The aisles are lofty and are cross-groined with transverse ribs from each pier to attached wall-shafts. The triforium is covered with the half-barrel, or quadrant vault described above; small slits give it light, and it opens to the nave with triple arcading of

[1] This tower is a modern restoration, though a very satisfactory one. I have seen an old print which shows nothing above the roofs of nave and transepts but a small wooden belfry.

columns carrying the horse-shoe trefoiled arches which are a characteristic of Auvergne and Burgundy. *Notre Dame du Port*

The apse is barrel-vaulted with a semi-dome, and has a *chevet* with an ambulatory which is cross-groined without transverse ribs. Four semi-circular chapels project from this, the central bay eastwards having a window instead of the usual chapel. This arrangement occurs also at the church of Chamalières on the way to Royat.

There is a crypt below the choir with a double descent, and at the west end is a gallery over a vaulted porch, opening to the nave and aisle, which also is a favourite feature of the Auvergnat plan.

All the capitals are carved with figures of sacred subjects, both inside and out of the church[1]. *The sculpture*

The south door (Plate CXVIII) is beautiful, and very characteristic of the style. The pedimental lintel reminds one of some of the Byzantine doorheads, such as that of Bishop Handegis at Pola. In the centre of it is carved a conventional temple with altar and hanging lamp; next to it on one side is a group of the Presentation, and beyond it the Baptism with angels holding towels. On the other side is the Virgin with the Infant Saviour, to whom the three Magi approach with offerings. Inscriptions in hexameter verse describe the subjects. Above under a horseshoe arch is a seated figure of our Lord between two six winged Seraphs recalling those in the mosaics at S. Sophia. Right and left of the door are single figures on brackets under a hood, but not niched into the wall, and above are two groups of small figures, one of which is much perished.

The sculpture on the lintel is very deeply cut, and sunk in the solid: the other figures are planted on the

[1] *v.* Illustrations in the *Musée du Trocadero*, Plates 181, 330, 332.

Notre Dame du Port

face of the wall in a manner typical of the style. The wall has been much restored but the figures are not touched, and it would seem they are in their original position.

The side walls are arcaded outside, and studded in the head of the arches with sections of basaltic columns. The east end is more richly decorated with rough mosaic work in lava and white stone than any other church of this Auvergnat style (Plate CXVII).

Issoire

The church at ISSOIRE (Fig. 105) is the largest of the

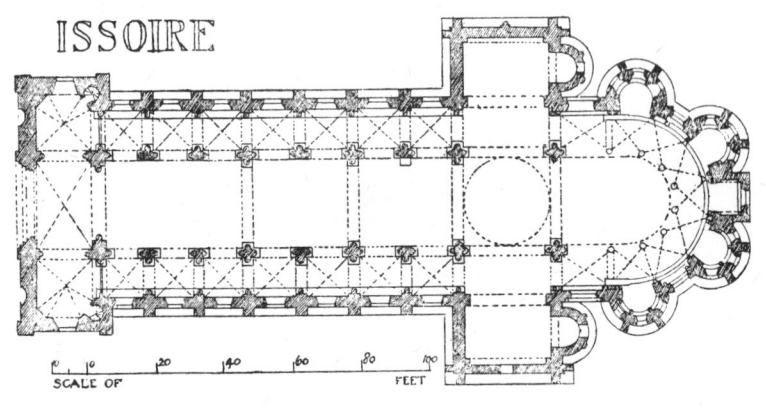

Fig. 105.

group, but the description of the construction at Notre Dame du Port will apply almost word for word to this building also. The nave is lofty and barrel vaulted, the piers are square with attached shafts, of which that on the nave side runs up, but there is no transverse rib to rest on it. There is a western tower, and a gallery over a porch across the front; the transept is of two heights, and over the crossing is an octagonal dome on squinches, but here it is little more than a square with the corners taken off. The choir as at Clermont and Brioude is lower

Plate CXVIII

NOTRE DAME DU PORT—CLERMONT-FERRAND

Plate CXIX

S. NECTAIRE

than the nave, which allows the central tower to be well seen. The four arches of this tower are adapted to the height of the choir and not that of the nave, so that over them on all four sides is room for a triple arch, that on the east being a window while the others are open arcades looking into nave and transepts. The nave has a triforium with horseshoe trefoiled arches, and the upper part is very dark.

In one respect Issoire differs from Clermont: it has a chapel at the east end of the *chevet*, instead of a window. This central chapel is square unlike the other four which are semicircular. Rude sculptures are dotted about the exterior walls, and the capitals are storied as at Notre Dame du Port.

S. NECTAIRE (Fig. 106) has the smallest church of this group. It is situated on a lofty rock in scenery that is almost Alpine, and is reached by a drive of about two and a half hours from Issoire, through a fine country. The construction here is exactly like those already described, with barrel vaults to nave, quadrant vault over triforium, cross-vaulted aisles, west gallery opening by arches over a porch into nave and aisle, *chevet* with ambulatory, semi-circular chapels, and exterior mosaic, and a central tower with dome. A single roof as usual covers both nave and aisles in an unbroken slope. Here however instead of compound piers the nave has cylindrical columns, with simple Corinthianizing capitals, and the storied capitals are confined to the east end. There are two towers at the west end which give this church an individual character among its fellows. On the whole the interior of S. Nectaire struck me as the most pleasing of all these Auvergnat churches (Plate CXIX).

BRIOUDE (Plate CXVI, *sup.* p. 130) is the latest of the

Fig. 106.

group in date, and has not only suffered a good deal of renovation in modern times like the rest, but was also a good deal pulled about in the 14th century, when the nave was ceiled with rib and panel vaulting. Two bays of the nave next the crossing remain in their original state: one has three blank arches where the triforium should be, and a circle above; and if this is original it would have prevented a barrel vault. The other bays have a clerestory into which Gothic traceries are inserted. The central tower over the crossing rests on four pointed arches, and is open as a lantern to the floor. The transepts do not outrun the aisles, and are vaulted in two heights, forming a gallery, with a barrel vault above and a cross-groined vault below constructed in ashlar. There is a western tower as at Issoire, and a porch and gallery at the west end. On the south side is a fine porch of simple design.

Brioude

The capitals are mostly Corinthianizing, but some are storied, and some of the pilasters are fluted, which is not common in Auvergne. The advanced style of this church appears in the windows, which instead of the plain round-headed openings of Clermont have two orders of shafts and arches.

The west front is very plain and simple, and this is characteristic of all these Auvergnat churches, in which the attention of the architect seems to have been chiefly bestowed on the eastern end with its chapels, and the central tower.

Simplicity of Auvergnat façade

The little church of CHAMALIÈRES, in a village now joined by lines of houses to Clermont, has escaped restoration, but is in a sadly dilapidated condition, and a good deal hidden by houses built up against it. It has an ambulatory and four apsidal chapels, with an east

Chamalières

Chamalières — window in the centre. The nave has the original barrel vault, but the choir has rib and panel vaulting and flying buttresses. Three arches at the west end open into what may have been a porch or narthex as at Notre Dame du Port and the other churches like it, but at present there is no exit and the church is entered by a side door. In other respects the building conforms to the Auvergnat type.

S. Saturnin — At S. SATURNIN, as shown by a photograph, for I have not seen it, is a church with central tower, transepts, an apse inlaid with mosaic, and an ambulatory, in all respects like the other churches that have been described, except that there are no apsidal chapels attached to the ambulatory aisle.

Royat — The church at ROYAT is peculiar. It is cruciform, square ended, single aisled, and barrel vaulted. The choir is raised by nine steps above a vaulted crypt. There is a central tower, square, surmounted by an octagonal stage carried on squinches. The east end has a triplet of round-headed windows and above them a cusped sex-foil circle of the 13th century.

Fortified church — The outside of the building is regularly fortified like a castle with parapet and machicolations, and on the south side is a castle yard or bailey. The crypt is extremely interesting. It consists of three aisles four bays long, cross-groined without ribs, and the columns have capitals of an early type.

Le Puy en Velay — The cathedral of LE PUY, as has been said above, has characteristics of the styles both of Auvergne and Aquitaine. To the influence of the latter school belongs the domical construction of the nave which has been described in a former chapter. To that of the former may be traced the polychrome decoration of the masonry

Plate CXX

LE PUY

which forms so important a part of the design, both of the exterior and interior.

The cloister at Le Puy on the north side of the nave (Plate CXX) is one of the most charming in France, though it has suffered a good deal from the severe restoration of M. Mallay. It is not all of one date, the southern walk next the church being the oldest, and dating according to Viollet-le-Duc from the 10th century; the other three were re-built in the 12th, that on the west side being the latest. The columns are diminished in the classic fashion, and carry round arches of three orders in the earlier walks, the middle order in the later arcades being replaced by a singular band of ornament like an exaggerated bead and reel. The voussoirs are of black basalt and white stone alternately, and the spandrils are filled with a rough mosaic of basalt and red brick in various patterns. Above, is a cornice delicately carved with scrolls, heads, and figures of men and animals, that in the older walks being simpler than the others. The keystones of the outer order of the arch are ornamented with little figures, among which is a mermaid, holding her tail in her hand. The cloister is covered with plain cross-groining.

Cloister, Le Puy

The capitals are rude and distant copies of Roman Corinthian, and in the earlier part have the leaves raffled in the Roman fashion with distinct pipings. In the decoration by polychrome masonry however one may suspect a trace of Byzantine influence, and both here and in the church are capitals with a curious resemblance to some we have described at Ravenna and Salonica. A capital in the north transept (Fig. 107) follows, though at an immense distance, the construction of one at S. Demetrius in Salonica (Plate VIII) with the selfsame convex band

Fig. 107.

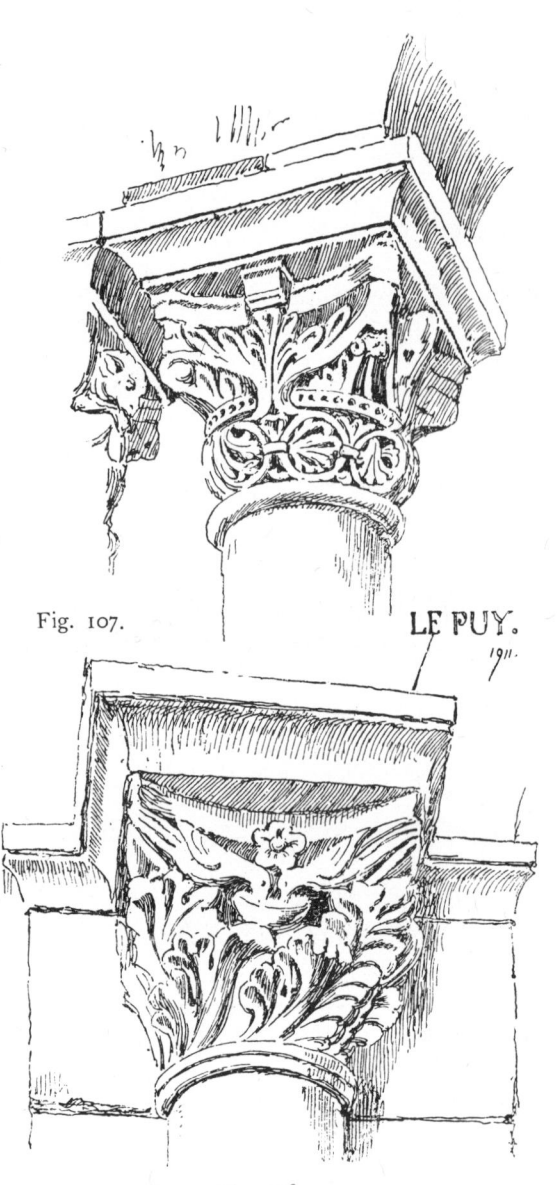

LE PUY.
1911.

Fig. 108.

Plate CXXI

South Porch—LE PUY

Plate CXXII

Capitals of South Porch—LE PUY

of scroll work below the stage of the volutes; and in a capital from the cloister at Le Puy (Fig. 108) with its Byzantinesque birds dipping into a cup, and its leaves thrown sideways, is it too fanciful to detect a suggestion from the blown leaf capitals of S. Apollinare in Classe at Ravenna, and those in S. Demetrius and S. Sophia at Salonica? (Plate III, vol. I. p. 52).

One of the most remarkable features of this church is the south porch, with its singular detached ribs within the true arches of the construction (Plate CXXI). They spring from columns, like themselves detached from the main jambs. The capitals of these columns and of the whole group of shafts carrying the arches are very strange, and unlike any other French examples known to me, and in their semi-barbarous richness remind one of Indian work rather than that of any other school (Plate CXXII). Some of the shafts are fluted, others are covered with small reticulations of sunk chequer-work, and one resembles on a huge scale the ornament that has been noticed in the cloister like an exaggerated version of the classic bead and reel. *Le Puy, south porch*

Close by this porch is the great campanile (Plate CXXIII), which dates from the end of the 11th century. It is built mainly of the lava of the district, and is remarkable for its extreme diminution as it rises storey by storey. This is managed by four interior pillars which rise through all the stages till they take the reduced structure of the upper part, so that it has no false bearing. These pillars are steadied by being united to the outer walls with arches and vaults forming galleries round the interior of the tower. It has in the upper part the same steeply pedimented windows which occur in the steeple of Brantôme near Périgueux, and those of *The campanile*

S. Leonard and S. Junien in Aquitaine, and which are found also in the steeple of Vendôme and the old steeple at Chartres, farther north. Lower down in the tower are windows with the horse-shoe trefoil heads which occur at Notre Dame du Port, Issoire, and the other Auvergnat churches, and are to be seen farther east at Vienne and Valence in Burgundy.

Fig. 109.

Distinct as the schools of these several provinces are in the main, they nevertheless overlap in minor details such as these. Another instance of it is afforded by the steeple of Uzerche (Correze) in Aquitaine, which has the high pedimented window of Brantôme, Chartres, and Le Puy, and also at the corners of the square stage the horns, like those of a Roman sarcophagus, which have been noticed above at Lyons and in Dauphiné[1].

[1] *v. sup.* p. 117.

Plate CXXIII

LE PUY

Plate CXXIV

S. MICHEL DE L'AIGUILLE—LE PUY

On a wonderful pinnacle of basaltic rock (Fig. 109) that rises in a suburb of Le Puy is perched most picturesquely the little church of S. MICHEL DE L'AIGUILLE, dedicated to the saint of such airy sites, which was originally founded by a dean of the cathedral about 963[1], though the present building can hardly be older than the 11th or earlier part of the 12th century. Its plan is adapted to the irregular shape of the summit, which it occupies entirely, but contrives to have something like a central tower and a semi-circular aisle. A lofty tower rises at one corner.

S. Michel de l'Aiguille

The ascent is by a long flight of steps cut in the rock, and room is found on the summit for a narrow walk round the building defended by a stone parapet.

The entrance (Plate CXXIV) is by a door at the head of a steep flight of stairs under a horse-shoe trefoiled arch, and the whole of the little façade is decorated with mosaic of basalt, white stone, red brick and little bits of white marble. Grotesque beasts project on consoles, mermaids are carved on the lintel, and above is an arcaded cornice with figures in each little arch, springing from corbels which are formed of human hands. The same device occurs in the cathedral porch.

The interior has tapered columns carrying capitals resembling those in the cloister, but with a stronger spice of Byzantine feeling (Figs. 110, 111). Some have birds

---

[1] See *Gallia Christiana*, vol. II.; Dioc. *Aniciensis* (Le Puy), where the deed of foundation is preserved. "...quoniam ego Truannus Aniciensis ecclesiae Decanus, in quadam praealta silice quae usitata locutione vulgi Acus vocatur, prope Aniciensem urbem sita, ubi quondam vix agilium hominum erat adscensus ecclesiam collocare gestiens, etc., etc....sic enim viam ampli itineris in praedicta silice constituens, in honore Sti Michaelis Archangeli ecclesiam intuitui cernentium gratam, Christi faventi auxilio, in Acu fundare studui." It was afterwards an Abbey: then annexed to the Cathedral and allotted to one of the Canons.

in the angles. The vaulting is of plain cross-groining without ribs (Plate CXXV).

Sculpture in Auvergne

During the Romanesque period sculpture, it will have been noticed, does not play so important a part in the school of Auvergne as in those of Provence and Burgundy, or even that of Aquitaine. Examples of statuary are very rare, and the sculptor's art is confined chiefly to capitals, which are very largely carved with figure subjects, especially in the eastern part of the churches. Painted decoration appears to have been common, and

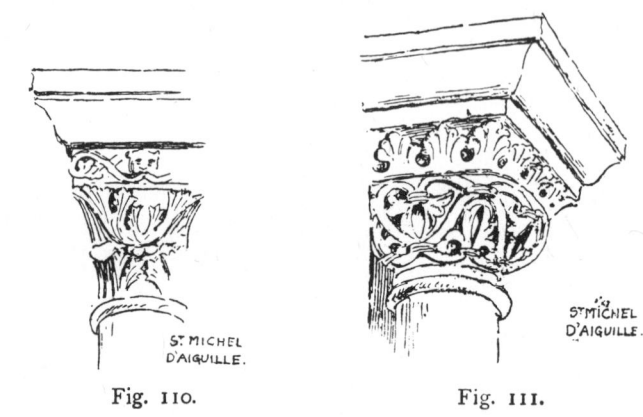

Fig. 110.

Fig. 111.

there seems to have been some warranty even for the excessive modern painting at Issoire and elsewhere[1]. It was however in architecture that the Auvergnats excelled, and they developed within their province a distinct style of their own, so original and so satisfactory that one regrets the wave of Gothic architecture that came to sweep it away. In such able hands one might have imagined it would have led to some further development of surpassing interest.

[1] At various times down to the 15th century the Capitular hall of Le Puy was painted with admirable frescoes, still in a great measure preserved.

Plate CXXV

S. MICHEL DE L'AIGUILLE—LE PUY

And yet the style is so complete in all its parts that one does not see an opening for anything to proceed from it; and in this respect it may resemble the art of Provence, which after splendid achievement in its early days sank into stagnation and decay. At all events the Auvergnat churches are so nearly all of a date, and so very closely designed on one model, without any of those variations which appear in the successive schools of Gothic to prepare the way for a new departure in art, that it is doubtful whether the style had not played its part, and done all there was in it to do. *Perfection of Auvergnat style*

Gothic architecture however never established itself generally in this part of France, and the great Gothic cathedral at Clermont, comes upon one as a surprise, and seems out of place. Nor does it gain by contrast with the Romanesque of the province. After spending some weeks among the robust round-arched churches that we have been describing, one finds the Gothic of the cathedral at Clermont thin and unsatisfactory. It is undeniably a fine church, though I am not sure that the west front with which Viollet-le-Duc has completed the imperfect nave is not the best part of it; but one misses the broad simplicity, the generous solidity of column arch and wall, the grandeur of unbroken surface that gives the earlier Romanesque a dignity, and at the same time a geniality that one fails to find in the more scientific construction of the later style. *Gothic rare in Auvergne* *Romanesque and Gothic contrasted*

One feels the same at Limoges on entering the great Gothic cathedral there after wandering among the Romanesque buildings of Poitou, the Limousin and Perigord. Indeed in these provinces and in the south of France generally one may forget Gothic, for one finds Romanesque work everywhere, and except in certain isolated places Gothic buildings are exceptional. And when you do come across them, if I may judge by my own experience, you will find that the stalwart Romanesque has put you out of conceit with them. The intrusion of Gothic at Limoges causes surprise; at Clermont it seems almost an impertinence. Here, at all events, the passage from Romanesque to Gothic is disenchanting.

CHAPTER XXIV

NORMANDY

THE Normans were the last and most ferocious of the barbarian races who conquered and founded settlements in western Europe. Repressed with severity by Charlemagne, the Danes or Normans returned and ravaged France under his degenerate successors; and in England after a long struggle with the Anglo-Saxons they obtained from Alfred a settlement of half his kingdom. Rollo, or Gang-Roll, a fresh leader in the 10th century, declining a contest with the English, invaded northern Gaul, where he committed the most disastrous ravages. Towns were pillaged, Paris itself was besieged, and churches and monasteries were rifled. Pagans themselves, the Normans paid no respect to the sanctities of the Christians; the abbot of S. Denis was carried off and held to ransom, and had to be redeemed with 685 pounds of gold; and the treasuries of all the abbeys were exhausted either by rapine of the Danes, or by exactions for purpose of defence.

<small>Norman invasion of Gaul</small>

In 918 the French king, Charles the Simple, followed the example of Alfred of England, and ceded to these freebooters the province they had already conquered, requiring only an act of feudal homage for it, which was accorded with difficulty, and performed with insult[1].

[1] Jussit (Rollo) cuidam militi pedem regis osculari, qui statim regis pedem arripiens, deportavit ad os suum, standoque defixit osculum, regemque jecit supinum. Willelm: Gemmet: *Hist. Normann.* Lib. II. Cap. XVII. The Normans shouted with laughter, which the Franks did not venture to resent.

Settlement of Normandy

Here the Normans settled down and this part of the province of Neustria became Normandy. Rollo and his men became Christians, and with that extraordinary adaptability which was a Norman characteristic, they soon became Frenchmen, and melted into the body of the people, just as in England they became English and in Italy Italians. Of all the barbarian settlers in France the Normans who had been perhaps the most savage showed the greatest capacity for orderly government, and though they had been remarkable for their ferocity towards the priests they became in the second generation most devout Christians. The conquerors took French wives—they had, says Hallam, made widows enough—and their children were brought up in Christian ways, and learned the French tongue which rapidly superseded the old Norse language.

Norman adoption of Gallo-Roman styles

With such a history it would be vain to look for any architectural remains in Normandy older than the 11th century. The earlier barbarian inroads had desolated the country, the buildings were probably all in ruins, and the new settlers brought no art of their own from their old rude homes. But no sooner were they firmly established in their new country than they adopted the arts of the conquered race, as they did their culture, their religion, and their language; and within a century and a half they had covered the land with buildings, both civil and religious, of unusual splendour. Viollet-le-Duc observes the energy with which they pushed their enterprises to an end, so that their buildings are not left half-finished but are completed, differing in that from those of the southern races in Gaul. To all they did they imparted a distinctive character. "They found," says the same writer, "in the conquered territory remains of Carlovingian

Energy of Norman builders

CH. XXIV] FRANCE—NORMANDY 149

art, but they infused into it their national genius, positive, grand, a trifle savage but nevertheless free and unfettered[1]." The 11th century was the period of the utmost expansion of the Norman race. They had planted themselves firmly in the conquered province of France; they had made themselves masters of Sicily and Apulia, and shaken the throne of the Eastern Empire; and in the latter part of the century they conquered England, and became a great European power. Their peculiar style of architecture which they afterwards brought with them to England, where it almost wiped out all traces of the older Saxon work, is a fitting monument of their greatness and activity.

Norman conquests

Byzantine architecture had not made any impression on the northern provinces of France, and the Norman style was based originally on Gallo-Roman examples. Provincial Roman work declined in quality as it receded farther and farther from the Capital, and the buildings which the Normans had to guide them were no doubt very inferior to those of Provence. In particular the sculpture would have been coarse and inartistic, and there would have been but little of it. The figures and ornaments found in the Roman baths at Bath are probably favourable specimens of what art could do in the northern provinces of the later empire. There was therefore nothing to inspire the northern architect to rival the portals of Arles or S. Gilles, and figure sculpture is either wholly absent from Norman work, or if present barbarous. In decorative carving also the same sterility shows itself. There are no foliaged capitals like those of S. Trophime, or Avallon, but in the earlier Norman work only plain cushion capitals, made by squaring and

Poverty of Roman remains

Character of Norman ornament

[1] V.-le-Duc, vol. I. 138.

truncating an inverted cone or hemisphere: and when in later instances attempts were made to produce sculptured capitals the result was for a long while extremely rude and inartistic. The ordinary ornament which gives a decided richness to early Norman work is purely conventional, consisting of arcadings, diapers, billets, zig-zags, rosettes, bosses, and channellings, more the work of the mason than the sculptor, but it is used with skill and feeling, and though it cannot claim a high place in the scale of architecture it serves its purpose.

Influence of Byzantine fabrics

Several writers point out the analogy between the more advanced Norman ornament and the patterns of oriental stuffs. The Norman settlements in Italy and Sicily would tend to familiarize their kinsmen in the north with the products of the East; and the trade with Venice and the Levant, which has been described in a preceding chapter, brought the fabrics of Syria and Constantinople to Poitou, Anjou, and the borders of Normandy if not into the duchy itself. On these the Norman ornaments are based, and the case was the reverse of that in Aquitaine, for instance at S. Front, where though the architecture is Byzantine the sculpture is Gallo-Roman, whereas here the architecture is Gallo-Roman while the ornament is derived from Byzantium.

Instruction sought from Burgundy

When the Normans had established the rule of order and acquired a taste for culture they sought instructors from the more settled parts of France. Duke Richard I (943–996), scandalized by the dissolute life of the canons of Fécamp, invited Majolus, Abbot of Cluny, to come and reform the convent to the rule of S. Benedict. This fell through owing to the extravagant conditions required by the abbot. The next duke, Richard II (996–1027), repeated the invitation to William, Abbot of S. Benigne at Dijon, of whom we have heard already. Abbot William was at first afraid to go. He said "he had understood that the Norman Dukes, men by nature cruel and savage, were more used to overthrow churches than to build them, to destroy and drive away rather than to collect and cherish congregations of spiritual men. Also the journey was long, and he had no horses or beasts of burden for transporting the brethren and their chattels." The Duke, hearing this, sent saddle horses and pack horses, and William, overcome by his perseverance, having gathered a suitable number of monks, went with them to Fécamp, where the Duke received him "as an angel from heaven, and sending away the menials, waited himself on the godly man at table[1]."

Abbot William of Dijon

William, as we know, was an Italian, and a great builder, and his influence was felt not only in the reformation of the monastery, but in the architecture[2]. Many other religious houses were put under his rule by the Duke, among them that of Mont S. Michel which was burnt that same year 1001, and in the re-building of which Abbot William's hand may no doubt be detected. The influence of the Lombard school was thus introduced into this part of France, and was probably maintained under Abbot John, whom at the duke's request William appointed to the abbey of Fécamp, when he retired to his native Italy in his old age, for John came from the parts about Ravenna[3].

Abbot William's influence

Influence of the Lombard school

[1] Mabillon, *Annales, Ord. S. Benedicti*, vol. IV. p. 152.
[2] His personal direction of the building of the abbey at Bernay is recorded. Haec enim auctore Guillelmo Abbate Fiscamensi...qui in locandis fundamentis non modicum praestiterat consilii auxilium. *Gallia Christiana. Dioc. Lexoviensis (Lisieux).*
[3] Mabillon, *Acta Sanctorum S. Benedicti*, vol. VI. pars I. p. 302. William and his brothers founded an Abbey on their paternal estate of Volpiano in a "solitary place, four miles from the Po," "ut fructus bonorum operum quae

In the 10th century art throughout France was very rude and backward, and Normandy, the last province to become settled, was naturally the most backward of all. A letter from the abbey of Fécamp implores the monks of Dijon to send them craftsmen, of whom they had great need to enable them to finish the buildings they had begun. The earliest churches in Normandy were extremely plain. If the aisles were cross-vaulted in stone the nave was originally roofed with wood, which was not replaced by stone till a later age.

The churches of MONT S. MICHEL and CERISY-LE-FORÊT date from the earlier part of the 11th century, and the latter has the peculiarity of a gallery at the triforium level across the transept ends, which is found also in the cathedral of Winchester. Something like it occurs at Le Puy in Auvergne, but with a difference, and it may be regarded as especially a Norman feature. It appears also in the fine church of S. GEORGES DE BOSCHERVILLE, which was founded between 1050 and 1066. The architecture seems too advanced in its style for so early a date, and Sign. Rivoira[1] believes it to have been re-built about 1116 in its present form, which has remained almost untouched by later work. Here, among cushion capitals, are others rudely carved with angle volutes distantly derived from ancient example, though barbarous enough in design and execution. But in the entrance to the chapter house, which is in a later style, we find human figures attenuated serving as colonnettes like those of a king and his queen at Rochester (Plate CXXVI).

The transept gallery

S. Georges de Boscherville

ibi gerunt sibi et illis esset abolitio peccatorum...Unde et Fructuariensis ille locus est vocatus" (*Ibid.* p. 286). Sign. Rivoira illustrates the tower of Fruttuaria which is all that remains of William's church. He returned to die at Fécamp.

[1] Rivoira, vol. II. p. 171.

Plate CXXVI

S. GEORGES DE BOSCHERVILLE

Plate CXXVII

ABBAYE AUX HOMMES—CAEN

CH. XXIV] FRANCE—NORMANDY 153

The abbey of JUMIEGES on the Seine was begun in 1040, and consecrated in 1065 in the presence of Duke William II, the conqueror of England. Of the original building the west front and the nave still remain. The aisles are cross-groined, but the nave was roofed with wood. The capitals are of the plain cushion type and the ornament is confined to simple billets or dentils: but in its simplicity it is a majestic piece of work. Jumieges

The connexion between Normandy and Lombardy was continued when Lanfranc of Pavia came to France and settled in the Duchy with a train of scholars and associates. In 1042 he retired to the abbey of Bec, a foundation which in him and his successor Anselm was destined to give the see of Canterbury two of its most famous prelates. A Lombard, like his predecessor Abbot William of Dijon and Fécamp, Lanfranc was a great builder, and in 1077 the new abbey of Bec was consecrated, with which he replaced the more modest structure of the rude Norman knight and monk Herluin. Under his rule Bec became a seat of learning famous throughout Christendom, and the arts were not neglected, as Lanfranc showed both there and afterwards when he came to England and re-built his metropolitan cathedral. We may detect his influence in the Conqueror's buildings at Caen, the two great abbeys founded by Duke William and his queen Matilda to reconcile the Pope to their marriage within the prohibited degrees. Lanfranc of Pavia

Abbey of Bec

The ABBAYE AUX HOMMES, or S. Étienne, was consecrated in 1077, and Lanfranc was its first abbot. It has been a good deal altered in later times; the choir was re-built and the wooden roof of the nave replaced by stone vaulting in the 13th century, but in the lower part of the west front and in the nave arcades and triforium Abbaye aux Hommes, Caen

Abbaye aux Hommes, Caen

we still have the earlier work. The façade is of the sternest simplicity: two tiers of three wide round-headed windows light the west end of the nave, which is flanked by a tower on either hand flush with it, and with similar windows below the eaves level. Above this is a storey simply decorated with plain strips of masonry carrying narrow semi-circular arches. The next two stages are in a later and more ornate style of Romanesque, dating apparently from the first quarter of the 12th century. Above rise the two splendid spires of 13th century work which are the dominating features of the town of Caen (Plate CXXVII).

Progress of the Norman style

In the interior, in spite of its abstract severity, we find the Norman style already advanced toward a greater degree of refinement. The capitals are carved with some attempt at Roman example. Under the heavy spreading super-abacus which answers to the Byzantine pulvino, we find the angle volutes, the coronal of leaves, the hollow sided abacus, and a block representing the rosette of the Corinthian capital. They are carved with some skill, and are not devoid of architectural beauty and propriety. It is only when the sculptor wanders away from these foliated designs and attempts the figure of man or beast that he betrays a hopeless childishness and imbecility.

Proportion of triforium and arcade

The proportion of the triforium to the arcade below is different from that in any French work we have hitherto considered, for the triforium arch is as wide as that below it, and not much less in height, the lower arch being about 22 ft. high and the upper 17. This nearly equal proportion of the two storeys is one characteristic of Norman work in England, as for instance at Ely, Peterborough, Norwich, Southwell, and Winchester. It is significant of the Lombard connexion that there is something like the same proportion in the church of S. Ambrogio at Milan, which was finished in its present form during Lanfranc's lifetime. A somewhat similar arrangement occurs nearer home in the nave at Tournai where the triforium arches are actually larger than those of the main arcade and are surmounted by a row of small openings forming a second triforium (*v. sup.* Fig. 72, p. 23). The nave at S. Étienne had originally, like those of all early Norman churches, a wooden roof, but the aisles were vaulted, and the triforium is covered with a quadrant barrel vault like those of Auvergne, with an underlying transverse arch at each bay springing from an attached pilaster on the outer wall. The Norman triforium at Gloucester cathedral is covered with a similar half-barrel vault on transverse ribs.

The other foundation of the Conqueror and his wife, the ABBAYE AUX DAMES, or La S. Trinité at Caen has been more thoroughly altered than the Abbaye aux Hommes, and is now mainly a 12th century building. The crypt however, which has Corinthianizing capitals like those described above, is perhaps of the original date. The church is transeptal with a central tower and at the west end two flanking towers, ancient below, but finished with an incongruous and ugly upper part. The choir is aisleless, and ends in an apse covered with a semi-dome, a feature which one is surprised to encounter so far north. Two tiers of five arches each surround the apse. They have deep soffits and are carried by detached columns with a narrow passage behind them. The capitals are rude imitations of Corinthian, and the arches are decorated with a kind of embattled fret on the face of the outer order in the lower storey, and with

<small>Abbaye aux Dames, Caen</small>

Abbaye aux Dames, Caen

other conventional ornaments, as well as a roll-moulding elsewhere. There was originally a wide round-headed window in each bay both above and below but the lower lights have been blocked. There are two bays between the apse and crossing, the lower storey a blank wall, the upper with lofty round-headed windows and a passage in the wall continued from that round the apse (Fig. 112). The bays are divided by a wide transverse rib springing from a wall shaft, and the groining is plain quadripartite without diagonal ribs.

The nave has three storeys, the triforium being represented by a series of narrow openings, six in a bay, which are not very interesting, and the great arches are decorated with the embattled fret that occurs in the choir.

S. Nicholas

There are other Romanesque churches of interest in Caen and the neighbourhood. S. NICHOLAS is the most remarkable of them, with its curious lofty semi-cone over the apse, rising like the half-section of a steeple above the roof.

S. Michel de Vaucelles

The church of S. MICHEL DE VAUCELLES in the suburbs has a beautiful tower and spire in the later style of Norman architecture, when the workmen had gained greater skill and freedom in dealing with their material and the style had begun to abate its severity (Plate CXXVIII). The belfry stage with its richly shafted and moulded windows would seem to be coeval with the upper storeys of the towers of S. Étienne, while that below has the plain square sunk panelling between narrow strips of pilasters which mark the Conqueror's work on the same building.

S. Contest

The village of S. CONTEST, a few miles off, has a tower and spire of the same date and style, with a similar

ABBAYE·AUX·DAMES.
CAEN.
BAY OF CHOIR.

Fig. 112.

circular stair-turret at one corner surmounted by a spirelet of its own growing out of the larger one.

<small>The Norman style in England</small> The Norman style however may be studied as well in England as in Normandy, if not better, for no sooner had the invaders settled themselves firmly on the conquered soil than they set to work to cover the country with vast buildings on a scale not only far beyond what they found there but even greater than those they had left behind them in their own country. It is therefore unnecessary to dwell longer on the Romanesque of Normandy itself, which does not differ appreciably from that which the Normans transported to the other side of the Channel. <small>Distinctive character of Norman architecture</small> In either country it has a distinct character of its own, differing not much more widely from the Saxon work in England than from the other schools of Romanesque architecture in France. It has none of the wealth of sculpture which plays so large a part in Provence, Toulouse, and Burgundy; it challenges none of the constructional problems solved in Aquitaine with its domes, or in Auvergne with its barrel vaults; what little ornament it has is abstract, conventional, and restrained, and it relies for effect on a sturdy straightforward practical mode of construction, not looking much to preceding styles for example, but working out a satisfactory result with simple means, and honest building. It is a style full of originality and pregnant with promise of a great future: and in its magnificent simplicity and ponderous majesty it gains in one way what it loses in another by comparison with styles more refined and ornate.

Plate CXXVIII

S. MICHEL DE VAUCELLES—CAEN

CHAPTER XXV

THE ISLE OF FRANCE

THE royal domain during the Romanesque period was confined within narrow limits, though the king exercised a more or less shadowy supremacy over the great feudatory dukes and counts whose dominions and power exceeded his own. When Louis VI (Le Gros) came to the throne in 1108 the royal domain scarcely extended beyond the cities of Paris, Orleans, Bourges, and the adjacent districts. His territory comprised only the modern departments of Seine, Seine et Oise, Seine et Marne, Oise and Loiret[1]. The six great peers of France were the Count of Flanders, whose territories reached from the Scheldt to the Somme, the Count of Champagne, the Dukes of Normandy and Burgundy, the Count of Toulouse, and the Duke of Aquitaine who included in his domains Poitou, Limousin, most of Guienne and the Angoumois, and latterly Gascony. The Counts of Anjou, Ponthieu and Vermandois and others had held directly from the Carlovingian kings, but were more or less independent or had passed under other allegiance. The firmer establishment of royalty began with Louis VI. His grandson Philip Augustus took Artois and Vermandois from the Count of Flanders, and Normandy, Maine, and Anjou from John of England. His son Louis VIII conquered Poitou and attacked Guienne; the Albigensian

The royal domain

The great feudatories

---

[1] Guizot, *Civilization in France*, Lect. XIII.; Hallam, *Middle Ages*, chap. I.

wars brought Toulouse into subjection in the 13th century; the English were driven out of Guienne in 1451; but it was not till the latter part of the 15th century that Burgundy, Dauphiné, and Provence were finally united to France by Louis XI and his son Charles VIII, who also acquired Brittany by marriage.

Philip Augustus

During the whole period of the Romanesque style therefore the royal domain was of very limited extent, and its boundaries bore no comparison with those of the greater feudatories. The expansion of the monarchy under Philip Augustus and his father and grandfather was marked by a corresponding expansion of the art of architecture, which brought the Romanesque style in that part of France, and before long in other parts as well, to a conclusion. The royal domain, l'Ile de France, was the cradle of French Gothic architecture, and the reign of Philip Augustus, 1180–1223, saw the foundation of the cathedrals of Paris, Chartres, Bourges, Laon, Soissons, Meaux, Noyon, Amiens, Rouen, Cambrai, Arras, Tours, Seez, Coutances, and Bayeux, nearly all of which were finished before the close of the 13th century[1].

Scarcity of Romanesque work in l'Ile de France
The Norman ravages

There are therefore comparatively few remains of Romanesque architecture in this part of France. In the 11th century the territory had been laid waste by the terrible Normans, who besieged Paris and ravaged the country round about, and spared neither church nor monastery. But the absence of earlier monuments is due still more to the extraordinary outburst of building which has just been referred to, which swept away all the principal churches in the older style, and replaced them by structures in the new style of the day, which

---

[1] V.-le-Duc, *Dict. Rais.* I. 140.

Plate CXXIX

LE MANS

Plate CXXX

LE MANS

was worked with a passionate earnestness that excites our wonder.

The BASSE ŒUVRE at BEAUVAIS would seem to be the nave of the cathedral, of which Bishop Herve laid the foundation in 990, though according to some it was built originally in the 6th or 7th century, and according to Viollet-le-Duc in the 8th or 9th. It is so plain and devoid of detail that in the absence of any documentary evidence we can only say it might have been built at almost any time within those centuries. It is a basilica in plan with nave and aisles, divided by piers of plain square masonry carrying round arches which are not moulded. Each bay of the aisle and of the nave clerestory has a wide round-arched window, the voussoirs being of stone alternating with tile. The roofs were and are of wood. The front has probably been altered at a later time. Only three bays of the building remain, and they have been so extensively restored as to have lost nearly all trace of antiquity. The walls are faced with the *petit appareil* of Roman work.

LE MANS did not strictly belong to the royal domain when the nave was built in the 11th century, but it may be taken in this connexion. It is a good example of well developed Romanesque. The west front is simple but impressive, with a round-headed doorway surmounted by a great window opening, recessed within several receding orders. The upper part is faced with reticulated masonry enriched with bands or mouldings in relief, arranged to form patterns (Plate CXXIX).

The nave aisles have some very simple wall-arcading, consisting of plain round arches resting on square pilasters with no capital, but only an impost moulding at the springing[1]. The capitals of the nave columns (Plate

[1] It is illustrated by V.-le-Duc, *Dict. Rais.* vol. I. p. 89.

CXXX) are of a Corinthianizing character, preserving the tradition of angle and intermediate volutes, which shows that the influence of classic art was felt here very differently from what we found in Normandy, although in this part of France the remains of Roman art must have been far fewer than in the south, and of inferior execution. The same influence may be detected in the ruined abbey of S. EVREMOND (Plate CXXXI) on an island in the river at Creil, which has by way of buttresses piers with classic capitals, recalling those of the cloister at Arles, and the apses at Valence.

The development of the buttress, which plays so large a part in the succeeding style of the 13th and following centuries, was only arrived at by very timid and tentative steps. The Romanesque buttress was a flat pilaster, wide but with very little projection. It was often so shallow that it was taken up to the eaves and stopped against the cornice or corbel course. Sometimes it was rounded like an attached column, thus preserving the Roman tradition of the theatre of Marcellus or the Colosseum, and the arenas of Nîmes and Arles. When a greater projection was given to it the architect was evidently puzzled to know what to do with it at the top. Having the attached column still in his mind the natural thing seemed to him to be to crown it with a capital, and this is what he did with the square buttress-piers outside the cloister of S. Trophime at Arles (Pl. CVII, p. 72).

That however is evidently an unsatisfactory finish, for the capital, logically, is a member of support, whereas in this case it carries nothing, but is merely a sort of unmeaning finial. The next step was what we see here at S. Evremond: we have the pilaster pier, and the capital as before, but above the capital there is a sloped

Plate CXXXI

S. EVREMOND

Plate CXXXII

S. DENIS

weathering taken back to the main wall, which clearly is a great improvement not only in appearance but in construction, for the raking weathering throws the water off, which would otherwise lie on the flat top and do harm. But the architect seems to have thought his new device wanted some sort of explanation or apology, and so, as its slope reminded him of the roof of a house, he carved it with scolloping in imitation of roof tiles.

At Valence some of the buttress-piers are square and some round, but they all have the weathered top, though without the imitation of tiling.

With the abbey of S. DENIS, the burying-place of French kings from Dagobert to the Revolution, we bring the tale of Romanesque architecture in France to a close. The original church, founded or perhaps re-founded by Dagobert, fourth in descent from Clovis, about 625, was an apsidal basilica. Several worked stones and foundation walls were discovered by Viollet-le-Duc in 1859 during the restoration under his direction, which consisted to a considerable degree in undoing the injudicious repairs and false embellishments of his pre-decessors. These debris, he says, which had belonged to a Gallo-Roman edifice, "had been used in building a church of which the foundations of the apse have been found, and which must be that of Dagobert. There might still be seen, on the inside of the apse walls, traces of painting representing draperies very coarsely drawn in grey on a white ground.... Of precious marbles not the least fragment, but a construction indifferently put together, composed of debris, and covered with an ill-made coat of plaster[1]." This Merovingian church had become ruinous in the 8th century, and was re-built

Abbey of S. Denis

[1] *L'Église Abbatiale de St Denis*, Vitry et Brière.

S. Denis about 750, but not completed and dedicated till 775 in the presence of Charlemagne. Though sacked by the Normans in 856 and 858, and again in 886 during the siege of Paris, when the monks had to fly for safety to Rheims, the Carolingian church lasted till the 12th century, being probably better built than its Merovingian predecessor, which it seems also to have surpassed in size and adornment.

Abbot Suger In 1122 the famous Suger was elected Abbot of S. Denis. A contemporary of S. Bernard, Abelard, and Arnold of Brescia, Milman classes him in the quartette of Saint, Philosopher, Demagogue, and high Ecclesiastical Statesman which represents the age. Attached from his youth to the royal interest he became the chief counsellor of the king, and during the absence of Louis on the crusade he was for two years Regent of the kingdom. In his time, and owing partly no doubt to his wise administration, the regal authority over the great feudatories began to be something more than nominal, and grew, as M. Guizot[1] points out, to be a public power to control and regulate feudalism, in the interest of justice, and for the protection of the weak. The abbey of S. Denis became the political centre of France, and S. Bernard, alarmed at the part it played in secular affairs, wrote to reprove the abbot for his worldliness. "The abbey," he says, "is thronged not with holy recluses in continual prayer within the chapel, or on their knees within their narrow cells, but with mailed knights; even arms were seen within the hallowed walls." Suger himself, however, practised the austerities of a monk in his own person, inhabiting a humble cell, and observing all the severe rules of the cloister.

[1] *Civilization in France*, Lecture XII.

As soon as he became abbot he began to contemplate the re-building of his church on a sumptuous scale worthy of its famous relics. Pilgrimages to adore shrines and relics were great sources of wealth to monastic communities, and generally supplied the motive for re-building and enlarging the cathedrals and abbeys of the Middle Ages. The vast concourse of pilgrims to Canterbury after the murder of Becket demanded the eastward extension of the cathedral to "Becket's crown." The cult of S. Swithin at Winchester brought such crowds thither that Bishop de Lucy at the beginning of the 13th century built what is practically an additional church at the east end of Walkelyn's cathedral. Abbot Suger writes that on the days when the relics were exposed the pilgrims crowded and crushed one another to get near the shrines, women shrieked, and the monks could hardly resist the pressure of the faithful or protect their treasures. To avoid this inconvenience, and to glorify the martyrs whose relics were so attractive and profitable, he re-built his church on a magnificent scale. The first stone was laid by King Louis VI (Le Gros)[1] and the building was finished with such rapidity that in 1144 it was consecrated with great pomp in the presence of Louis VII (Le Jeune). As Louis le Gros died in 1137 the re-building must have taken at least seven years, and if it was begun as some think in 1132, five years more. Even nowadays twelve years would be little enough for so great an undertaking, and for that time the speed was marvellous and, as it turned out, injudicious.

Suger's re-building of S. Denis

His new abbey church

[1] Ipse enim Serenissimus Rex intus descendens propriis manibus suum imposuit, hosque et multi alii tam abbates quam religiosi viri lapides suos imposuerunt, quidam etiam gemmas ob amorem et reverentiam Jhesu Christi, decantantes "Lapides pretiosi omnes muri tui." Suger, *Letter.*

Viollet-le-Duc asks "Why this haste?" and suggests that Suger anticipated the decline of the monastic system, and felt that "the glory of the royal abbey must be renovated by some great undertaking; that something more, and something other must be done than what the Clunisians had effected," on one hand, and that on the other hand, instead of decrying art with the Cistercians and S. Bernard, the religious orders should be in the van of progress and new ideas, and lead the way to a "display of art hitherto unknown[1]."

Suger's writings show the immense importance he attached to his building, which he wished to rival the splendour of the Eastern basilicas, with their wealth of gold, mosaic, and precious stones. But it is not only by its scale and magnificence that S. Denis occupies a foremost place in the ranks of mediaeval buildings: it is still more remarkable as the place where the adoption of the pointed arch, and the system of Gothic construction was first shown on a grand scale. From its social and political importance the abbey of S. Denis gave a powerful impetus to the new school which was beginning to free itself from the classic traditions of Romanesque art to which the monastic orders persistently clung. In the façade (Plate CXXXII) round and pointed arches appear together, but in the construction the pointed arch gains on the other, and it may fairly be said that although pointed arches had been used elsewhere, and tentatively, it was at S. Denis that they first appeared as the ruling motive of design on a large scale.

One is naturally curious to learn what part Suger himself had in this artistic revolution. The question may be widened to include all the famous churchmen

[1] Viollet-le-Duc, *Lectures on Architecture*, Lect. VII.

whose names are connected with great building movements that led to fresh departures in art, like Hugh of Avalon at Lincoln, and William of Wykeham at Winchester. One reads in Suger's life that he gathered round him "from different parts of the kingdom workmen of all kinds, masons, carpenters, painters, smiths, founders, goldsmiths, and lapidaries, all renowned for skill in their several arts." He tells us that he watched and surveyed the work with the greatest care, that he went himself to choose the materials, the stone from Pontoise, and timber from the forest of Yveline, and that he directed the sculptured and other ornament, giving their subjects to the carver, the glass painters, the goldsmiths, and supplying the inscriptions. He seems to have been at S. Denis what Justinian was at S. Sophia, who is described as haunting the work, dressed in white linen with a handkerchief round his head and a staff in his hand. But though Procopius, like a good courtier, attributes to Justinian some sagacious suggestions which he does not scruple to say must have come by divine inspiration, for the emperor was not skilled in construction[1], he attributes the design to the real architects Anthemius and Isidorus. One may imagine that Suger played a similar part at S. Denis: that he watched and directed the work and gave many useful suggestions for plan, arrangement, and decoration: but it is not likely that any amateur, however accomplished, should be the author of a fresh constructional movement in architecture. The suggestion must have come from some practical master mason, the real architect of the building, who was to Suger and Bishop Hugh what William Wynford was to William of Wykeham. These enlightened prelates

S. Denis

Abbot Suger's part in the building

---

[1] οὐ γάρ ἐστι μηχανικός. Procop. *De Aedif.*

S. Denis are nevertheless entitled to the credit of having recognized and valued and eagerly seized the opportunity for a forward step in art, instead of ignoring it and adhering to strict formula of tradition as the monastic schools would have done. In this way they may be regarded as instrumental in opening a new chapter in the history of art, though not themselves the inventors of the new system.

Remains of Suger's building Of Suger's work, whether owing to accident, or more likely to imperfect building carried out with too great haste, and badly put together, is uncertain, nothing now remains but the west front with the two bays that form a sort of narthex, and at the other end the ambulatory round the apse with its radiating chapels and the crypt below. The whole of the church between these two extremities was re-built from the design of Pierre de Montereau, and the work which was begun about 1231, and not finished till 1281, is of course in fully developed Gothic. In the earlier work of Abbot Suger, we find traces of Romanesque ornament, but the construction may fairly be called Gothic. The chapels are fitted between radiating buttresses, and have each two single-light windows, which have pointed arches though those of the crypt are semi-circular.

Beginning of pointed architecture In the construction the system of equilibrium of forces, which is the main principle of what we call Gothic architecture, is fully recognized. Till the adoption of the pointed arch this principle could only be applied imperfectly, as we see at Vézelay; the round arch not lending itself, as may easily be understood, to combinations of arches with unequal span. With the pointed arch came the opportunity of adaptation to any span and any height, and the greater elasticity thus attained led on rapidly to all the infinite varieties of vault that followed. The old-fashioned barrel vault disappeared: a square bay was no longer necessary for setting out a cross vault: if the semi-circular arch were retained, as it was at first, for the diagonal rib, the rest being pointed could be raised to the same height if necessary, and they were generally raised to a height not much less, leaving the vault to be only slightly domical. With all these changes the art passed rapidly into a new phase, and in the great burst of cathedral building which marked the reign of Philip Augustus we find Romanesque tradition has little or no place.

Development of the Gothic vault

If we look round the other parts of France in the middle of the 12th century, when this movement towards a new style took place in the central domain, we find Romanesque art still running its course. In Burgundy, though the pointed arch had been admitted in the narthex of Vézelay, the general design still clung to ancient tradition, and the round arch still ruled the design. In Auvergne the round arch still reigned supreme, but the admirable skill of the architects of that province had refined and developed it into a style of their own so interesting and original that one regrets the Gothic invasion, which indeed never achieved more than a partial triumph over the native art. In Aquitaine and Anjou the domed style still prevailed, and may be traced to Loches in Touraine where as late as 1180 the church was covered by what is practically a series of hollow spires. In Normandy the sturdy round-arched style followed a line of its own, owing but little to Roman tradition, practical, dignified, and severe, into which sculpture hardly enters at all. Lastly in Provence no movement at all had been made in the direction of

Summary of French Romanesque

Gothic: classic tradition was strong, and Romanesque held its own. The portals of Arles and S. Gilles date from the middle or latter part of the 12th century and show no sign either of decline or of further development.

Coincident social changes

The passage of architecture into a new phase was one incident in the social revolution that was taking place in other departments. The 12th century was an age of an intellectual upheaval—of aspiration after liberty both of thought and civil life: for it was marked by the movement for enfranchisement of the communes, and also by the teaching of Abelard; and though the two had little in common, they arose at the same time from the same stirring of the human mind. With Louis le Gros began the new royalty. He first undertook to police the kingdom, by repressing feudal outrages and "taking or reducing to submission the castles conspicuous as haunts of oppression." He first of the Capetians made royalty a real power, different from feudalism and superior to it, being intent, says Suger, on the real needs of the Church, and showing a care, long neglected, for the security of the labouring people, the artizans, and helpless poor. Feudalism was thus reduced to something like obedience. The enfranchisement of the commons attacked feudalism on another side: and since the monasteries had long given up the pretence of poverty, and had become great feudal potentates they came in for their share of popular odium. As the towns grew in wealth and power their assistance became valuable, and was bought in many cases by grants of charters from their feudal lord. The Count of Nevers, who disputed with the Abbot of Vézelay the suzerainty over the burghers of that town, granted them a constitution to attach them

The new royalty

Enfranchisement of the Commons

to his side[1]. When they complained that the monks in revenge would not grind their corn or bake their bread, the Count told them if anyone hindered their baking they should put him on the fire, or if the miller opposed them, grind him in the mill. "I wish," he said, "the monks were gone and the abbey destroyed"; and plucking a hair from his raiment "Were the whole hill of Vézelay sunk in the abyss, I would not give this hair to save it." With this encouragement the burghers attacked the monks and sacked the convent, in spite of the thunders of the Pope, threats of excommunication against Count and people, and reproofs addressed to the Bishop of Autun whom the Pope accused of being the instigator of the outrage[2].

Revolution at Vézelay

For the bishops and secular clergy had long been jealous of the regulars, who were exempt from episcopal control, and responsible to the Pope alone. The decline of monastic and feudal influence in the 12th century, and the rise of popular communities gave the bishops an opportunity of which they were not slow to avail themselves. The great outburst of cathedral building throughout France at the end of the 12th, and beginning of the 13th century, was a popular movement. The bishops ranged themselves on the side of the burghers, and the cathedral became a civic institution, an emblem of popular independence. Unlike the conventual church, from the principal parts of which laymen were rigidly excluded, the cathedral was open to all, a building

Antagonism of secular and regular clergy

Cathedral building sign of popular enfranchisement

---

[1] Constituitque illis Principes vel Judices quos et Consules appellari censuerunt. *Spicil. Hist. Vizel.* III.

[2] D'Achery, *Spicilegium Hist. Vizeliacensis*, Lib. I. Epist. XVII; *Eugenius, etc. Episcopo Eduensi...*omnes molestiae atque vexationes quas dilecto filio nostro Pontio Abbati Vizeliac. Burgenses ipsius villae ausu nefario praesumpserant, per instinctum et incitationem tuam habuerunt exordium.

in which the burgher could take pride, as being his own[1].

Practice of architecture passes into lay hands

Architecture now passed from the cloister to the lay guilds of workmen. They were originally trained no doubt in the convent workshop, for though the monks had at first been their own workmen when all skilled labour was in their hands, they had long given that up and had trained craftsmen to work for them. Working now under free conditions and in a freer atmosphere the builders and master-masons gave new life to the art, discovered new methods, and developed a new style, new both in outward form and inward principle. Romanesque art in France was mainly a monastic art: only in the shelter of the cloister could art have survived in the confusion of the dark ages: and with the decline of monasticism it passed into other phases more expressive of the tendencies of the age. The change was most rapid and complete in the royal domain, the centre of the new social and political movements, and though in the remoter provinces Romanesque art lingered longer and in some parts can hardly be said to have quite disappeared, the new art finally triumphed and made itself felt from the English channel to the Pyrenees.

[1] V.-le-Duc, *Dict. Rais.* III. 227. "Les cathédrales ... à la fin du XIIe siècle avaient à la fois un caractère religieux et civil: et là, sauf l'autel qui était entouré de ses voiles, rien n'obstruait la vue."

This is disputed by M. Luchaire (*Social France at the time of Philip Augustus*) who thinks the secular canons in the new cathedrals enclosed their choirs from the first with tapestries if nothing more.

The two views do not seem irreconcileable. M. Luchaire is no doubt right in not believing that the bishops had any democratic sympathies. But this would not prevent their siding with the popular party, as the Popes did with the Guelfs, for political reasons, without any affection for their principles.

CHAPTER XXVI

ENGLISH ROMANESQUE BEFORE THE NORMAN CONQUEST

WHEN in the reign of Honorius the Romans finally withdrew from this island, after having governed and colonized it for 400 years, a period as long as that from the reign of Henry VIII to our own day, it will readily be understood that they left behind them traces of their rule not only in the civil constitution of the towns, which was modelled on the Roman system, but also in the architecture and other arts which they had brought with them and cultivated for so long a time. The whole country was dotted with Roman villas; many considerable towns had arisen under Roman protection, some of which possessed regular municipal privileges[1]. Colchester, Lincoln, Gloucester and York were *Coloniae*, and Verulamium (S. Albans) was a *municipium*. Gildas, whom Bede follows says there were twenty-eight cities besides some castles[1]. It is even supposed that in the cities of Southern and Eastern Britain, if not in the rural districts, Latin was becoming or had become the vernacular tongue[2].

Romano-British architecture

The remains of towns and country houses throughout England testify to the refinement of society under Roman government. Excavation at Silchester has brought to light a British Pompeii; similar discoveries have been made at Caerwent, and in the stations along the Roman wall, and await us at Verulam. The houses were large, handsomely finished with mosaic floors, and comfortably warmed by hypocausts. They show also by the difference between their plan and that of Italian villas that their design was accommodated to the climate.

[1] ...bis denis, bisque quaternis civitatibus ac nonnullis castellis...decorata. Gildas, *Prologus*.
[2] Haverfield, *The Romanization of Roman Britain*.

British disorder

Of the mysterious period of British history that followed the departure of the Romans, when the natives were left to their own resources, we know just enough to tantalize us. A corner of the veil only is lifted for a moment by the monk Gildas, who wrote during the lull that interrupted the career of the Saxon conquest, after the invaders had been checked by the British victory at Mount Badon, and while the issue of the struggle was still doubtful. From him we gather that the Britons were with difficulty united in the presence of the enemy, and turned their swords against one another when the general danger was removed[1]. Writing forty-four years after the British victory at Mount Badon Gildas describes the country as laid waste and the cities no longer inhabited as formerly, but deserted and ruined, for though foreign wars had for the time ceased, civil wars took their place[2].

In such a state of society there was no room for the arts of peace. Buildings left by the Romans might be turned into defences against the Saxons, or castles for marauding chieftains, but it would be vain to look for any native architecture. *Britons not Romanized* The Britons had not assimilated Roman culture like the Gauls, and it is not likely that many Romans, if any, let the legions go without them. Among the princes whose vices Gildas castigates we find side by side with the Celtic names of Vortiporius, Cuneglasus and Maglocunus, the Latin Constantinus and Aurelius; but there is nothing to tell us whether they were Romans who had stayed behind, or Italianized Britons. All foreign artizans had probably departed

---

[1] Moris namque continui erat genti, sicut et nunc est, ut infirma esset ad retundenda hostium tela, et fortis esset ad civilia bella, et peccatorum onera sustinenda. Gildas, *Epistola* § 19.

[2] *Ibid.* § 26, he tells us he was born in the year of the battle of Mount Badon, which was 520, so that his history was written in 564.

CH. XXVI] ROMAN BRITAIN 175

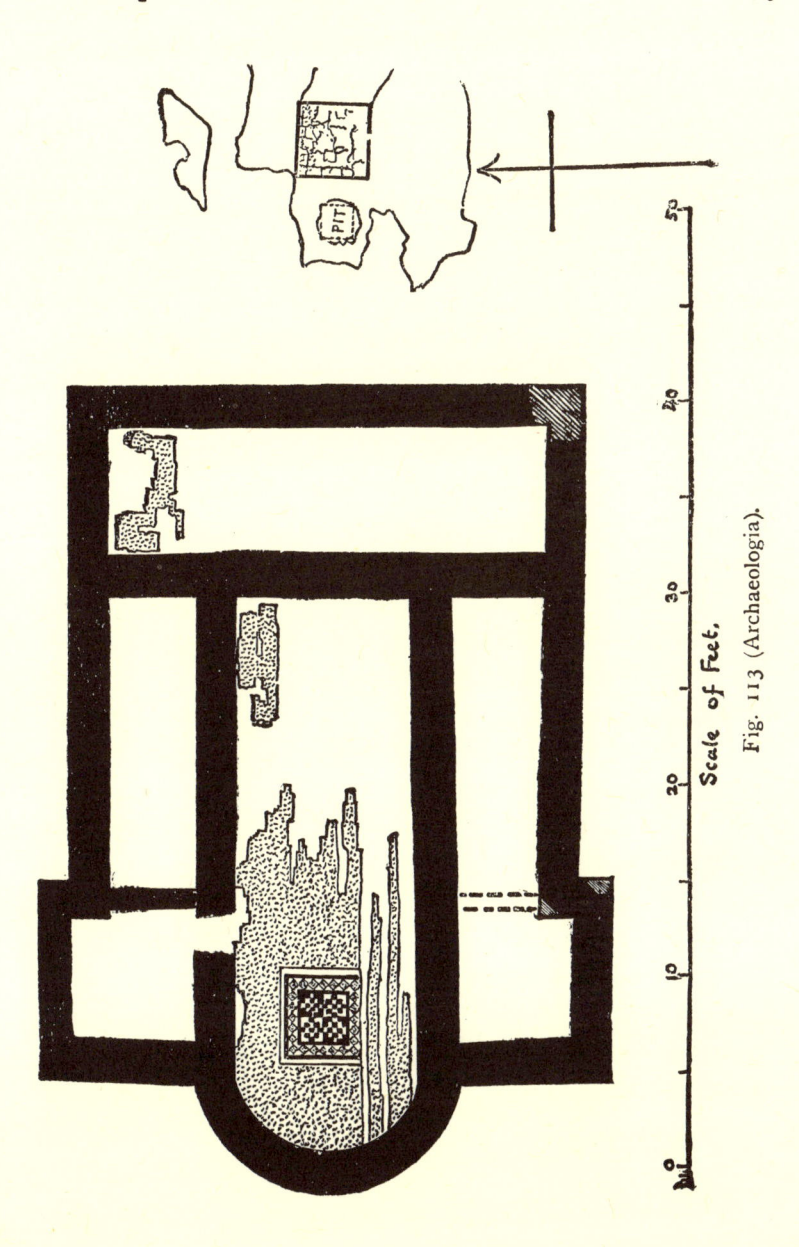

Fig. 113 (Archaeologia).

British churches

Silchester

with the rest, and few if any of the Britons were able, even if their civil wars gave them leisure, to carry on the arts and industries that had flourished under Roman rule. The Britons it was true were Christians, and had churches of which some remains have come down to us, but they show only very humble architectural skill. Excavations at Silchester in 1893 exposed the foundations of a small basilican church, which dating as it must from some time between Constantine's Edict of Milan in 313 and the departure of the Romans in 411, may fairly be considered the earliest ecclesiastical building in England of which we have any trace. Small as it is, only 42 ft. in length with a nave 10 ft. wide, it is in miniature a perfect basilica, with nave and aisles, apse, narthex, and transepts. The walls are 2 ft. thick, of flint rubble with tile coigns (Fig. 113)[1]. Conformably to primitive rule the apse is at the west and the entrance at the east end, and the altar was on the chord of the apse, the position of the priest being behind it, facing the people and looking eastward. Both church and narthex are paved with mosaic of plain red tesserae, except for a square with an elegant pattern before the apse, on which or in front of which the altar would have stood.

Although two churches of British Christendom were found at Canterbury by Augustine and repaired and restored to use, most of them had, no doubt, been swept away at the return of Paganism with the Saxon conquest. In S. Martin's the traces of Roman work are dubious, but the plan of the little church of S. Pancras (Fig. 114) can be made out, though if any part of it be Roman it was a good deal altered after the arrival of Augustine.

---

[1] *Archaeol.* vol. 53, p. 563, etc. I am indebted to the Society of Antiquaries for this illustration.

CH. XXVI] ROMAN BRITAIN 177

The earliest church in Britain according to tradition Glaston-
was at Glastonbury, where a legend, of which Bede is bury
ignorant, has it that Joseph of Arimathea built a humble
fane of wattle and daub. Such a structure apparently
existed in Dunstan's time, and was so highly revered
that he enclosed it in his new church. And when after
the conquest the abbey was again re-built an inscription
was placed on a column to record the exact size and
position of the primitive chapel. Its dimensions, 60 ft.

ST PANCRAS.
CANTERBURY

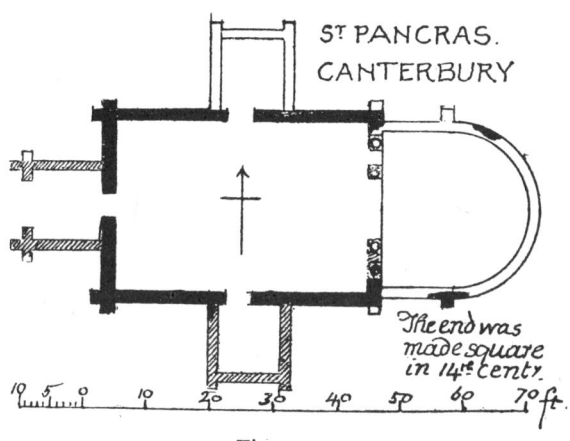

The end was made square in 14th centy.

Fig. 114.

by 26, seem to have been taken by S. Patrick as the
model for several churches in Ireland. Sir Gilbert Scott
says they are nearly the same at the Saxon churches of
Brixworth, Worth, and Dover[1].

During the two centuries which it took the Saxons to The
complete their conquest the remains of Roman architecture Saxon
must have suffered considerably; and as the Saxons, like invasion
the Slavs in Eastern Europe, were a rural and not an

[1] *Mediaeval Architecture*, vol. II. p. 19.

Neglect of Roman cities

urban people, hating towns and living in the country, as the many "ings, hams, and thorpes" among our villages testify, the Roman cities were probably left to decay, except so far as some of the old British population may have been allowed to linger there. Bishop Stubbs says that London and York preserved a continuous life as well as some other cities; and when the land was ravaged by Danish invasion the Saxons were driven to take refuge in the towns and restore their fortifications.

When the time came for re-building, and the need of architecture made itself felt once more, the land must still have been covered with examples of Roman work to inspire the efforts of the builder, although in Britain, the remotest province of the Empire, Roman art, as might be expected, failed to reach the standard of Provence and Southern Gaul. Many of its remains are of very rude workmanship, but at BATH, where the Roman Thermae were on a really magnificent scale, the architecture and its decoration are not inferior to the contemporary work of the later 2nd or 3rd century at Rome itself. The tympanum of the temple (Plate CXXXIII), dedicated, it is supposed, to Sul-Minerva (*Deae Suli Minervae*), is very irregularly composed. The helmet on one side, with the scalp of some wild beast drawn over it, would have been ill-balanced on the other by the little crouching human figure whose left hand holding a staff remains in front of the owl's wing. Other miniature figures appear to have filled the corners of the pediment, quite out of scale with the large "Victories" that support the disc. But though the tympanum does not reach a very high classic standard in point of composition or execution it is the work of no mean craftsman, and the great Corinthian capital which belongs to it is excellently modelled. Nothing nearly so

Roman Thermae at Bath

PEDIMENT OF
ROMAN TEMPLE
AT BATH

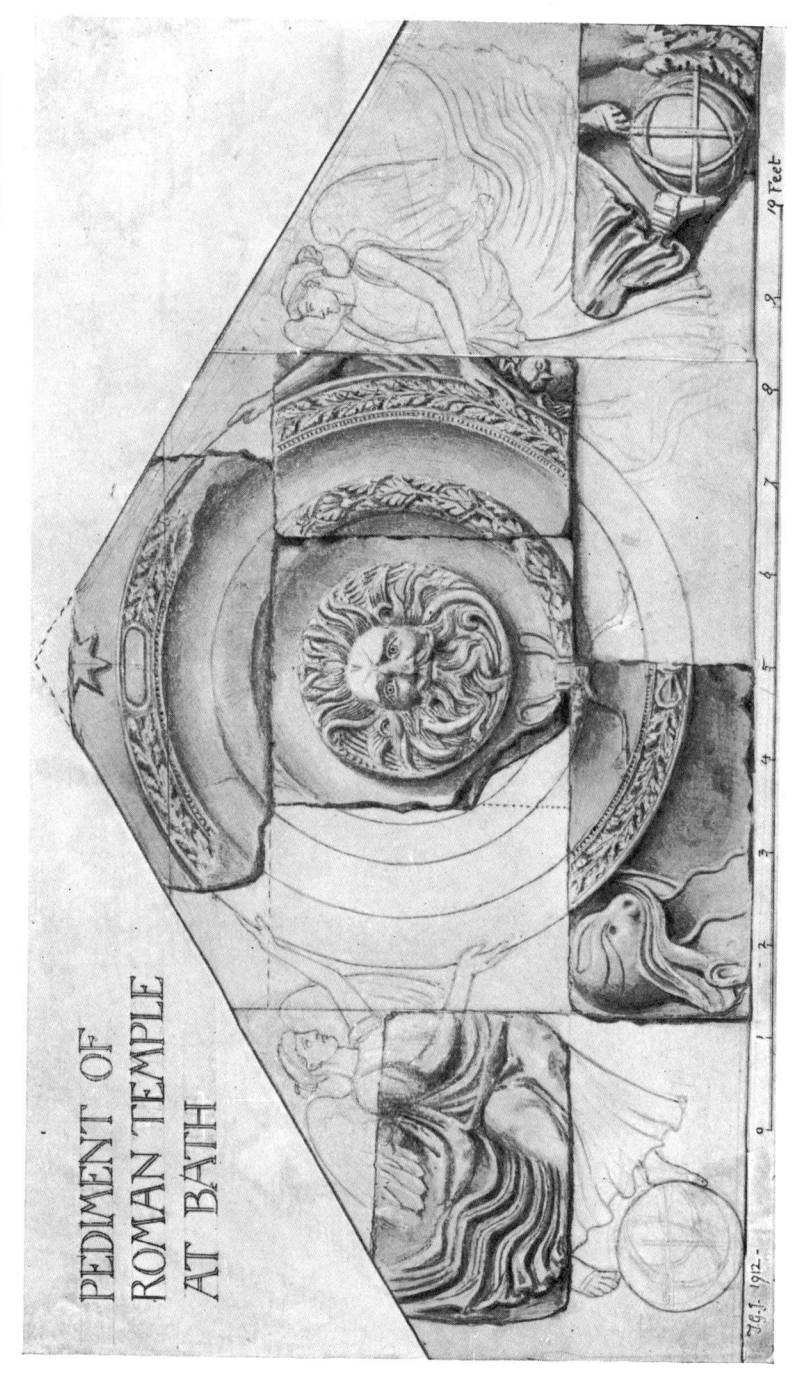

good was done in Britain during the next nine hundred years[1]. _{Temple at Bath}

The Roman buildings at Bath were no doubt wrecked by the Saxons, as well as those in other parts of the Kingdom; but their ruins must have been for many succeeding centuries sufficiently imposing to excite admiration.

Giraldus Cambrensis describes the city of Caerleon-upon-Usk, the old Urbs legionum, and the centre of Arthurian romance, as still retaining in 1188 much of its Roman magnificence, though apparently in ruins. "Here you may see," he says, "many traces of former magnificence; immense palaces that once with gilded pinnacles of their roofs imitated the splendour of Rome, having been originally erected by Roman princes, and adorned with fine buildings; a gigantic tower; magnificent baths; remains of temples, and places for theatrical shows, all enclosed by fine walls partly still standing. You will find everywhere, both within the circuit of the walls and without, subterranean buildings, ducts of water and channels underground; and what I thought especially noteworthy, you may see everywhere stoves contrived

_{Caerleon-upon-Usk}

---

[1] In the central head some see Sul, the native deity of the hot springs, whom the Romans, after their fashion, identified with the Minerva of their own mythology, just as Caesar makes Mercury the chief deity of the Druid Pantheon. The owl is appropriate to Minerva, but Sul was a female deity, and the head is a male one. Others see in it the Gorgon, on the strength of the snakes in the hair, but Medusa has no need to add wings and a pair of moustaches to her other charms. Some think it the Sun, from the confusion of Sol and Sul, which led to Bath being called *Aquae Solis* instead of *Aquae Sulis*: but this does not explain the snakes and the star. I venture to suggest Aesculapius, the proper president over the healing waters, on the ground of the snakes, and the star into which Jupiter turned him after killing him with a thunderbolt, and for which the other theories do not account. The wings, I confess, still need explanation.

with wonderful art, so that certain lateral and very narrow passages secretly exhale the heat[1]."

Roman art as the model

It was therefore natural that in England, as in France and Germany, the ambition of the infant schools of architecture, as soon as they came into being, was to revive that art of Ancient Rome which was their only model, and which even in this remote province, though it had none of the grand structures of Southern Gaul to show, was very far beyond their feeble powers of imitation.

Wooden architecture of the Saxons

The earliest Saxon buildings were of wood, a material so abundant in England as to influence our architecture down to almost modern times. The Saxons' word for to build was *getymbrian*, and in dealing with timber they probably showed greater facility than they did in masonry, having been originally a seafaring folk like their cousins the Northmen. In 627 king Edwin was baptized at York in the church of the Apostle Peter, which he had built hastily of wood[2]. Soon afterwards, however, under the advice of Paulinus, who as a Roman had experience of more solid work, he replaced it by a larger and more splendid basilica of stone. This the Saxons proudly called building *more Romanorum*, while that in wood was described as in *more Scottorum*. So when Finan, bishop of Lindisfarne, in 652 built his church of timber and thatched it with reeds Bede says it was done in the manner of the Scots[3].

---

[1] Giraldus Cambrensis, *Itinerarium Cambriae*, Cap. V. Henry of Huntingdon (Book I) writing about 1135 says "Kair-Legion in qua fuit archiepiscopatus tempore Britonum, nunc autem vix moenia ejus comparent," and Giraldus on the strength of this passage is accused of exaggeration. But he says he saw these things, and we know he was there with Archbishop Baldwin recruiting for the third Crusade.

[2] Quam ipse de ligno...citato opere construxit. Bede, *Eccl. Hist.* II. xiv.

[3] Quam tamen, more Scottorum, non de lapide sed de robore secto totam composuit, atque arundine texit. Bede, *Eccl. Hist.* III. xxv.

CH. XXVI] ENGLAND—SAXON PERIOD

The first efforts of the Saxons in masonry were naturally not very successful. In 30 years Edwin's church at York had fallen into disrepair, and in 669 Wilfrid repaired it, covered the roof with lead, replaced the linen or pierced boards of the windows with glass, and whitened the walls above the whiteness of snow. *Wilfrid's work*

Even the tombs and shrines of saints were made of wood. In 672 Ceadda, bishop of Lichfield, was buried in a wooden tomb, shaped like a little house[1]. At Greensted near Ongar in Essex there still exists a humble church of timber, not indeed of this early date, but perhaps the wooden church near Aungre mentioned in the chronicle of Bury as receiving the relics of S. Edmund in 1013. Its wall consists of balks of timber set close together side by side and resting on a wooden cill. *Greensted church*

The first serious step towards a Saxon Romanesque style was taken in 674 when Benedict Biscop[2], on his return to his native Northumbria from a third journey to Rome, was charged by king Egfrith to build a monastery at the mouth of the river Wear. After a year's work in laying foundations, Benedict, in despair of finding masons in England, crossed to Gaul where he succeeded in finding them, and brought them back with him[3]. Such speed was made that within a year service was held in the new church. Again, when the building was ready Benedict *Benedict Biscop at Monkwearmouth* *Artizans from Gaul*

---

[1] Tumba lignea in modum domunculae facta.

[2] Florence of Worcester (anno 653) calls him Benedictus cognomento Biscop, regis Oswiu minister, nobili stirpe gentis Anglorum progenitus. Kemble (*Proceedings of the Archaeol. Inst.* 1845) says the surname is curious in one who was not a bishop, but it occurs in the ancient genealogy of the kings of Lindissi, to whom he may have been related. Benedictus he thinks may be a name earned by the frequent pilgrimages to Rome.

[3] Caementarios, qui lapideam sibi ecclesiam juxta Romanorum, quem semper amabat, morem facerent, postulavit, accepit, attulit. Bede, *Opuscula*, ed. Giles, p. 366.

Monk-wearmouth

sent messengers to Gaul to bring glass-makers to glaze the windows of both church and monastery, the art of glass-making being unknown in Britain at that time. "It was done: they came; and not only did the work required of them, but taught the English how to do it for themselves." From abroad also this *religiosus emptor* purchased the sacred vessels of the altar and the vestments for the clergy, for nothing of the sort was to be had at home.

Church furniture from Rome

But even Gaul did not furnish all he wanted for the furnishing and adornment of his church. Benedict himself made a fourth journey to Rome, and brought back an "innumerable quantity of books and relics: he introduced the Roman mode of chanting," and even persuaded John, the arch-chanter of S. Peter's and Abbot of S. Martin's, to return with him to teach the English clergy. Among his pupils was the youthful Bede who tells the story[1].

Benedict also brought back from Rome many pictures for the adornment of his church and the edification of an illiterate people: a painting of the Virgin and the Apostles, which stretched from wall to wall, pictures of the gospel-story for the south wall, pictures of the Apocalyptic vision for the north, "so that all who entered the church, even if ignorant of letters, whichever way they turned should either contemplate the ever lovely aspect of Christ and his Saints, though only in a picture, or should with more watchful mind revere the grace of our Lord's incarnation; or else having as it were the trial of the last judgment before their eyes they might remember to examine themselves more strictly."

Rome was at this time under Byzantine rule, and

---

[1] *Hist. Eccl.* Lib. IV. c. xviii. *Vita*, ed. Giles, vol. I. p. cl.

CH. XXVI] ENGLAND—SAXON PERIOD 183

Byzantine influences were strong there as may be seen in the mural paintings of the lately excavated church of S. Maria Antica, with their Greek names and inscriptions[1]. These paintings which Benedict brought back from Rome would probably have been Byzantine works.

Byzantine pictures

In a fifth journey to Rome, which shows how much more people travelled in those days than we are apt to suppose, Biscop brought back further treasures.

Eight years later, in 682, a fresh endowment by king Egfrith enabled Benedict to found a second monastery, which he dedicated to S. Paul, five miles off at Jarrow, where the Venerable Bede lived and died, removing thither as soon as it was built, from Monkwearmouth.

Church at Jarrow

These contemporary accounts,—for Bede was born three years before Biscop brought over his French masons, and entered the new convent when he was seven years old,—give a lively picture of the state of the Arts in England in the 7th century. Roman tradition was gone, the Saxons had no native art of their own and had to begin again and build one up afresh. Masonry was a forgotten art: wooden walls, thatched roofs, windows closed with linen or shutters, a floor probably of bare earth strewn with rushes,—this till Biscop and Wilfrid came to the rescue, was the best they could do. The new art progressed but slowly. S. Cuthbert built a monastery at Lindisfarne in 684, surrounded by a circular enclosure made of rough stone and turf, and the dwellings within were of earth and rough timber covered with thatch[2]. In Ireland, even as late as the 12th century,—though Mr Petrie thinks there were stone churches

Early Saxon architecture

Irish churches

---

[1] *v. sup.* vol. I. p. 204. See Papers of the British School at Rome, vol. I. p. 17.
[2] Bede, *Vita S. Cuthberti.*

S. Malachy at Bangor — as early as the time we are speaking of,—when S. Malachy, archbishop of Armagh, who died in 1148 began to build a chapel of stone at Bangor near Belfast, the natives exclaimed in astonishment "What has come over you, good man, that you should introduce such a novelty into our country? We are Scots, not Gauls. What levity is this? What need is there of such proud unnecessary work? How will you, who are but a poor man, find means to finish it, and who will live to see it brought to perfection?"

Monkwearmouth church — Benedict's church at MONKWEARMOUTH, as the place came to be called, was no doubt the wonder of the age in England at that time, though according to our ideas it was a modest enough achievement. It remains to a great extent to this day. The plan was simplicity itself. The nave, an unbroken rectangle about 60 × 19 ft. inside, and 68 × 22·8 ft. outside, exactly three times as long as its width, was preceded at the west end by a porch over which was a tower (Fig. 115). It is orientated, and no doubt *The square east end* ended square, but the original Saxon chancel was pulled down and re-built by the Normans, together with the chancel arch[1]. The square end and western porch conform to the primitive type of British church architecture. The little oratories of Scotland and Ireland, which go back to the time of S. Patrick, are rectangular chambers squarely ended; and in the square end of the English church, which has continued as a national characteristic to the present day, we have a survival of the primitive Christian temple such as the oratory of Gallerus and the

[1] It has been suggested that two blocks, carved with lions, now fixed in the vestry wall, were the imposts of the Saxon chancel arch, *Original church of S. Peter, Monkwearmouth*, G. F. Browne. The tower arch of S. Bene't's at Cambridge has two beasts at the springing, and so has the chancel arch at Deerhurst

CH. XXVI] ENGLAND—SAXON PERIOD 185

rude chapels on the western isles of Ireland illustrated by *Monkwearmouth*
Mr Petrie. The length of the church at Monkwearmouth corresponds almost exactly with the dimension of 60 ft. prescribed by S. Patrick for one of his churches, a

Monk Wearmouth.
before restoration
Fig. 115.

dimension probably imitated from the primitive Christian chapel at Glastonbury.

The western part of the church, including the west doorway, is now generally admitted to be Biscop's work, but only the lower part of the tower is original, for *The porch*

186 ENGLAND—SAXON PERIOD [CH. XXVI

Monk-wear-mouth

marks in the masonry show that it finished with a gabled roof above the second storey: the upper part, however, is still Saxon work though of the 11th century.

The porch under the tower has a barrel vault, with its axis east and west, and doorways on all four sides, the western one having very remarkable baluster shafts in

Monk Wearmouth West door
Fig. 116.

the jambs (Fig. 116). They carry a massive impost block from which the arch springs, and they rest on upright slabs reaching through the wall and carved with two curious serpentine creatures intertwined and with beaked heads. A frieze sculptured with animals, now much defaced, runs across the wall above.

In the tower wall above this archway was apparently

a figure carved in relief about 6 ft. high. It would have been a valuable specimen of Saxon art, but it has suffered the fate of similar Saxon sculptures at Headbourn-Worthy, Bitton, and Deerhurst, and been defaced.

Monk-wearmouth

The proportions of the church are very lofty, and the pitch of the roof is very steep, in both respects contrasting very strongly with the usual proportion of the churches in the Norman style that succeeded. This feature of great height both in the body of the church and in the tower is a characteristic of Saxon architecture.

Lofty proportion

The same lofty proportions are found at the Saxon church of DEERHURST on the Severn, between Tewkesbury and Gloucester (Fig. 117), which was founded before 800, but probably altered a good deal in the 11th century when it was restored after being damaged by the Danes. It has a western tower 70 ft. high, of which however the lower half only is original, and a narrow and lofty nave, to which aisles were added in the 12th and 13th centuries, though there seem to have been Saxon aisles before them. The tower arches are small and semi-circular, springing from simple impost blocks. There seems to have been a western gallery, the door of which, now blocked, appears in the tower wall. Above, still looking into the nave, the tower has a two light window with straight-sided arches like the arcading at Lorsch (*v. sup.* p. 6, Plate LXXXIII) the resemblance being increased by the fluted pilaster which divides the lights. Three triangular openings in the west and side walls of the nave are difficult to explain.

Deerhurst church

The chancel was originally square, with an arch to the nave, and another to an apsidal sanctuary which has now disappeared. The arrangement looks like preparation for a central tower, but the wall and arch separating the chancel

188   ENGLAND—SAXON PERIOD [CH. XXVI

Deerhurst from the nave which would have formed the west side of the central tower has disappeared and there is now no division (Plan, Fig. 118). A similar square compartment or chancel, for a central tower, occurs at the Saxon

Fig. 117.

churches in Dover Castle and at Repton. Mr Micklethwaite believes that these and other Saxon churches of the same type had two towers, the central one for interior

CH. XXVI] ENGLAND—SAXON PERIOD 189

dignity, the western for a campanile, and possibly for habitation in the upper part. At the church at Ramsey built in 969 there were two towers "quarum minor versus occidentem...major vero in quadrifidae structurae medio," &c., &c.[1] At Dover the place of a second tower at the west end is supplied by the Roman Pharos, which was once connected to the nave by a short passage.

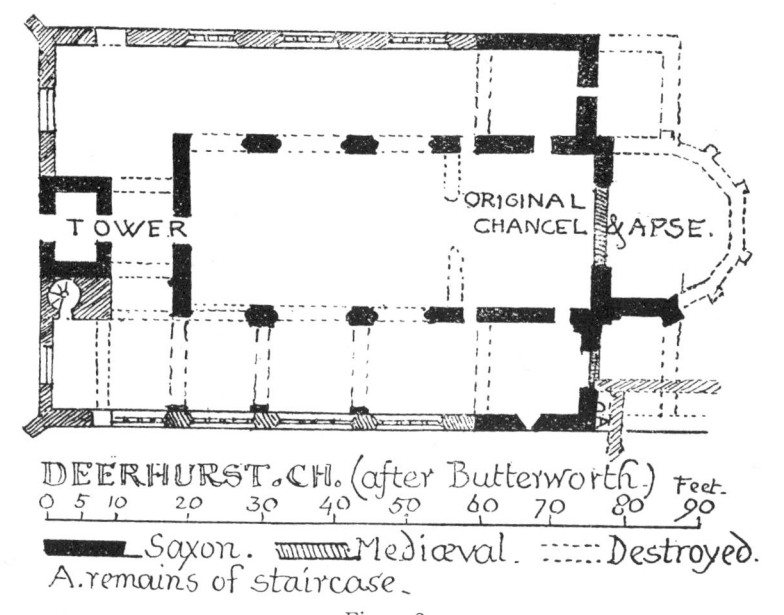

Ramsey

Dover

DEERHURST CH. (after Butterworth.)
▬▬ Saxon. ▒▒▒ Mediæval. ┄┄┄ Destroyed.
A. remains of staircase.
Fig. 118.

Deerhurst has another Saxon building, the chapel of Duke Odda, dedicated to the Trinity by Bishop Aeldred in 1056[2]. It consists of a nave and chancel communicating by a round arch on plain jambs with imposts blocks simply chamfered on the under side. The arch has a

Duke Odda's chapel Deerhurst

---

[1] *Hist. Ramsiensis*, cited Micklethwaite, *Arch. Journal*, Dec. 1896.
[2] The date and name of the founder are preserved on an inscribed stone now preserved in the Ashmolean Museum at Oxford.

plain unmoulded label, and the entrance doorway is like it. The windows are splayed both inwards and outwards. The total length is 46 ft., the chancel is 11 ft. wide, and the nave 16 ft. wide and 17 ft. to the plate. The coigns are of the long and short work frequent in Saxon building, though not peculiar to it, for I have seen some at a church in the Val d' Aosta, and the same construction has been noticed at Pompeii, at Tours, and round about Caen[1]. It consists of alternate courses, one being long and narrow, set upright, like a small post, and the next a broad flat stone set on its bed and bonding back into the wall. These long and short coigns are not found in the earlier Saxon churches, and are a sign of later date.

Long and short work

A lofty tower at the west end of the nave is almost an essential feature of the later Saxon churches built in the 10th and 11th centuries. It occurs at Earl's, Barton, Barton-on-Humber, Barnack, Brixworth, Wittering, Corbridge, and Clapham in Bedfordshire. At S. Andrew's the tower of S. Regulus or S. Rule has a strange likeness to the Lombard Campaniles, and might have been transplanted bodily from Italy (Plate CXXXIV).

The Saxon tower

S. Rule

Like the Lombard towers the English pre-conquest towers have no buttresses, but rise four-square from base to summit. It appears that in some cases they formed the actual nave of the church, which was completed by a square chamber on the west, and another square chamber on the east, one being the baptistery and the other the chancel. The upper chamber in the tower, often as at Deerhurst furnished with windows looking into the church, and treated with some attention, may have been

The Tower church

---

[1] Baldwin Brown in the *Builder* of 1895. *Notes on Pre-conquest Architecture in England*, No. VII.

Plate CXXXIV

S. RULE—S. ANDREWS

Plate CXXXV

EARL'S BARTON

CH. XXVI] ENGLAND—SAXON PERIOD 191

used for habitation[1]. The church at Barton-on-Humber seems to have been of this form originally[2].

The decoration by slightly projecting strips of stone sometimes arranged in various patterns, is a very curious

Strip-work decoration

Fig. 119.

feature of Saxon architecture. Although strip-work of a kind is to be seen in German Romanesque the way it was employed by the Saxon architects is quite original and

[1] Mr Micklethwaite who elaborates this theory credits the tower church to Danish influence.

[2] *Earlier history of Barton-on-Humber*, R. Brown, F.S.A., with illustrations by Prof. Baldwin Brown.

national, and it owes nothing to Roman example. The best specimens of it are at the two Bartons that have been just mentioned, and in the tower at EARL'S BARTON (Plate CXXXV and Fig. 119) it is so profusely used that it almost deserves to be called splendid. It occurs also in the little Saxon church of CORHAMPTON in Hampshire,

Earl's Barton

Corhampton

S LORENZO IN PASENATICO.   BARNACK NORTHANTS.

Fig. 120.

where the strips are framed round the doorways with rudely moulded bases and capitals. They are six inches wide, and project three inches from the wall face. Attempts have been made to see in this strip-work decoration a survival of the forms of timber construction, to which however it seems to bear no resemblance. It is

Plate CXXXVI

BARNACK

CH. XXVI] ENGLAND—SAXON PERIOD 193

no doubt only a device for decorating the wall, like the Cor-
blank arcadings of Toscanella and those of the brick hampton
buildings at Ravenna, and may possibly have been suggested by them. The bases and capitals of the wall-strips
at Corhampton show that what was in the architect's mind
was not a wooden post, but a stone pilaster.

Fig. 121.

The Saxon tower of BARNACK (Plate CXXXVI), near Barnack
Stamford, with its beautiful 13th century upper part, is
decorated with this strip-work, and has window slabs of
pierced stone very like one I saw and sketched at

S. Lorenzo in Pasenatico, far away in Istria (Fig. 120). The tower arch, with its curious imposts of several courses of thin stone unequally projecting, is very remarkable.

S. Bene't's, Cambridge

The Saxon church of S. BENE'T at CAMBRIDGE has a tower with baluster shafts in the windows, and a fine tower arch with two animals at the springing (Plate CXXXVII).

The Saxon baluster

The use of these dumpy balusters in the windows is another special feature of Saxon architecture. They are turned in a lathe, of which the stone bears distinct marks. Those in the doorway at Monkwearmouth are placed in pairs side by side, and measure 21 inches in height by 10 inches in diameter. Many more of the same kind are now built into the vestry wall, and two others are preserved in the Library of Durham cathedral. Baluster shafts are not unknown in Roman work, and they may have given the suggestion for these. They are often used as mid-wall shafts, as in the tower of S. Bene't's at Cambridge, and that of S. MICHAEL in the Cornmarket at OXFORD (Fig. 121), which though built probably after the conquest is obviously the work of Saxon hands. Nothing like the Saxon baluster has been found out of England, so that here again we have a distinct national feature.

Bradford-on-Avon

The most perfect and remarkable pre-conquest building is that at BRADFORD-ON-AVON, where Bishop Adhelm founded a church in 705. The existing building with its strange sculpture and arcaded walls is unique as a complete example of Saxon art. It consists of a nave and chancel, with a porch on the north side (Fig. 122). And probably it once had a corresponding porch on the south which has disappeared. It is well built with fine

Plate CXXXVII

S. BENE'T'S—CAMBRIDGE

Plate CXXXVIII

BRADFORD-ON-AVON

CH. XXVI] ENGLAND—SAXON PERIOD 195

large masonry, faced both within and without, and the exterior is decorated handsomely with shallow blank arcading of round arches springing from dumpy flat pilasters, some of which are fluted. These arcadings are not really constructed like arches, but are sunk in the surface of the coursed ashlar of the wall. The roof is of wood (Plate CXXXVIII).

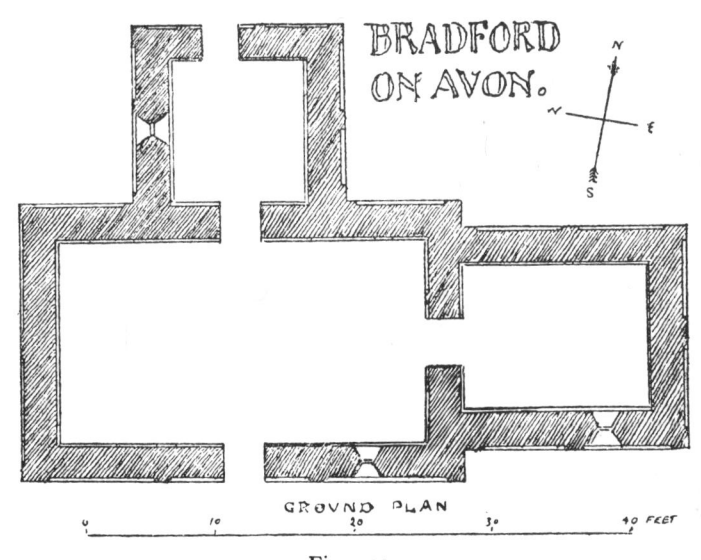

Fig. 122.

The interior is narrow and has the usual lofty porportion, and the nave and chancel communicate by a low and narrow opening with a stilted round arch springing from a plain block impost (Plate CXXXIX). The porch door is similar, and both arches have something like a rude version of the classic architrave round them.

High up in the wall over the chancel arch are fixed two remarkable sculptures of flying angels (Plate CXL) holding napkins in their hands, which perhaps belonged to

Sculpture at Bradford

a rood or crucifixion, on each side of which they might have been fitted. Doubt has been thrown on the antiquity of these figures, and Rivoira thinks, they are not coeval with the church but date from the 13th century. But there certainly was a school of sculpture in Saxon England, influenced by the foreign workmen who were introduced by Biscop and Wilfrid. Wilfrid's church at Hexham was painted and carved with histories and images in the 7th century. These figures at Bradford have a very Byzantine look, and have nothing of the grotesque which came in with northern Teutonic influences. Somewhat similar figures of angels with their hands similarly draped with napkins occur in the 12th century mosaics at the Martorana, Palermo, where they are proved to be of Byzantine origin by their Greek legends[1]. Four of them fly round the figure of Christ in the dome, but a pair are placed face to face like these at Bradford, ready to receive the soul of the Virgin which the Saviour is offering them. These figures however are in a much later style than those at Bradford.

The latter were no doubt copied from some ivory or woven stuff of Eastern looms, and so acquired a character and style in advance of English art before the conquest. The same thing has been observed in other instances: it explains the excellence of the figures on the stone crosses at Ruthwell and Bewcastle, far beyond the ordinary standard of British art at the end of the 7th century. The date of the Bewcastle cross is fixed by an inscription in 670–671, and that of Ruthwell is coeval or nearly so. In both of them the figures are modelled in a good style, the draperies are well composed, and the proportions are correct. The cathedral library at Durham contains

[1] Illustrated in Dalton's *Byzantine Art and Archaeology*, pp. 409, 665.

Plate CXXXIX

BRADFORD-ON-AVON

Plate CXL

BRADFORD-ON-AVON

CH. XXVI] ENGLAND—SAXON PERIOD 197

examples of ornamental work not less surprising. The cross of Acca, a bishop of Hexham who died in 740[1], is enriched with an arabesque pattern of singular delicacy and beauty, instead of the usual knot-work (Fig. 123). Canon Greenwell attributes this astonishing burst of artistic achievement in the Northern Kingdom to Italians introduced by Wilfrid and Biscop, but I know nothing to compare with it in Italian art of the same period, and I think it was inspired by the art of eastern rather than that of western Rome. It is confined to the Northumbrian school, and only lasted a short time there: the crosses found under the foundation of the Chapter House at Durham, which must be dated between 995 and 1130 are barbarous enough[2]. *The cross of Acca*

Decline of Northumbrian school

It has been observed "that there was an epoch when ivory carving was almost alone in maintaining the continuity of classical tradition in plastic art, and that to the lessons it was able to teach, the men who laid the foundations of Romanesque sculpture may have owed no small part of their capacity[3]." *Influence of Byzantine ivories*

The influence exercised by these smaller Byzantine works on the sculpture of the south of France has been noticed in a previous chapter[4]. There can be no doubt that it made itself felt also within our shores. Nor must we forget the effect which would be produced by the Byzantine paintings which were brought hither from

[1] Corpus vero ejus (sc. Accae) sepultum est, duaeque cruces lapideae mirabili caelatura decoratae positae sunt, una ad caput, altera ad pedes ejus. Symeon, *Hist. Regum.*
[2] See on this subject *Transactions of Durham and Northumberland Architectural and Archaeological Society*, vol. IV. Also *Catalogue of Sculptured and Inscribed Stone in the Cathedral Library, Durham*, Haverfield and Greenwell. Also Professor Lethaby in the *Architectural Review*, Aug. 1912.
[3] *Catalogue of Ivories in the British Museum*, Introduction, p. xxxiii.
[4] *v. sup.* ch. XX. p. 70.

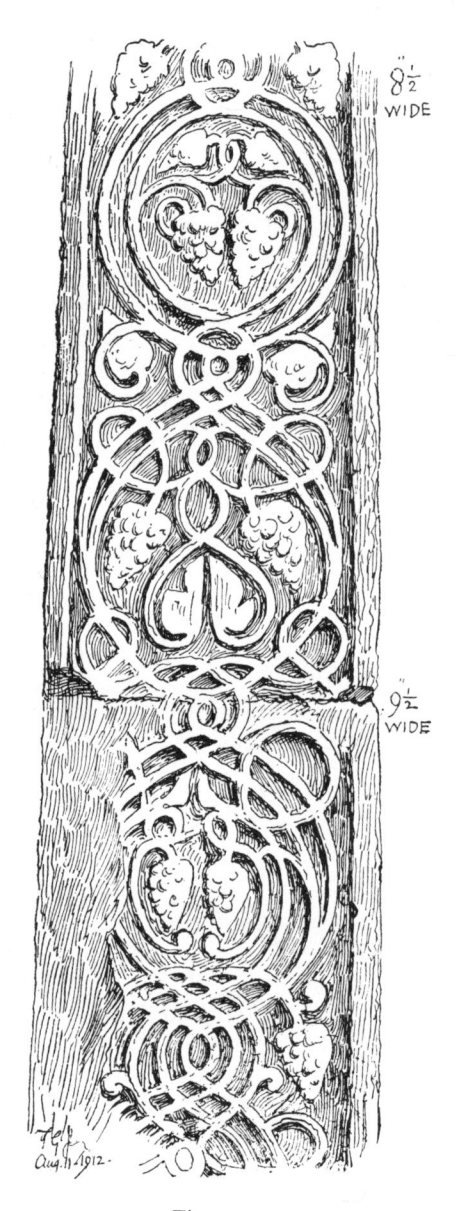

Fig. 123.

Rome by Biscop, whose example was no doubt followed by others as opportunity offered. For all hieratic decorative work the schools of the East seem to have set the example throughout Europe.

The date of the Bradford building itself is very uncertain. To judge from the design, which shows considerable architectural skill, and the execution of the masonry which is excellent, the work seems far too mature for the date of the original foundation by Bishop Adhelm about 705. One would naturally date it as well as the sculptures about the end of the 9th or even in the 10th century. And yet William of Malmesbury, writing within a century after the conquest, a monk of Adhelm's kindred foundation only a few miles away, who must have known the building well, says positively that this is Adhelm's church[1].

Date of Bradford-on-Avon church

Among the plans of Saxon churches two types appear. One has the square east end of Bradford-on-Avon, and includes Monkwearmouth, Escomb, Wittering, Repton, and Dover, the last having a transept. The other is basilican, ending in an apse, and either without a transept like Brixworth, Reculver, and S. Pancras the primitive church at Canterbury, or with one as Worth, and the curious little church at Silchester which has been described already (Fig. 113, p. 175).

Types of Saxon churches

Professor Baldwin Brown places in the oldest class those which have narrow naves and square ended chancels, some of them non-Roman, and others Romano-British and apsidal like Silchester and perhaps S. Pancras[2]. Those

Classification of Saxon churches according to date

---

[1] "Et est ad hunc diem eo loco ecclesiola quam ad nomen beatissimi Laurentii fecisse predicatur." (*Gesta Pontif. Angl.*) Micklethwaite, in the paper above cited, holds that the existing building is Adhelm's.

[2] Notes in *The Builder* as above.

with a cruciform plan, and those with towers like Brixworth which was built by Peterborough monks in 680, Reculver and Monkwearmouth belong to the 7th or early part of the 8th century. But the majority of the extant churches of Saxon workmanship probably date from the 11th century, when Canute after his conversion set to work to repair the havoc wrought by his father and his ancestors; and in this class would be the churches of Bosham, Wittering, S. Bene't's Cambridge, Corhampton, Stow, Worth, Norton, Deerhurst and Wootten-Wawen.

Two sources of plan— Roman and British

The difference in the termination, square or apsidal, introduces another classification. The round end speaks of Roman influence, either that of existing Roman buildings, or that of the Italian monks who came in with Augustine, and who naturally inclined to the form of basilica they were familiar with at home. The square end on the contrary was derived from the old British church on one hand, and from the Scotch missionaries from the north on the other.

The triple chancel arch

The ruined church at RECULVER (Fig. 124), which dates from 670, had between nave and apse, instead of a single wide arch, a triple arch supported by the two columns now standing in the garden on the north side of the cathedral at Canterbury. The church of S. Pancras at Canterbury had a similar triple arch, but there were four columns (Fig. 114, p. 177 *sup.*). The same arrangement has been traced in other early Saxon basilicas. Rivoira[1] says the remains which have been identified with the church of S. Cesario on the Palatine have the same feature, and that as this church was close to the convent whence Augustine came he must have been familiar with it, and may have imported the design to England. It is curious,

[1] *Origini dell' Arte Lombarda*, etc. vol. II. pp. 232—236.

CH. XXVI] ENGLAND—SAXON PERIOD 201

and perhaps more than a coincidence that Kent, where these two examples occur, possesses two instances of a triple chancel arch of later date, one in the fine early English church of Westwell[1] and another in the little church of Capel-le-Fern near Dover.

We can only judge of the architecture of the large Saxon churches from description, for they have all disappeared, and the style is known to us only from smaller buildings. The great minsters built by Wilfrid

The larger Saxon churches

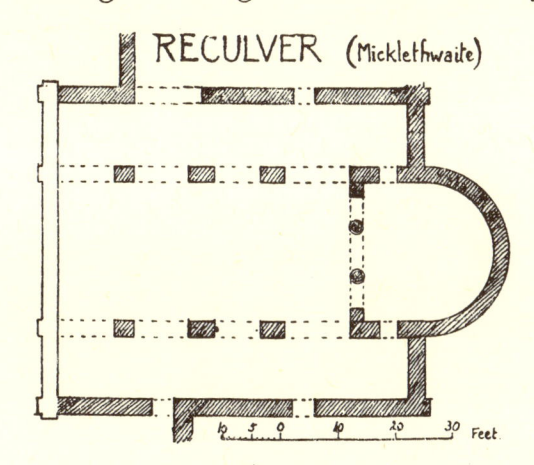

RECULVER (Micklethwaite)

Fig. 124.

at Hexham and Ripon are described in glowing language by Saxon and even by Norman writers. They dwell at length on the wonderful complexity of the fabric, on the chambers below ground of marvellously polished stones, the intricate building above supported on various columns, the wonderful height and length of the walls; on the capitals, and the sanctuary adorned with histories and images carved and painted, displaying a pleasing variety and wonderful beauty: on the pentices and porticos; on the three storeys, and the upper galleries with their winding

[1] Illustrated in my *Gothic Architecture in France, England and Italy*, vol. II. pl. LXXXI.

stairs so that a multitude might be there without being seen from below. From this we gather that the great Saxon churches had the triple construction of arcade triforium, and clerestory, which prevailed in all the larger churches of the succeeding styles during the middle ages.

Foreign workmen

It would seem also that they owed a good deal to foreign workmen, for Wilfrid no less than Biscop,—both of them strenuous promoters of the authority of the See of Rome, —imported workmen from Italy of various trades to help in carrying out these great structures.

Roman tradition

This will partly account for the presence of a much stronger classic feeling in Saxon buildings, such as that of Bradford-on-Avon, than in the Norman style which superseded it.

Canterbury, the Saxon cathedral

Roman influence showed itself remarkably in the original cathedral of Canterbury (Fig. 127) to which we shall have occasion to refer in the next chapter. Edmer who had seen both says it resembled the church of S. Peter at Rome. It appears from his description to have had an apse at each end, that to the west being no doubt the original Roman sanctuary, and that to the east being probably formed subsequently. But there was another instance of an English church with an apse at each end like those on the Rhine: the abbey church at ABINGDON, founded in 675, was 120 ft. long and was round both at the east and west end[1]. It is remarkable also that it had a round tower, like those at Ravenna and in Ireland.

Abundance of Saxon remains

It is unnecessary however to dwell at greater length on a style which has not very much artistic value though historically it forms a fascinating subject. Examples of it are found in all parts of the country, and there is no

---

[1] "Habebat in longitudine C et XX pedes et erat rotundum tam in parte occidentali quam in parte orientali." *Chron. Monast. de Abingdon*, cited Micklethwaite, *Archaeol. Journal*, 1896.

doubt that every town and village had its church before the conquest. In Lincolnshire alone it is said there were two hundred village churches, without counting those in Lincoln and Stamford, or the monasteries[1]. Careful observation is constantly adding to the list of those that remain: the first edition of Rickman doubts whether there are any; the third edition of 1835 mentions twenty, Parker's later edition names eighty-seven, and this number might now be increased.

The style has many points of difference both from the Roman work which preceded, and the Norman which followed it. The absence of buttresses, the enormously high proportion of the walls in comparison with the length and width of the building, the slender lofty tower, the small western porch, the balusters, the strip-work, the long and short coigns, and the triangular arches are all features peculiar to the style, and justify us in claiming it as a native art however much it was at first inspired by the ambition to build *more Romanorum*. {Characteristics of Saxon work}

Saxon architecture suffered from two great waves of destruction, the inroads of the Danes and Norsemen who burned houses and churches indiscriminately, and the much more thorough sweep made by the Normans after the conquest, inspired not by mere love of destruction, but by artistic passion, and a spirit of pride, which impelled them to despise the architecture of the conquered race, and replace it by their own vigorous work, which contained the seed of all future development of English architecture. {Destruction of Saxon buildings}

Saxon art seems to have sunk into a sort of Byzantine immobility. When we remember that a period of 464

---

[1] Churton's *Early British Church.*

<small>Unprogressive character of Saxon architecture</small>

years passed between the coming of Augustine and that of the Normans, and that there is but little difference between early Saxon buildings and late; and when we think of the next 464 years with the tower of London at the beginning and Wolsey's Palace of Hampton Court at the end of that period, we cannot but feel that in art as in politics the Norman conquest, with all the suffering and misery it caused for a time, was a necessary, and in the end a wholesome awakening.

CHAPTER XXVII

NORMAN ARCHITECTURE

THE Romanesque art of Normandy passed over to England before the conquest, and made its first appearance in the building which is the centre of all English History.

Edward the Confessor had been reared as an exile in Normandy during the reign of the Danish kings, and when he returned to England he was more a Norman than an Englishman. When therefore he resolved to re-build the Abbey at WESTMINSTER on a more splendid scale he adopted the Norman style with which he was familiar[1]. From early times there had been a Western minster of S. Peter, so called to distinguish it from the Eastern minster of S. Paul. Eastward of this, to avoid interruption of the services, Edward's new church was raised in a style never before seen in England (Fig. 125). It had a round apse, a transept with apsidal chapels on its east side, a long nave, and two western towers. A nearly contemporary account written between 1065 and 1074[2] speaks of two storeys of vaults over the aisle, and a central tower with winding stairs covered with a roof of timber and lead. Such a tower is shown in the representation of the church in the Bayeux tapestry,

The Confessor's Abbey at Westminster

---

[1] In the Record office Report, (cited Lethabye, *Westminster Abbey*, etc. p. 102) the Architect appears as Godwin called Great Syd, Cementarius of the church, which seems to make him a Saxon.

[2] *Life of Edward the Confessor*, Rolls Series; *v. Gleanings from Westminster Abbey*, ed. Sir G. G. Scott. It has generally been thought that the confessor did not live to complete the nave: but Dean Robinson doubts this. *v. Archaeologia*, vol. LXII.

206 ENGLAND—NORMAN PERIOD [CH. XXVII

Remains of the Confessor's building

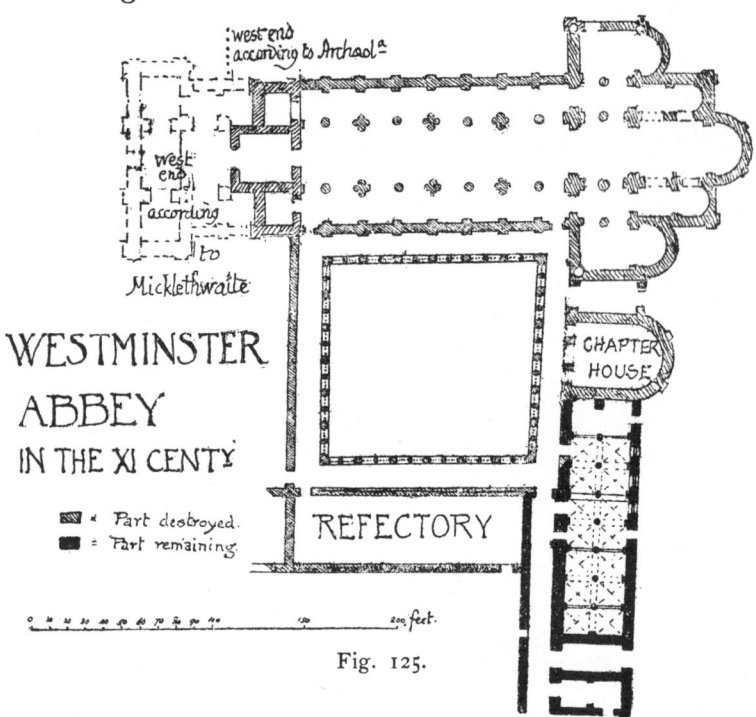

which however is no doubt very conventional. Though the Confessor's Church[1] has disappeared a long range of his monastic building remains, between the south transept and Dean's Yard. The upper storey, once the monks' dormitory, is now occupied by the library and the great school of Westminster. Below it is a

WESTMINSTER ABBEY IN THE XI CENTY

■ = Part destroyed.
■ = Part remaining.

Fig. 125.

low vaulted building with a row of massive columns down the middle from which the groining springs to either side, with plain flat transverse ribs, but no

[1] The plan in my first edition shows Mr Micklethwaite's conjectural restoration of the Saxon church. Excavation has since proved that there was no columned apse with an ambulatory. The present plan (fig. 125) shows the apse of which foundations have been found, and Dean Robinson's conjectural restoration of the transepts and their chapels, which he bases on the plan of Jumieges. v. *Archaeologia*, vol. LXII. part I.

CH. XXVII] ENGLAND—NORMAN PERIOD 207

diagonals (Fig. 126), like the crypts of Mainz, Speyer, and many others described in former chapters. Nothing can be plainer than the workmanship. The capitals are thick flat slabs with a simple ovolo below, and the base is similar. Some of the capitals have been roughly decorated in Norman times on one side leaving the other square, showing probably that there were partitions

Fig. 126 (from *Gleanings &c.*).

against them. There is a little better finish in the windows of the upper storey, which have an outer order with jamb shafts and cushion capitals. But there are signs that it is later than that below.

The effect of this building, reinforced by the Norman conquest that followed, was to revolutionize the art of the country. William of Malmesbury, writing less than

Spread of the Norman style

a century later, says the church "which Edward was the first to build in England in that kind of design, was now emulated by nearly all in sumptuous outlay." "Now," he says in another place, "you may see in villages churches, in towns monasteries rise in the new style of building[1]."

The Norman re-building

No sooner were the Normans established here than they began to pull down the existing churches and re-build them on a more magnificent scale. There could have been no necessity for this re-building: most of the Saxon churches only dated from the time of Canute, and could not have fallen into disrepair in so short a time, for the Saxon masonry is on the whole as good if not better than that of the Normans, much of which is very bad. The general re-building was dictated by the ambition of impressing themselves visibly on the conquered soil, and leaving behind them an unmistakeable mark of their superiority to the conquered race in art as well as in arms. The Saxon buildings were small compared with those the conquerors had left behind them in Normandy.

The size of Norman buildings in England

But they were not content to build here as they had built there: their work on the conquered English soil should be still vaster and grander. The churches they began and to a great extent finished within half a century after the Conquest,—Lincoln, Durham, S. Albans, Winchester, Gloucester, S. Paul's in London, Norwich and many more—are far bigger than the Norman buildings over the sea. The Abbey Church at Bath, built about 1100 by John de Villula, the first bishop of Bath and Wells, was so vast that the site of the nave alone contains the present building[2]. When one

[1] Will. of Malm. II. 228.
[2] v. Paper on the Norman Cathedral of Bath by J. T. Irvine. *Brit. Archaeol. Association*, 1890.

thinks of the number of buildings done in so short a time, of the enormous scale of most of them, and compares them with the scanty population which even two hundred years later is estimated at less than two million, and with the few appliances and slender resources of the 11th and 12th centuries, one feels amazed at the enterprise of these Norman builders, who could not only conceive but actually carry out undertakings apparently so far beyond their means.

It is not to be supposed that all the traditions of the older English architecture suddenly disappeared: on the contrary the Saxon mode of building went on for a long time side by side with the Norman, which was itself largely influenced by it. Professor Freeman observes that Edward's dark cloister at Westminster is more Saxon than Norman; he traces the more Roman character of Saxon work in the vast round piers of Gloucester and Durham, and derives the curious spiral channelling of the columns at Durham, Norwich, and Waltham from classical flutings[1]. Church towers continued to be built like those at Deerhurst and Cambridge. The castle tower at Oxford is Saxon in character, and so is the tower of S. Michael's in the Cornmarket (Fig. 121) with its baluster shafts, placed mid-wall like those at Earl's Barton and S. Bene't's at Cambridge. The crypt of S. Peter's in the East at Oxford is very like Wilfrid's Confessio at Hexham and those at Repton and Ripon, and traces may still be seen of the two descending passages and the central tomb or relic chamber between them which exist in the earlier structures. The square east end of the Norman churches at Romsey, S. Frideswide's, S. David's and S. Cross speak of Saxon influence, and the same

Survival of Saxon architecture

Influences of Saxon art on Norman architecture

[1] Freeman's *Norman Conquest*, vol. V.

210 ENGLAND—NORMAN PERIOD [CH. XXVII

national tradition in time supplanted most of the apses with which the Norman cathedrals began.

Lanfranc's cathedral at Canterbury

The second Norman church in England was the cathedral of CANTERBURY. Lanfranc the Italian monk, abbot first of Bec, and afterwards of S. Étienne at Caen, whom William made his archbishop, was a native of Pavia. During his youth he would have seen rising in his native city arcaded walls, rich in marble and sculpture, of the fine Lombard Romanesque. The humble church of Augustine satisfied neither him nor his master, and just before his arrival an opportune fire had completed the ruin into which it had fallen from age. "But though the greatness of the misfortune drove him to despair, he recovered himself, and relying on his strength of mind, he disregarded his own accommodation and completed in haste the dwellings needed by the monks. The church which fire and age had made unserviceable he pulled down to the foundations, desiring to build a more noble one[1]." The re-building was accomplished by Lanfranc in seven years.

Saxon cathedral at Canterbury

What Lanfranc destroyed was the ancient Roman church, which was recovered to Christian use by Augustine in 602, and enlarged, re-roofed, and restored by Odo about 950. A description of it has been left us by Edmer who saw it pulled down and its successor built. He had been to Rome with Anselm, and had seen Constantine's church of S. Peter there, and he says the church at Canterbury was in some part imitated from it. The resemblance between two churches so vastly different in scale and execution could only relate to points

[1] Ecclesiam Salvatoris, quam cum prefatum incendium tum vetustas inutilem fecerat, funditus destruere et augustiorem construere cupiens, etc. Edmer, cited Willis, *Architectural History of Canterbury Cathedral.*

CH. XXVII] ENGLAND—NORMAN PERIOD 211

of ritual arrangement; and if we compare the plan of S. Peter's (*v. supra* vol. I. p. 19, Fig. 2) with that of the Saxon church at Canterbury which Willis has constructed from Edmer's account (Fig. 127), it would seem to be confined to the presbytery, which Edmer tells us was raised over a crypt or confessionary like S. Peter's, and had to be reached by many steps from the choir of

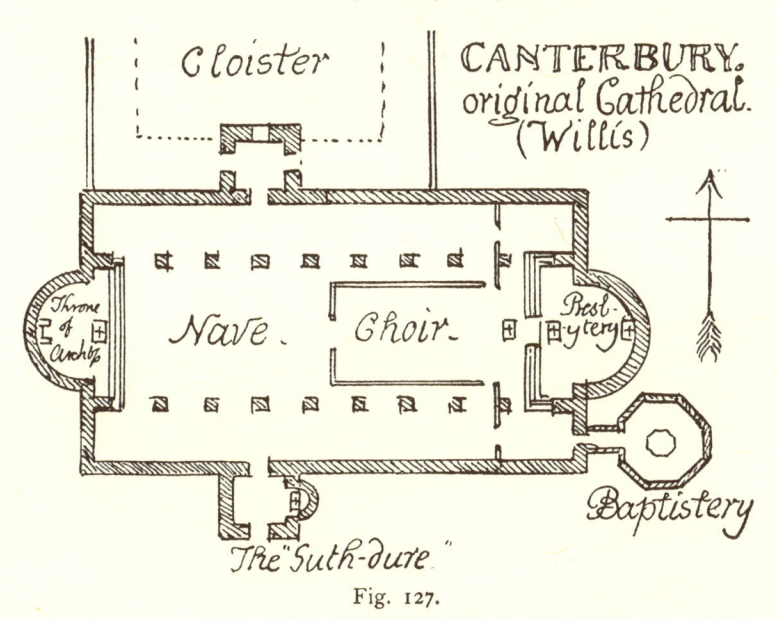

Resemblance to S. Peter's at Rome

Fig. 127.

the singers. This *chorus cantorum* was in the nave like those at S. Clemente and S. Maria in Cosmedin in Rome and the excavated basilica of Salona in Dalmatia[1]. The two flanking towers have nothing in common with S. Peter's. At the west end Edmer tells us was the altar of the Virgin, raised some height and reached by steps, and behind it against the wall was the Pontifical

[1] Chorus psallentium in aulam ecclesiae porrigebatur, decenti fabrica a frequentia turbae seclusus. Edmer, cited Willis.

14—2

212 ENGLAND—NORMAN PERIOD [CH. XXVII

Canterbury

chair[1]. Willis conjectures that this implies a western apse, which may have been the original presbytery before orientation became the rule.

The new cathedral

Lanfranc's new cathedral was a basilica ending in an apse with transepts, and a central tower over the crossing. On the east of each transept was an apsidal chapel, and the whole plan was very like that at Westminster (Fig. 128). Willis observes that the dimensions of the new Cathedral so far as can be ascertained, correspond very closely with those of S. Étienne at Caen, of which Lanfranc had been the first abbot, and which was built under his direction. Nothing however is now to be seen of Lanfranc's

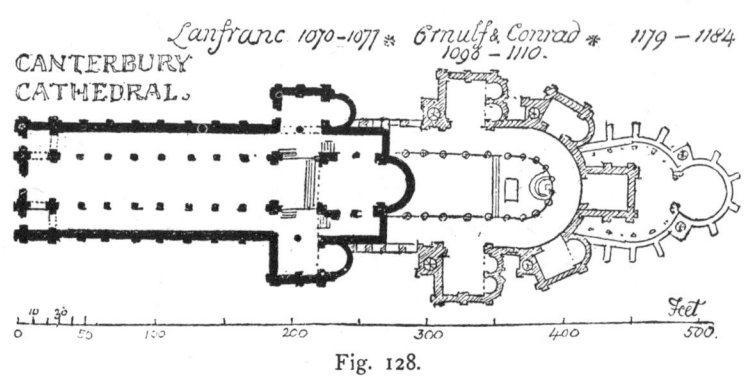

Fig. 128.

Ernulf and Conrad's glorious choir

cathedral but a few patches of masonry opposite the spot where Becket fell. The choir was pulled down twenty years after its completion and re-built on a much grander scale by Priors Ernulf and Conrad between 1096 and 1110. To them we owe all the Norman work now visible above ground (Plate CXLI), and the greater part of the crypt. In the slender jamb-shafts of the windows and the rich interlacing wall-arcades we see an

---

[1] Ad hoc altare cum sacerdos ageret divina mysteria faciem ad populum qui deorsum stabat ad orientem versam habebat. Edmer, cited Willis.

Plate CXLI

CANTERBURY—South-east Transept

Plate CXLII

CANTERBURY—The Crypt

CH. XXVII] ENGLAND—NORMAN PERIOD 213

advance of the style towards greater delicacy and refinement. Some of the colonnettes are twisted, some octagonal, and others are enriched with diaper ornament. Some of the capitals are rudely carved, but most are of the cushion form though often relieved by fluting.

Canterbury

The crypt (Plate CXLII), the finest in England and among the finest in Europe, is vaulted with cross-groining carried on monocylindrical pillars with plain transverse ribs between the bays. Many of the shafts are enriched with fluted patterns, scaled, zigzaged or twisted, and the capitals are either plain cushions, or carved with rude Corinthianizing foliage, or storied with grotesque beasts. On one a devilish goat plays the fiddle to another, who is riding on a fish and blowing a trumpet. This Norman crypt of about 1100 extends under the smaller transept, and stops at the eastern apsidal end of Prior Conrad's choir. The rest of the present crypt eastwards is of the later building after the fire of 1174.

The crypt

The great church at WINCHESTER had been re-built for the third time by Kynegils king of Wessex on his conversion in 635, and it became a cathedral shortly after when the see was transferred thither from Dorchester in Oxfordshire. As usual various miracles attended its erection. A mason named Godus fell from top to bottom of the structure, but no sooner touched the ground than he rose unhurt, wondered how he got there, signed himself with the cross, mounted the scaffolding, and taking his trowel continued his work where he left off[1]. It is described in an elegiac poem of 330 lines by

Winchester cathedral

---

[1] *Annales de Wintonia*, Rolls Series. These miracles are not peculiar to Christian legends. A workman on the Parthenon who fell from a height was cured by a medicine which Pallas revealed to Pericles in a dream. (Plutarch, *Life of Pericles*.)

Winchester, the Saxon cathedral

the monk Wolstan, who following the similar descriptions of Wilfrid's churches at Ripon and Hexham, enlarges on the mysterious intricacy of the fabric. The stranger arriving in the courts knows not which way to go, so many doors stand open to invite him; and casting a wandering eye hither and thither he stands transfixed with amazement at the fine roofs of Daedalian art, till some one familiar with the place guides him to the threshold. Here he marvels, crosses himself, and with astonished breast wonders how he shall go out, so splendid and various is the construction. As Wolstan only conducts his visitor to the threshold of the church, all this mystification would seem to belong to an atrium before it, which may have had chapels or other monastic apartments opening from it to puzzle strangers.

Bishop Walkelyn's building

But all this was not good enough for the Norman bishop Walkelyn, a cousin of the Conqueror, who began a new cathedral in 1079. In 1086 it was ready for roofing. The king had given the bishop leave to take as much timber from Hempage wood as he could cut in three days and three nights, and Walkelyn managed to cut down and carry off the whole wood within that time. The king coming soon after was *quasi in extasi factus*. "Am I bewitched?" said he, "Had I not here a delightful wood?" On learning the truth he was *in furorem versus*, and Walkelyn only obtained pardon by the most abject humiliation[1].

The new church was finished in 1103 and consecrated in the presence of nearly all the bishops and abbots of England. The old Saxon church was still standing close

---

[1] Postremo Rex, "certe," inquit, "Walkeline, ego nimis prodigus largitor, et tu nimis avidus exstitisti acceptor." *Annales de Wintonia* (*Annales Monastici*, vol. II. p. 34, Rolls Series).

CH. XXVII] ENGLAND—NORMAN PERIOD 215

by, but its demolition was begun the next day. Till Winchester cathedral
then, there would have been the strange spectacle of
three great churches of cathedral size in one enclosure;
for a few yards away, so near that the services of one
church disturbed those of the other, stood Alfred's New-
Minster, which was not removed to Hyde outside the
town till a little later.

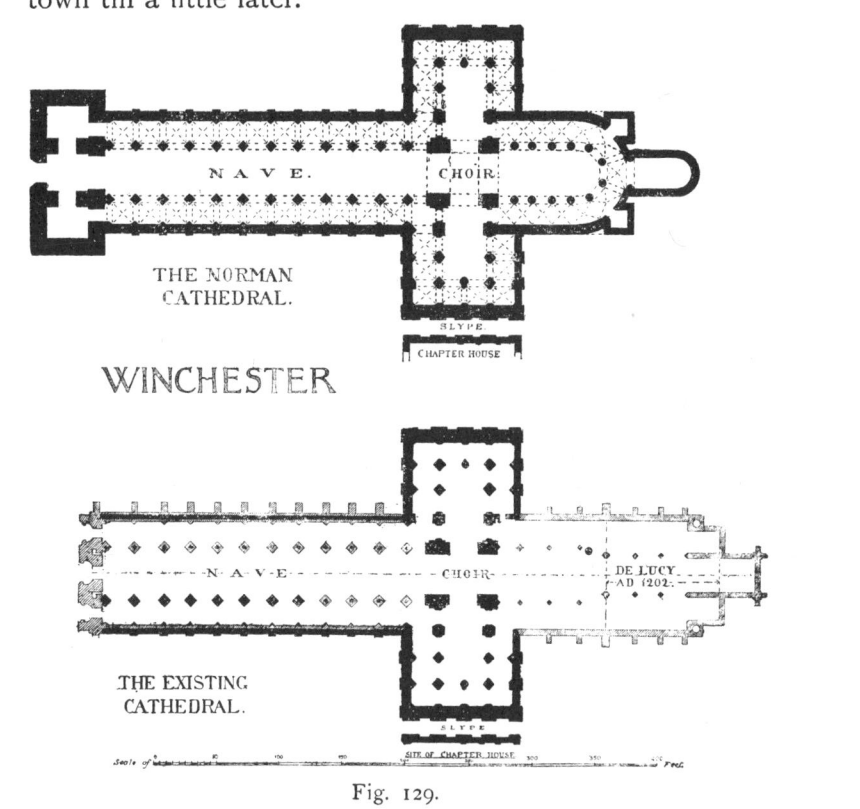

Fig. 129.

WINCHESTER cathedral is the longest or the longest Its size
but one in the kingdom, but Walkelyn's west front
reached 40 ft. still further westward (Fig. 129). Its
gigantic proportions were probably occasioned by the

216 ENGLAND—NORMAN PERIOD [CH. XXVII

Winchester, Cult of S. Swithin
great flow of pilgrims to the shrine of S. Swithin. This good bishop of Winchester was a very popular saint: Canterbury for a long while had no relics so attractive as his, and the monks were furiously jealous of the abbey in the older capital, which threatened their ecclesiastical supremacy. The possession of a great relic was the fortune of a convent. Gloucester for a long while was as badly off as Canterbury, till Abbot Thokey sagaciously begged the body of the murdered king Edward II, which from fear of the queen had been denied burial at Malmesbury and Bristol; and he was rewarded by a stream of pilgrims to the shrine of the Lord's anointed which filled the coffers of the Abbey to overflowing. It was even said that the monks of Canterbury regarded the martyrdom of Becket as a blessing in disguise, enabling them to eclipse all other places of pilgrimage in England, and almost in Europe.

The cult of S. Swithin however did not languish, and it was to accommodate the swarms of pilgrims that Bishop Godfrey de Lucy built the beautiful retro-choir, almost a church by itself, in the first years of the 13th century.

The transepts
The greater part of Walkelyn's fabric still remains, though disguised in the nave by Wykeham's Perpendicular casing: but the transepts and the crypt have preserved their original form unaltered (Plate CXLIII). The aisles were vaulted in rubble masonry, with transverse arches dividing bay from bay, but no diagonal ribs. The upper roofs were, and in the transepts still are ceiled with wood. The details are rude, almost barbarous; the masses of masonry enormous; the detail

Absence of sculpture
simplicity itself. No sculpture decorates it, the only ornament is a billet or dentil such as any mason could

chop out. The columns have mere cushion capitals Winchester cathedral
formed by squaring off the four sides of an inverted
and truncated cone or hemisphere. Those in the crypt
are strangely primitive, and seem rude imitations of
some Doric capital that may have survived from Roman
Venta Belgarum. Across the end of each transept (Plate
CXLIII) there is the peculiar feature of a gallery,
formed by returning the arches and vaults of the aisles The transept gallery
with nothing over them, so as to form a terrace from
triforium to triforium. The same feature occurs in
Normandy, at S. Étienne in Caen, at the fine church of
Boscherville and in that at Cerisy-le-Forêt, from which
it would appear to be a feature peculiar to Norman
architecture, though an instance of something like it
exists at Le Puy in Auvergne[1]. The isolated column in
the middle of the north transept, "the Martyrdom," at
Canterbury, which together with the vault it carried was
removed for the convenience of the pilgrims, belonged
to a similar structure; and there was a corresponding
one in the south transept. The two storeyed apsidal
chapel on the east side of the transept at the Priory
church of Christchurch suggests a similar arrangement
there.

The Norman design of the transepts, which once The large Norman triforium
extended to the nave, is a good example of the importance given to the triforium in northern Romanesque.
In the south of France, in Aquitaine, Provence, and
Auvergne, either there is no triforium or it is very small.
In Italy it is generally the same thing, at all events
during the Romanesque period, except where the church
was built under Byzantine influence as S. Mark's, and

[1] That at Le Puy however is not in its original state but has been brought forward.

218 ENGLAND—NORMAN PERIOD [CH. XXVII

Winchester cathedral

S. Vitale, though their galleries differ somewhat from the northern triforium. S. Ambrogio also is an exception. In the east and in the Greek church the gallery plays an important part as the women's quarter, but it is difficult to account for its appearance in the north, where women were not separately provided for.

The apse

From the crypt (Fig. 130) we can recover exactly the form of the eastern termination of Walkelyn's church. It was apsidal with a sweep of great mono-cylindrical columns; the base of one of them may still be seen in Bishop Gardiner's chantry. It had an ambulatory aisle, and seems to have been flanked on each side by a small square tower. Eastwards was projected a Lady-chapel, aisle-less, and apsidal. The canted end of the decorated choir is accommodated to the original apsidal plan, and the eastern piers rest in great measure, though not entirely, on the original Norman foundation. The piers of De Lucy's work bear on the walls of the Norman crypt below the original Lady-chapel.

Winchester, the crypt

The crypt is one of the largest in the kingdom (Fig. 130), built with immensely massive piers, from which spring flat plain transverse ribs, and cross-groining of rubble work, plastered. It has an ambulatory aisle like the superstructure and its continuation eastward under what was the Norman Lady-chapel, is divided down the centre by a row of columns, carrying cross-groining like the rest. There is no ornament of any kind, and the capitals are as simple as the rest of the work.

Winchester tower

Winchester had a central tower which like many Norman towers fell soon after it was built. The reconstruction was begun at once in 1107, and the new tower is beautifully decorated inside with Norman arcadings,

WINCHESTER—North Transept

Plate CXLIV

ELY—North Transept

CH. XXVII] ENGLAND—NORMAN PERIOD 219

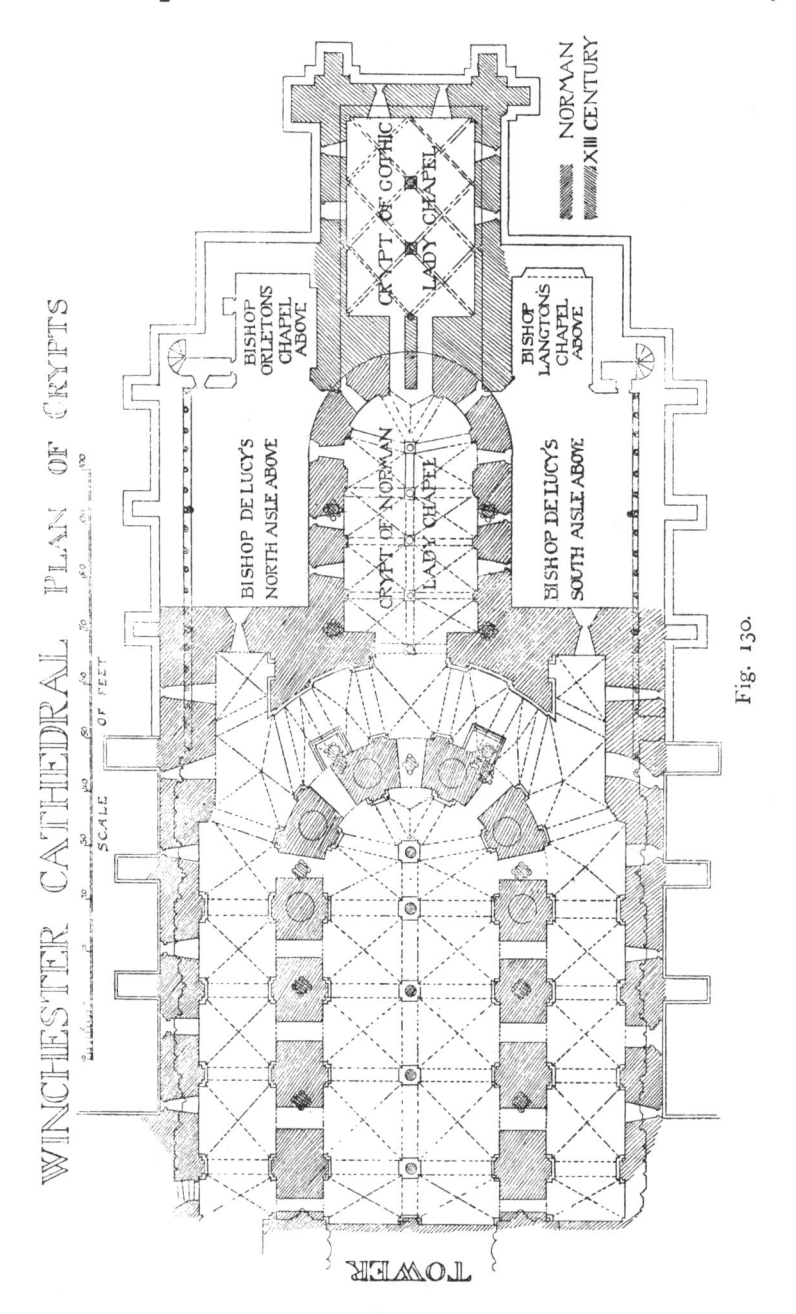

Fig. 130.

Winchester cathedral intended to have been seen as a lantern from the church, but now hidden by wooden groining of 1634.

Rude as the work is at Winchester the general effect of Walkelyn's building is magnificently impressive, and there are few façades so grand and so satisfactory as that of the south transept.

Ely cathedral ELY cathedral was begun at the same time as Winchester by Prior Simeon who was Walkelyn's brother, and as was natural there is a certain resemblance between the Norman work at the two places. At Ely one bay of the nave and one of each transept have been absorbed by Alan de Walsingham's octagon, constructed after the fall of the Norman tower in 1321. At Winchester the nave has lost one arch through the setting back of the west front of the nave by Bishop Edyngton in the middle of the 14th century. But originally both cathedrals seem to have had 13 arches in the nave, and four in the transepts. At both churches the transepts have aisles on both sides, both ended with a short choir and an apse, though Winchester alone had an ambulatory round it. There is even some ground for supposing that Ely had the same gallery from triforium to triforium, occupying the last bay of the transept.

Abbot Simeon however, who was 87 when he went to Ely in 1081, did not live to carry his walls very high, and the cathedral is in a later style of Norman than his brother's church at Winchester. Probably the only part of Simeon's work is the lower storey of the transepts (Plate CXLIV), which is in an earlier style than the upper part; but even there the capitals of the great round columns (Fig. 141 *inf.*) show an attempt at decoration beyond anything to be seen at Winchester. After Simeon's death in 1093 no abbot was appointed by

William II, and the office remained vacant till it was filled by Abbot Richard in 1100, who finished the eastern part, which is now superseded by a later building. The nave and the Norman stages of the western tower were completed by Bishop Riddell (1174–1189). Ely cathedral

The greater part of the nave and transepts is still of the original building, but the eastern limb was re-built and prolonged by Bishop Hugh de Northwold between 1229 and 1254 in the Early Pointed style, when the national square east end took the place of the Norman apse. The Norman pillars of the nave have shafts running up to the roof to mark the bays, but are alternately composed of clustered columns, and mono-cylindrical columns with small shafts attached. This gives an agreeable variety to the piers, which would, if all alike, have been monotonous. At the west end is a second transept of later Norman work, with a great tower in the middle of the west end of the nave; and the design included a wing on either side, of which only the southern one now exists, with an apsidal chapel on its eastern side and two round Norman turrets at the end. This is a singular feature, reminding one of the great churches on the Rhine, though the motive for a western transept, which is there supplied by a second apse and choir, is wanting here.

At Ely the nave and transepts never received their stone vaults, and are still ceiled with timber.

NORWICH cathedral was begun by Bishop Losinga in 1096 after he had moved the see thither from Thetford. It is built on a superb scale, and still remains a Norman church, with an eastern apse surrounded by an ambulatory aisle, and with two chapels attached to the sides of it like those at Canterbury and Gloucester. A similar chapel

Norwich cathedral

for Our Lady at the east end probably completed the original *chevet*, but it was replaced by a larger rectangular one in the 13th century which has in its turn disappeared. The central tower is crowned with a later spire which was added in the 15th century and this, with the apse and the flying buttresses that support the 15th century clerestory and vault of the choir, makes the exterior of this cathedral exceptionally picturesque. The nave is some half-century later than the eastern limb; it is enormously long and has 14 bays, and the choir, with four bays before the apse, is longer than the usual Norman proportion. If the nave was built by Bishop Eborard (1121–1145), as is supposed, its style is very archaic for that date. The pillars as at Ely are of two kinds, placed alternately. The principal piers are formed of a cluster of attached colonnettes with cushion capitals, some of which run up to the roof and serve as vaulting shafts. The intermediate pillars also now have attached colonnettes, but they have been cased and altered, the bases of the colonnettes that were added being of 15th century work. Originally they seem to have been huge mono-cylindrical columns without colonnettes attached, but with a single vaulting shaft only on the nave side starting above the capital. In the eastern bay of the nave on each side one column remains in its original state (Plate CXLV) with a simple spreading cushion capital and spiral flutings. The casing of another column has been cut into, revealing similar flutings behind it, and there seems no doubt that like those at Durham these huge round columns once alternated all down the nave. The triforium consists of great open arches, undivided into two lights by the usual central column, and is almost if not quite equal in height to the arcade below, resembling in this the proportion

Plate CXLV

NORWICH—South Nave Aisle

Plate CXLVI

DURHAM

of those noticed in preceding chapters at Tournai in Belgium, and in Normandy. The same stern simplicity reigns here as at Winchester and Ely: the capitals are of the plain cushion form, and the arches are little more than square-cut openings through the walls, which seems a survival of the Saxon method. The wide soffits thus formed give space for several attached shafts with cushion capitals set side by side, both below in the arcade and above in the triforium. *(Norwich cathedral)*

The exterior of DURHAM, with its three massive towers, its enormous bulk, and its superb position on a rocky promontory round which the river Wear sweeps in a grand wooded defile, makes perhaps the most impressive picture of any cathedral in Europe (Plate CXLVI). *(Durham cathedral)*

Terror of the Danes drove away the monks in 875 from Lindisfarne, where S. Aidan had been established by King Oswald, and where S. Cuthbert in 684 had built a monastery of rude huts of timber and earth, within an enclosure of stone and turf[1]. For eight years they wandered, carrying with them the precious body of S. Cuthbert, before they found a temporary resting place at Chester-le-Street; and it was not till 995 that they finally settled on the impregnable site of Durham. In 999 Bishop Aldhun built the first stone church there. *(The Saxon church)* This was destroyed by William of S. Carilef, the second Norman bishop, who laid the first stone of a new minster in 1093. Before his death he had completed the eastern part as far as the crossing, including the east side of the transepts; and the monks continued the work afterwards, completing the transepts and central crossing, and the first bay of the nave. The western side of the transept, *(The Norman church)*

---

[1] Bede, *Vita S. Cuthberti, v. sup.* p. 183.

224 ENGLAND—NORMAN PERIOD [CH. XXVII

Durham Cathedral — which is their work, is plainer than the other and has no aisle.

The choir now ends in an eastern transept, the "chapel of the Nine Altars," built in a vigorous Early Pointed style. Originally, as might be expected, it finished with an apse, and in 1875 it was discovered that instead of having an ambulatory like Winchester, Canterbury, and Norwich round the central apse, the church ended with three apses like S. Maria in Cosmedin at Rome, and the churches of the Greek rite. The two side apses seem to have been square externally though round within, as is the case at the Euphrasian basilica of Parenzo (*v.* vol. I. p. 182).

The choir — The Norman choir had four arches in two double bays east of the crossing: the main piers have attached half-columns, and are elongated as if they were segments of a side wall, and the intermediates are circular with spiral and zigzag flutings. A later bay occupies the place of the Norman apse. The details are plain, though the arches of the main arcade are rather richly moulded, an advance on those of Winchester (Plate CXLIII *sup.*) which are not moulded at all. The triforium has a moulded including order over two sub-arches with a central column. The clerestory windows are very plain and in the choir have no mural passage. The design of Carilef's work is continued in the transept (Fig. 131) where some of the original shafts remain, running up to the top of the wall, showing that though the aisles were vaulted the central span was intended to be covered by a wooden roof.

The capitals — The capitals are all of the cushion type, but those of the cylindrical columns are eight-sided, which makes them deficient in projection, and gives them a curious bluntness of effect.

Fig. 131.

226 ENGLAND—NORMAN PERIOD [CH. XXVII

Durham cathedral, The nave

The vault

The nave was built by the next bishop, Ralph Flambard (1099–1128), and shows an advance in technique on the earlier work. The simple clerestory of Carilef's building is handsomely replaced by a triplet, with a central arch opposite the window, and a narrow arch on each side carried by colonnettes; the triforium has two including orders instead of one; and the main arches are enriched with zigzags and other ornaments (Plate CXLVII). They are grouped in double bays, the intermediate columns being cylindrical, and fluted or enriched with channellings in chevrons or chequers. The stone vault, which is thoroughly developed with rib and panel construction, is supposed by some to have been finished before 1133[1]. I think it more probably dates from the 13th century or at the earliest from the time of Bishop Pudsey (1153–1195) the builder of the Galilee. It has many peculiarities. There is a heavy transverse arch dividing one double bay from another and between them are two quadripartite vaults with no transverse rib to divide them. The same plan obtains in the transept (Fig. 131). I am not aware of another instance of this arrangement.

The great transverse arches are pointed, but they are segmental: the height being given by the side walls and the round arch of the central tower, a pointed arch could only be got by dropping the springing. This again implies that the present vault was not the covering originally contemplated, but that as in the transept a wooden roof was prepared for.

[1] Canon Greenwell, *Durham Cathedral*, 1897, p. 36. He quotes Symeon of Durham, who says the monks completed the nave between the death of Flambard in 1128, and the succession of Galfrid Rufus in 1133. Eo tempore navis ecclesiae Dunelmensis, monachis operi instantibus, peracta est. Symeon, *continuatio*, Cap. I. Canon Greenwell argues that at the death of Flambard there was nothing but the vault left for them to do, but this seems a large assumption. M. de Lasteyrie shares my doubts and thinks these vaults coeval with those at S. Denis, i.e. 1144. *Arch. Rom.* p. 497. See further as to this my *Gothic Architecture in France, England and Italy*, vol. I. p. 184.

Plate CLVI

CASTOR

Plate CLVII

S. PETER'S—NORTHAMPTON

CH. XXVII] ENGLAND—NORMAN PERIOD 227

The Galilee chapel outside the west end, which overhangs the precipice, and where lie the bones of the Venerable Bede, shows what the Norman style was developed into when greater experience and riper constructive power enabled the builders to design in a lighter style and with more elegance (Plate CXLVIII). It was built by Bishop Pudsey about the year 1175, less than a hundred years after Bishop William laid the first stone of his ponderous arcades, and it shows a fairly rapid advance in architectural skill[1]. Indeed the architect reduced his supports dangerously. Of the present

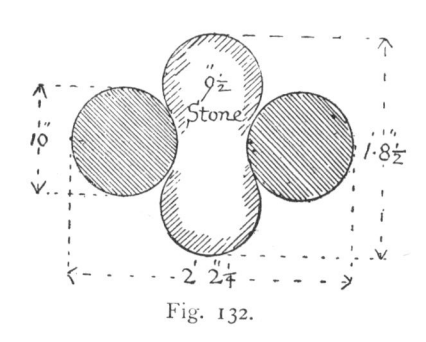

Durham cathedral, The Galilee

Fig. 132.

quatrefoil columns (Fig. 132) only the two marble shafts are original, and the stone shafts were added by Cardinal Langley (1406–1437) to strengthen them. The original arrangement remains in the responds, which have the two detached marble shafts without the addition. Some only of the capitals have the abacus broken out over the additional shafts; several still retain the simple straight abacus belonging to the two marble shafts, like the entablature over the coupled columns at S. Costanza in Rome (v. vol. I. p. 190, Plate XLIV).

[1] The names of Bishop Pudsey's architects are recorded,—Richard and William. They are called *ingeniatores*. Greenwell, *op. cit.* p. 48

15—2

228 ENGLAND—NORMAN PERIOD [CH. XXVII

Durham cathedral, The conventional ornament

The development of ornament however did not keep pace with that of the architectural form; in the Galilee arches we have still only the conventional Norman zigzag, and the capitals consist of four plain flat leaves which hardly amount to sculpture. In this respect the work at Durham lags behind that at Canterbury, where by this time Romanesque tradition had almost been forgotten.

Progress of the art from Winchester to Durham

Winchester and Durham between them furnish an epitome of Norman Romanesque. The plain unmoulded orders of Bishop Walkelyn are followed some 20 years later by Bishop William's well-moulded arcades at Durham; his simpler work is succeeded in less than another 20 years by Bishop Flambard's more ornate and refined work in the nave; and half a century later Bishop Pudsey's elegant Galilee brings us to the period of transition from Romanesque to lighter Gothic.

Improved proportion of the storeys

The advance at Durham on the transepts of Winchester is shown also by the infinitely better proportion of the three storeys. At Winchester the triforium and the great arcade are nearly equal in height. At Norwich they seem quite so. At Durham the great arcade is raised at the expense of the upper storeys with a magnificent result. In that splendid nave, with its huge towering columns, no artist can stand unmoved.

Pittington church

The interesting church of PITTINGTON, some five or six miles from Durham, is said to have been another work of Bishop Pudsey. The fluted and spirally adorned columns of the nave (Plate CXLIX) seem to have been inspired by the earlier work at Durham, but they are carried out differently. The spirals at Durham are chased into the cylindrical shaft, and do not mar the outline. At Pittington they are left in relief, and the ground is sunk instead, with the result that except where

Plate CXLIX

PITTINGTON

CH. XXVII] ENGLAND—NORMAN PERIOD 229

the spiral roll reaches it the capital overhangs the shaft Pittington church
disagreeably. The days of this spiral ornament were
really over, and the artist trying to do something original
in that way has bungled. The capitals even here do not
rise above a version of the cushion type (Fig. 133).

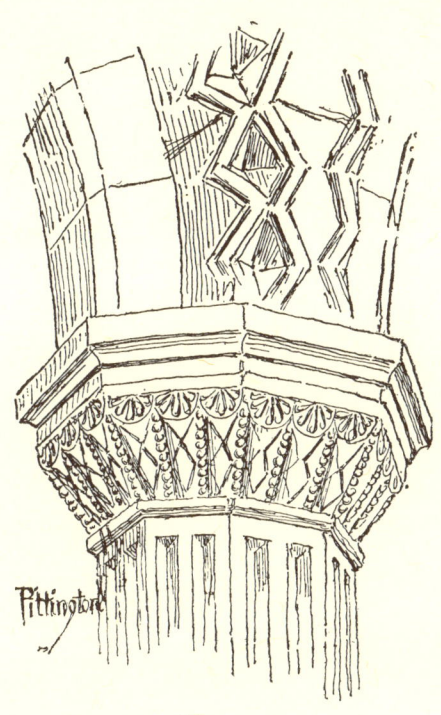

Fig. 133.

The sternest Norman work in England is that of the S. Alban's cathedral
Abbey at S. ALBAN's, of which the earlier part was built
by Abbot Paul between 1077 and 1088. Here there are
absolutely no mouldings on the edge of pier and arch.
The material employed had no doubt something to do
with this, being chiefly brick from the Roman city of
Verulam, and the remains of the Saxon church which

Abbot Paul pulled down. Among them are many of the balusters which have already been noticed as peculiar to Saxon architecture.

Elstow On a smaller scale the same simple unadorned Norman construction is shown in the fine church of ELSTOW near Bedford (Plate CL) where the square-ordered arches spring from a mere impost moulding, without even the usual cushion capital.

Peterborough cathedral PETERBOROUGH was not begun till 1118, and the nave was not finished till the end of the 12th century. It is

Fig. 134.

practically a Norman church still, though the primitive style of the nave at a period when elsewhere the style was changing into Early English is apparently an archaicism. The western part of the nave in fact was hardly finished in the Norman style before the well-known west front was begun in the Early Pointed manner. The church is basilican, and ended eastward in three apses like the original plan at Durham. The central apse still exists, though a good deal altered to make it harmonize with the Perpendicular retro-choir at the east end.

Plate CL

ELSTOW

GLOUCESTER—The Nave

CH. XXVII] ENGLAND—NORMAN PERIOD 231

The details show progress in refinement. The triforium arches are graceful and prettily decorated, and the aisle vaults have diagonal as well as transverse ribs of a heavy roll section. The nave retains its painted wooden ceiling of Norman times. *Peterborough cathedral*

The columns are massive and have attached colonnettes, some of them rising as vaulting shafts, others carrying the several orders of the arches, but in many cases, where the correspondence of order and shaft is not observed, the cushion capitals, which are universal in the Norman part, are broken out for the orders, though the main pier below remains a plain cylinder or octagon (Fig. 134).

The lofty proportion of the triforium stage which has been noticed at Winchester and other Norman churches is maintained here, though the gradation of the three storeys is more pleasing at Peterborough.

At GLOUCESTER on the other hand, which was begun by Abbot Serlo in 1089, and dedicated in 1100 much greater importance is given to the nave arcade; it attains a stately proportion at the expense of the triforium, which is diminished to very small coupled lights under an including arch (Plate CLI). The columns are enormous cylinders built of small masonry and with plain round capitals, which are neither moulded nor carved, but devoid of any ornamentation. From these capitals all the orders of the arch spring, unprepared for by anything below, and are decorated with plain roll mouldings, zigzags, and billets. The general effect, if a little severe and cold, is extremely impressive. *Gloucester cathedral*

TEWKESBURY Abbey has the same huge cylindrical columns in the nave, with plain round unornamented capitals, and arches of still simpler detail than those at *Tewkesbury*

Fig. 135.

Gloucester, and the triforium is quite unimportant, pinched up against the clerestory window-sill. The clerestory however is not original, and the Norman design may have been different. The magnificent west front with its deeply recessed arch of many orders and its two piquant pinnacles, together with the grand central tower over the crossing make this one of the very finest examples of Romanesque architecture in existence (Fig. 135)[1]. *Tewkesbury*

HEREFORD and MALVERN have the same massive cylindrical columns with simple round capitals; that at Hereford however having attached shafts on one side and surface carving on the ovolo of the capital. At Malmesbury the round capitals are scolloped in imitation of the cushion form, and there is a similar capital, still further enriched, at ABBEY DORE in Herefordshire. *Hereford and Malvern* *Malmesbury and Abbey Dore*

These cylindrical columns with a plain or nearly plain round capital at Gloucester, Tewkesbury, Malvern, Hereford, Abbey Dore, and Malmesbury, seem to form a distinctive west country type differing in many particulars from the cylindrical columns already noticed at Durham, Norwich, and Waltham, and others at Fountains, Buildwas, and S. Bartholomew's in Smithfield.

[1] I am indebted to Mr Raffles Davison for leave to reproduce his beautiful drawing.

CHAPTER XXVIII

ENGLAND—NORMAN PERIOD

Romsey abbey

OF the two great conventual churches which Hampshire boasts in addition to her cathedral, ROMSEY is remarkable among Norman churches for its square east end, which has the further anomaly of containing two windows, so that a pier comes in the middle instead of a light. The same peculiarity exists in the church of the Hospital of S. Cross near Winchester.

Christchurch priory

The other Hampshire church, the Priory of TWYNHAM or CHRISTCHURCH, which is on the scale of a cathedral, was probably begun by Ralph Flambard in the time of William Rufus. The nave and transepts (Plate CLII) of the original building still remain, but the eastern arm and the chapels beyond it were re-built with splendour in the 14th and 15th centuries. There was perhaps a Norman central tower which has disappeared, and a fine 15th century tower has been added at the west end. The aisles are vaulted, and the nave is roofed with wood. The Norman roof was replaced in the 14th century by a handsome one of timber, now much decayed, and hidden by sham vaulting of lath and plaster. The nave piers are very simple,—rectangular masses of masonry with attached colonnettes; and the triforium is divided by a central column into two sub-arches under an including one. The lofty proportion of the triforium here is like that at Winchester, Peterborough, and Ely.

Plate CLII

CHRISTCHURCH—PRIORY

Plate CLIII

CHRISTCHURCH—PRIORY—North Transept

One of the most remarkable features of the Norman work at Christchurch is the round staircase turret (Plate CLIII) at the N.E. angle of the north transept, which is richly decorated not only with arcading, but with roll mouldings in relief, forming a reticulated pattern on the surface, a feature of rare interest, which occurs also at Le Mans in France (*v. sup.* p. 160, Plate CXXIX). The capitals of the arcades on this buttress form an instructive series of early Norman carving. They have the square abacus and preserve the tradition of the classic volute.

The nave of ROCHESTER (Plate CLIV) which, in its present form, dates from 1115 and onwards, shows an advanced stage of Norman Romanesque by its clustered piers, in which the shafts correspond to the members of the arch they carry, and by the graceful enrichments of the spandrils of the triforium, or rather the arch which represents the triforium, for it has the peculiarity of being open to the aisle, so that both the lower arch of the nave arcade and that which should belong to a triforium look into the same side aisle, as they do in the Cathedral of Rouen and in S. Lorenzo at Genoa. Rochester cathedral

Professor Willis observes that originally the same peculiarity existed in the Abbaye aux Hommes, at Caen, though the aisles were subsequently vaulted at the level of the lower arches. He suggests that the same arrangement may have been adopted in Lanfranc's cathedral at Canterbury. At Rochester, there being no floor to the triforium, a passage way is formed through the piers at that level.

The chapel of S. Mary at GLASTONBURY (Plate CLV), which used to be known as S. Joseph's, represents the primitive church supposed to have been built by Joseph of Arimathea[1]. It stands at some distance west of the Glastonbury, S. Mary's chapel

[1] *v. sup.* p. 177.

Glastonbury, S. Mary's chapel

great church, to which it was joined by a Galilee porch. It was consecrated in 1186 and affords another instance of the conservatism of the monastic orders; for while at Canterbury English William was building in a style of advanced transition towards Early English, this chapel at Glastonbury is round-arched and adorned with interlacing Norman arcades, zigzags, and billet mouldings. The capitals alone betray a later taste, for they have discarded the convex outline of Norman work and adopted the concave form, and something of the springing character of the coming *cap à crochet* of Gothic architecture. The

Glastonbury abbey

same spirit of archaicism shows itself in the architecture of the great church which was built after this chapel; for though the arches are pointed, and trefoil cusps appear in the triforium, the mouldings are enriched with the zigzag and billet of the older art.

This brings us in fact to the meeting of the two styles, Romanesque and Gothic, and to the end of our period. At Malmesbury, Fountains, and Buildwas though we have the massive cylindrical columns of the Norman period

Attachment to the round arch

they carry pointed arches. The round arch nevertheless lingered on in unconstructional features, in doorheads, windows, and ornamental arcadings. The monks especially loved it best, and clung to it with conservative zeal, though in matters of construction the superior convenience

Fountains abbey

of the pointed arch could not be denied. At Fountains the clerestory windows are round-arched though the arcade below is pointed. The aisles there are vaulted in a very primitive way, by barrel vaults with their axis at right angles to that of the nave, springing from round arches turned from pier to wall.

Castor church

There is no richer example of late Norman architecture than the tower of CASTOR church in Northamptonshire

Plate CLIV

ROCHESTER—Nave

Plate CLV

GLASTONBURY ABBEY—S. Mary's Chapel

CH. XXVIII] ENGLAND—NORMAN PERIOD 237

(Plate CLVI). The church was dedicated in 1124, as a stone informs us which is built into the south wall of the chancel¹. It resembles the later work in the upper storeys of the steeples of S. Étienne at Caen (*sup.* p. 154, Plate CXXVII) and that at S. Michel des Vaucelles (Plate CXXVIII) and the tower of the south-east transept at Canterbury (Plate CXLI). It will be observed that the ornament however rich is purely conventional, more mason's work than sculptor's.

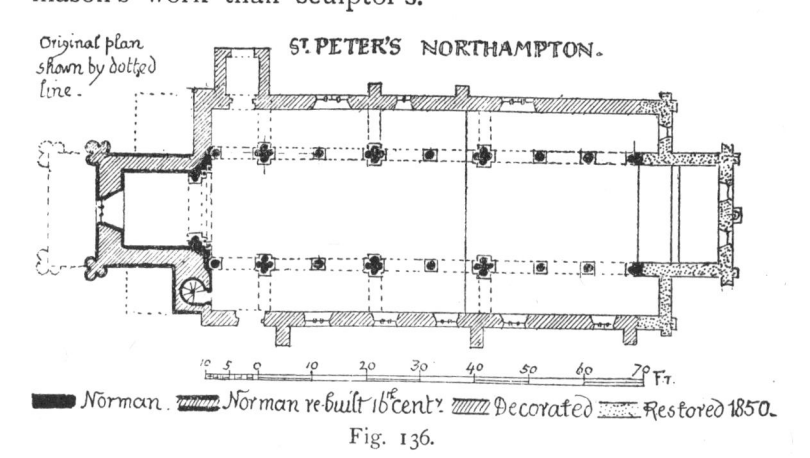

Castor church

ST. PETER'S NORTHAMPTON.
Original plan shown by dotted line.

■ Norman. ▨ Norman rebuilt 16ᵗʰ centʸ. ▨ Decorated ▨ Restored 1850.
Fig. 136.

The church of S. PETER at NORTHAMPTON, which Mr Sharpe dates as early as 1135, but others with more probability about 1180, is remarkable on many accounts. It is one of the very few instances in northern Gothic architecture where polychrome masonry is used as a mode of decoration. The strong orange-coloured iron-stone of South Northamptonshire is employed in conjunction with white free-stone in bands and alternate voussoirs, with a very happy effect. The church but for its square east end is a perfect basilica (Fig. 136), unbroken by

S. Peter's, Northampton

¹ This stone seems not to be in its original place or state. The last numeral is not in relief like the rest but scratched very rudely into the stone.

238 ENGLAND—NORMAN PERIOD [CH. XXVIII

S. Peter's, Northampton

any chancel arch, with round arches on columns, and wooden roofs. The principal columns are quatrefoil in plan, formed of four attached shafts, of which one runs up to take the tiebeams of the trusses, and they once had arches springing from them across the aisle. The intermediate columns are cylindrical, with an enriched and

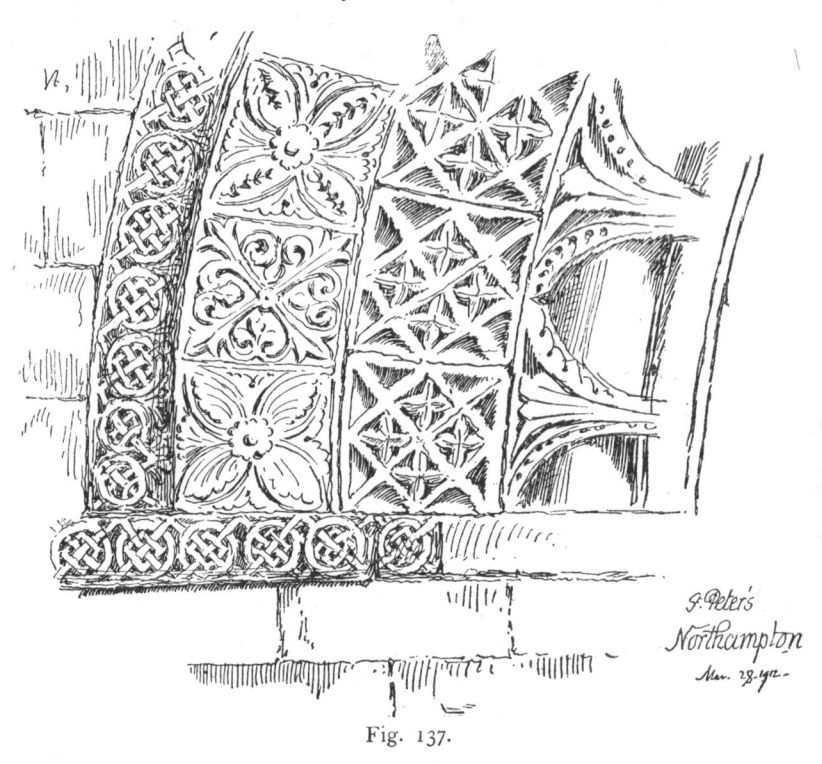

Fig. 137.

moulded band or ring surrounding them about mid-height. They all have stilted attic bases, which in some cases have toes. The tower (Plate CLVII) at the west end is not in its original state, but was re-built in the 16th century with old materials and not on the original site, but farther eastward, cutting off half of the next double bay. It has

Plate CXLVII

DURHAM—The Nave

Plate CXLVIII

DURHAM—The Galilee

CH. XXVIII] ENGLAND—NORMAN PERIOD 239

a magnificent Norman arch of many orders decorated, as are all the others in the church, with the zigzag. Another richly decorated arch of four rings and a label in the west wall once probably surmounted a west doorway (Fig. 137): but these rings are now merely inserted flat into the wall over a perpendicular window. Originally they would probably have been recessed as orders. The two western angles of the tower are buttressed each by a group of three round columns running up to the top stage which is of the 16th century. These buttress columns can hardly have been invented in the 16th century when the tower was pulled down and re-built, and in all probability they formed part of the original Norman structure; but they are so far as I know unique in England, and remind one of those of Notre Dame at Poitiers, and Civray in Poitou (*v. sup.* Plates C, CI). *S. Peter's, Northampton* *Columnar buttresses*

The clerestory on both sides is handsomely arcaded outside, and the arcades are carried on to the east end which has been reconstructed on the old foundations (Fig. 138) and on a design more or less conjectural[1].

The sculptured capitals of this church are interesting examples of what the early Norman artists could achieve. They are well proportioned, of a convex or cubical shape, and the carving takes the form of surface ornament as it did in Byzantine work. Some of them have figures of animals; others simple attempts at foliage, quite inartistically arranged; the best are covered with ornament half-way between foliage and strap-work. They have very little ordered arrangement such as classic example *Norman sculptured capitals*

---

[1] *History of the Church of S. Peter, Northampton,* by the Rev. R. M. Serjeantson. His book contains in an appendix Sir Gilbert Scott's report and account of the various stages of construction and reconstruction. The church is illustrated in Sharpe's *Churches of the Nene Valley.*

Fig. 138.

CH. XXVIII] ENGLAND—NORMAN PERIOD 241

would have taught. In the capital shown in this illustration (Fig. 139) there is to be sure a leaf to mark the angle, and the beasts are placed symmetrically, but the scroll-work wanders loosely over the surface, and the rudimentary idea of vegetable growth is ignored, for

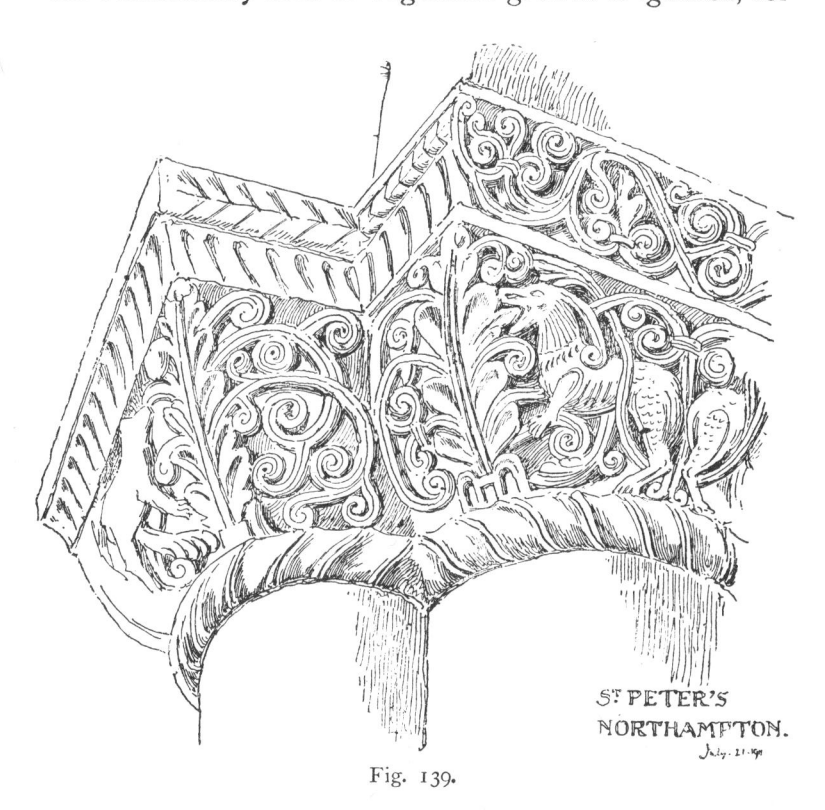

Norman sculpture

Fig. 139.

S^T PETER'S NORTHAMPTON.

while most of the sprays branch off as they ought in the direction of the main stem others start from it backwards.

In sculpture indeed the Norman school, whether here or in Normandy, lagged far behind those of the South of France and Burgundy, where the remains of Roman art afforded superior instruction. At first it was rarely attempted, and the earlier churches seldom got beyond cushion capitals, and billet or dentil mouldings. The next step in advance was the introduction of such simple conventional ornaments as the zigzag, which the carvers soon learned to treat with much skill and refinement. The front of CASTLE RISING church in Norfolk affords a pleasing example of this kind of decoration. Nowhere is it so lavishly employed as in the little village church of IFFLEY near Oxford, where its profusion is somewhat tedious. The early efforts of the Norman sculptors at the human figure are deplorable, and are like the efforts of the street boy with a piece of chalk on the palings, or shall we say the masterpiece of a post-impressionist painter. I have in former pages observed the same difficulty in dealing with the figure in the Lombard school, and it is only fair to say, that these figures (Plate CLVIII) at WORDWELL in Suffolk are not much worse than those at Cividale in Friuli[1].

The Norman attempts at animals are not much better: they are generally grotesque lions treated heraldically with tails that branch into foliage, barbarous enough, and showing but little promise at first of future excellence. In the tympanum at STOW LONGA, Huntingdonshire (Plate CLIX), there is a queer figure of a mermaid, with on one side an animal apparently mounting a pedestal or altar, and on the other what seems to be an Agnus Dei. It is attempted to read a symbolic meaning in these sculptures, but without much success. That at Wordwell has been variously interpreted to mean the sacrament of marriage, Christ giving the benediction, or Edward the Confessor and the pilgrim, and the same

[1] I have to thank Mr Keyser for Plates CLVIII, CLIX, and CLX from his work on *Norman Tympana and Lintels in Great Britain*.

Plate CLVIII

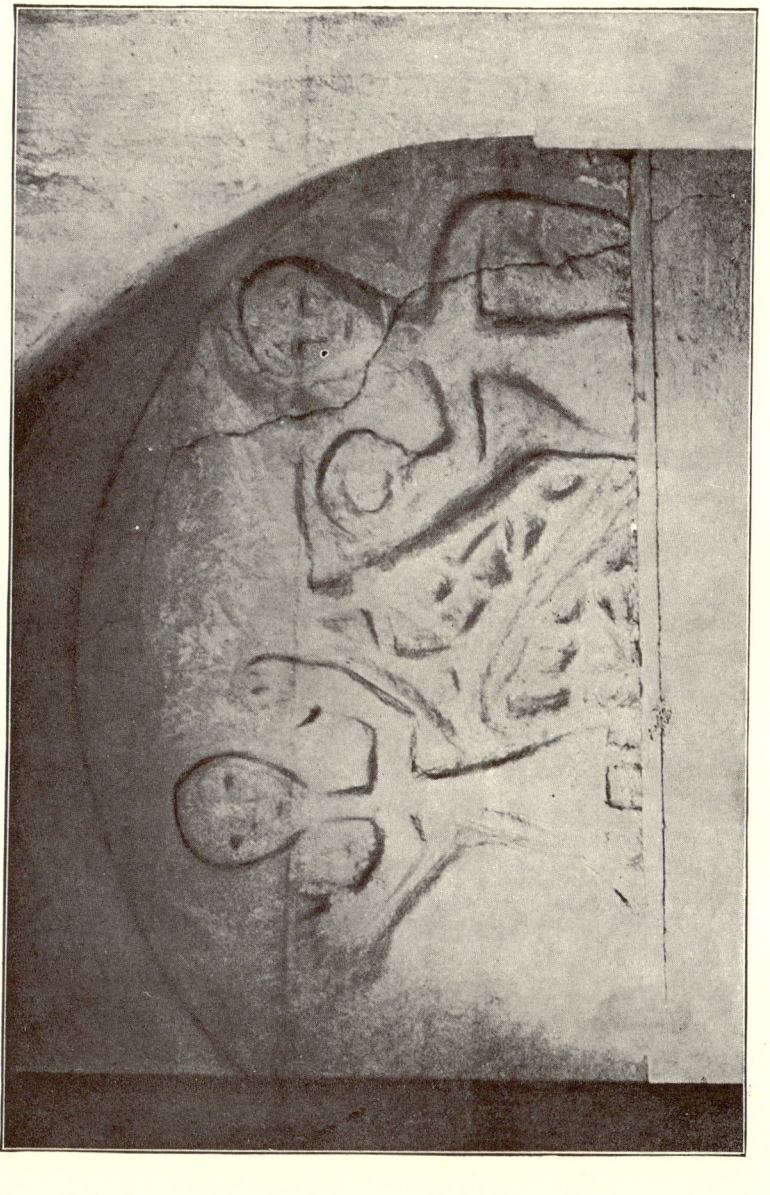

WORDWELL

Plate CLIX

STOW LONGA

CH. XXVIII] ENGLAND—NORMAN PERIOD 243

license of interpretation may be accorded to most of the Norman sculpture others. Subjects from the Old or New Testament are sometimes attempted with miserable success, and now and then the design seems based on Byzantine example. It will be observed, as for instance in the door-head from Stow Longa, how far superior in technique the purely architectural ornament is to the sculpture in the tympanum.

Fig. 140.

The capitals gradually grew from the simple cushion Improvement of the cushion capital type into something more artistic. At first the ornament was treated superficially like the cubical Byzantine capitals, of which the example given already from S. Peter's, Northampton, is a favourable instance. In many cases the ornament is applied without any constructive idea whatever. In the example from Castor (Fig. 140) there is no attempt to express decoratively the form and function of a capital, but the figures are placed on the surface anyhow; a leaf finishes one angle

16—2

244 ENGLAND—NORMAN PERIOD [CH. XXVIII

Unconstructive sculpture

with nothing to balance it on the other, and on the left-hand capital is an ill-designed piece of foliage at one corner with no resemblance to nature and no relation to anything. Nothing could be much more barbarous. An early rudimentary attempt to decorate the cushion capital is shown by Fig. 141 from ELY, where the corners are adorned by a very abstract form of leaf with a simple scroll turn-over. This is said to be part of Abbot

Fig. 141.

Simeon's work, but though nothing could well be simpler it is more advanced than anything by his brother at Winchester. There are precisely similar angle leaves in the capitals of Ernulf's crypt at Canterbury.

Enrichment of the cushion capital

The next step was to break up the cushion by fluting it, which marked a decided advance; and then the semi-circular ends of the cushion so divided were decorated by sunk carving as at Ludlow, in the arcading of the

CH. XXVIII] ENGLAND—NORMAN PERIOD 245

round chapel (Fig. 142). In addition the abacus was often enriched by diapers as at S. Peter's BEDFORD (Fig. 143) where also the shaft and the arch mould are decorated with spiral and zigzag mouldings studded with little jewel-like bosses. Later as in Peter de Leia's nave

Norman sculpture

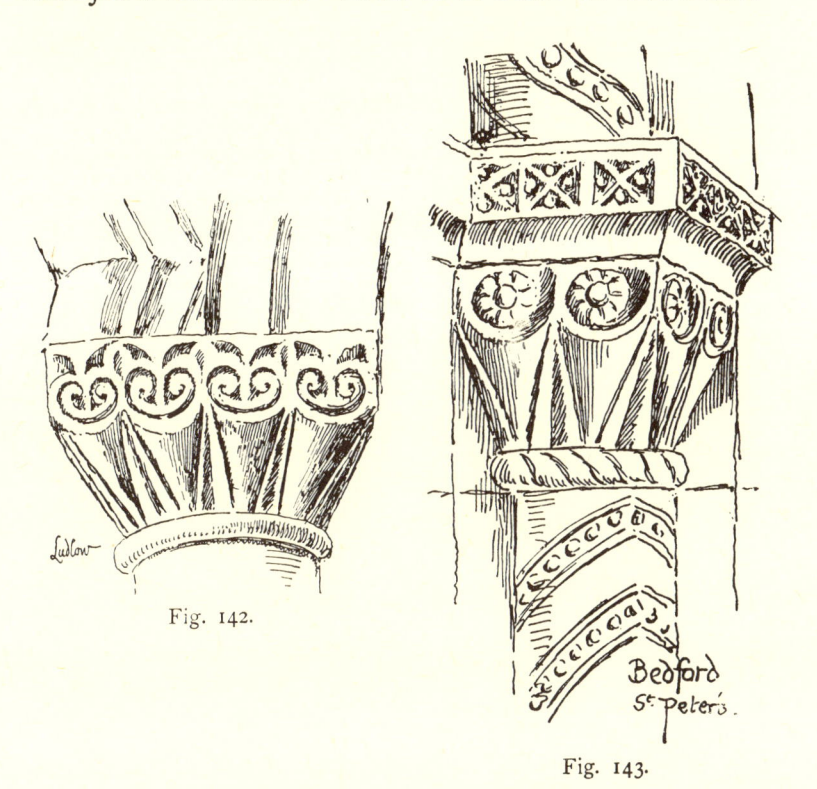

Fig. 142.

Fig. 143.

at S. DAVID'S (1176-1198) the divided cushion capital lost its convex form, and curled over on a concave line, the different divisions becoming almost stalks of vegetable growth; and the next step was to treat the rounded end as a plaque for sculpture (Fig. 144), suppressing the stalk altogether and substituting real foliage, in which

Abandonment of the convex form

Norman sculpture

appears that curious Early English trefoil leaf, of which I have never seen an example beyond these shores, except at Bayeux.

In conventional ornaments, such as diapers and panelling, the Normans showed great skill and ingenuity. Nothing in this way can be better than the ornament of the blank arch on the west face of S. Peter's tower at Northampton (Fig. 137), which has been referred to already.

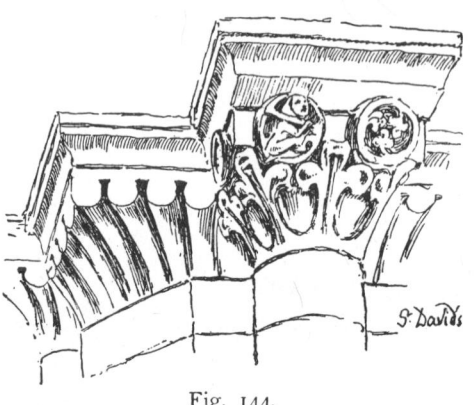

Fig. 144.

Gradually, though slowly, the school of Norman sculpture advanced to better things, and towards the end of the 12th century we find it more nearly abreast of the other schools. The splendid doorway at BARFRESTON (Plate CLX) in Kent was probably carved by workmen from Canterbury cathedral, where Romanesque architecture was already giving way to the pointed style. The capital, of which the four sides are shown by Plate CLXI, was lately taken out of the south aisle wall of WINCHESTER cathedral, where it had been used by William of Wykeham as a plain facing stone with the carved part inwards. Its finish is remarkable, almost like that of

Barfreston church

Capital from Winchester

Plate CLX

BARFRESTON

CH. XXVIII] ENGLAND—NORMAN PERIOD 247

an ivory carving, and allowing for the grotesque element in the fabulous creatures represented, they are well modelled. *Capitals from Winchester*

Another capital (Fig. 145), which was built into the wall in the same way with the carved part inwards, shows a refinement of the cushion capital, the sides being shaped

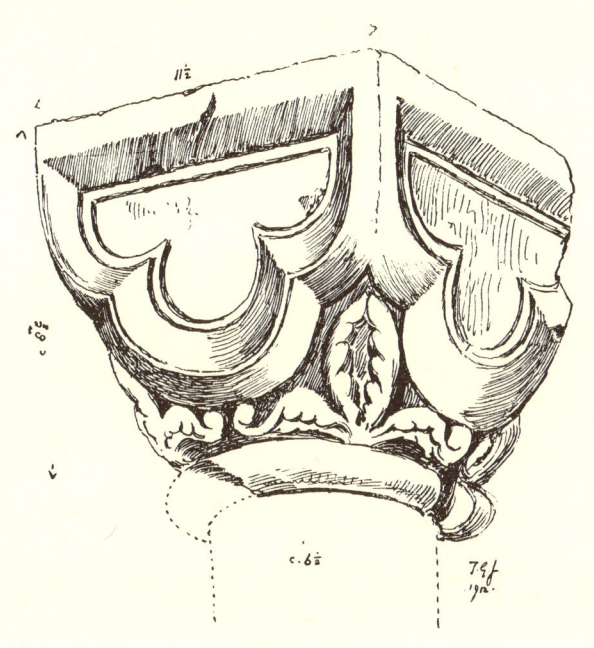

Fig. 145.

into a trefoil, of which the planes are cleverly managed. Fig. 146 shows a very similar capital from Ernulf and Conrad's crypt at Canterbury.

These two capitals at Winchester being carved on all four sides and prepared for slender colonnettes about $6\frac{1}{2}$ inches in diameter, may very likely have belonged to the original cloister of the abbey, though their style is much

248 ENGLAND—NORMAN PERIOD [CH. XXVIII

later than that of Walkelyn's arches which opened from the cloister to the chapter-house[1].

Symbolism in sculpture

The centaur shooting an arrow into the monster's mouth is said to be symbolical. One explanation is that it means the "Harrowing of Hell." Sagittarius is an emblem of Christ and the dragon's mouth is Hell-mouth.

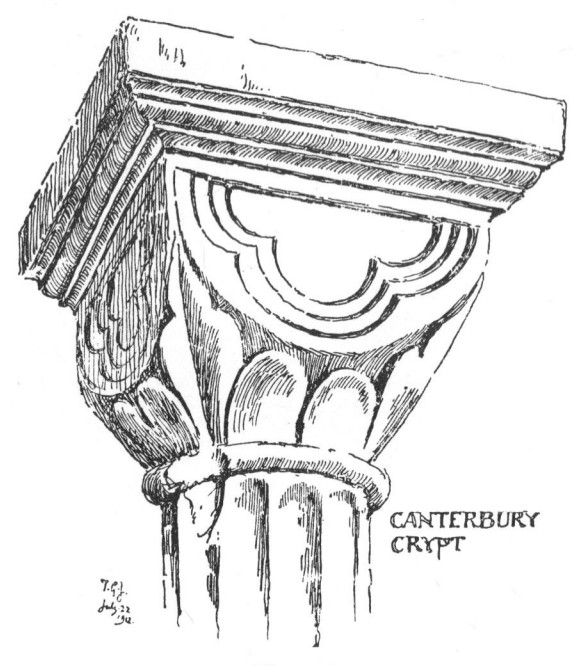

Fig. 146.

In the *Livre des Créatures* of Philip de Taun, written in the 12th century, Sagittarius drawing his bow is said to

[1] These carvings were discovered when the stones were drawn out to afford bond for my new buttresses in 1912. Wykeham's perpendicular facing of this wall is no doubt full of similar relics of the work of his predecessors. According to tradition the cloisters were destroyed in Queen Elizabeth's time: if so Wykeham may have pulled down the Norman cloister and built a new one, which was in its turn destroyed in the 16th century.

Plate CLXI

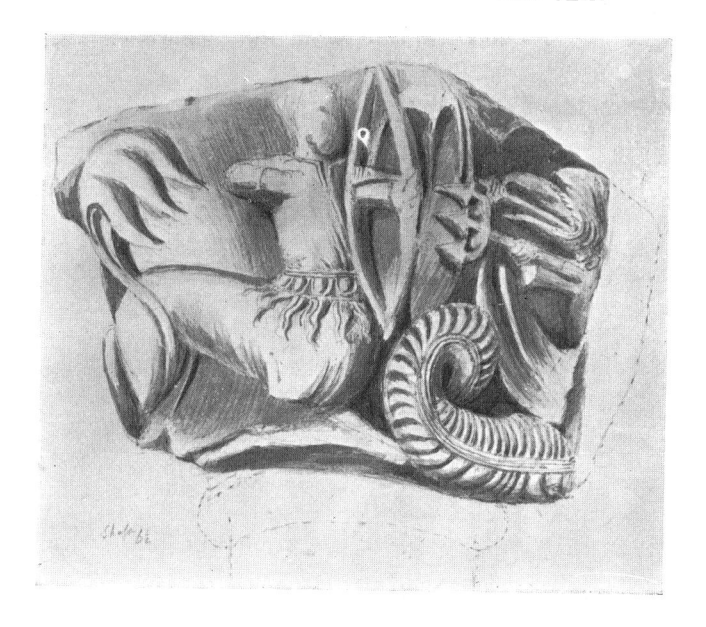

WINCHESTER

CH. XXVIII] ENGLAND—NORMAN PERIOD 249

express Christ's vengeance on the Jews, and his arrow points the way his spirit departs through Hell-mouth to the spirits in prison[1]. This far-fetched and confused theory at all events does not explain the griffin in this capital, who is shot in the chest, nor the trident with which the other monster is defending himself. One wonders whether most of this far-fetched symbolism was not invented by clerics to give a meaning to the sculptor's fancies, and whether the sculptor had anything

Symbolism in Norman sculpture

Fig. 147.

in his mind but a sporting subject. And yet it is curious that the centaur shooting into a dragon's mouth, as at Kencott in Oxfordshire (Fig. 147), should be of not uncommon occurrence.

In Mr Keyser's collection of Norman door-heads however there are many subjects with Sagittarii and other archers, which seem to have no symbolic meaning whatever. There is a Sagittarius in the portal of S. Gilles in Provence which has been illustrated above

[1] Papers by Mr George C. Druce in the *Archaeological Journal*, vol. LXVI. No. 264 and 2nd series, vol. XVI. No. 4, pp. 311—338.

(*sup.* p. 70, Plate CVI) who is shooting at an innocent stag; it would be difficult to draw any moral from that. The centaurs in Romanesque sculpture are among the barbarous figures which S. Bernard ridicules[1]. It is clear he attached no symbolical value to them.

Rochester west door The west doorway at ROCHESTER (Plate CLXII) marks the highest level to which Norman architectural sculpture attained. The logical correspondence of jamb to arch is recognized by the shafts below their respective orders, and the execution of the ornament shows the work of a skilled hand. The attenuated figures of Henry I and his queen, or perhaps Solomon and the Queen of Sheba, which serve as shafts to the inner order resemble those of the western portals at Chartres which are a little later, and those in the chapter-house doorway at S. Georges de Boscherville in Normandy (*sup.* p. 152, Plate CXXVI) which would perhaps be contemporary. The tympanum is occupied by a figure of Christ in an imperfect vesica supported by an angel on each side and the apocalyptic beasts. A frieze of little figures along the lintel resembles in miniature the arrangement at S. Gilles, Vézelay, and Arles.

Christ in Norman sculpture In Saxon architecture the representation of Christ on the cross is common, but in the earlier Norman sculpture any direct representation of our Lord seems to have been studiously avoided. It occurs in later examples as in the two last illustrations, but for the most part in earlier work Christ is represented by a symbol, a lamb carrying a cross, or even by a simple cross as for instance at Hawksworth in Nottinghamshire, where on the two extreme crosses are carved the figures of the thieves, but

---

[1] Quid ibi immundae simiae? Quid feri leones? Quid monstruosi centauri? Quid semi-homines? Quid maculosae tigrides?......Pro deo! si non pudet ineptiarum, cur vel non piget expensarum? *Apologia ad Guillelmum Theodorici abbatem*, Cap. XII.

Plate CLXII

ROCHESTER

Plate CLXIII

MALMESBURY ABBEY—South Porch

between them is a plain cross with no figure on it[1]. It will be remembered that the same unwillingness to attempt the divine portraiture was characteristic of the earlier Byzantine work[2].

MALMESBURY has a magnificently sculptured porch of late Norman work with figures of the apostles, six on a side, and in the tympanum of the doorway a figure of Christ, in a vesica supported by angels. The figures have draperies with thin folds, much convoluted, and an attempt has evidently been made to give them variety of attitude and expression (Plate CLXIII). Local tradition has it that the sculptures of the apostles are older than the doorway, and some have thought them to be Saxon. I see no reason to doubt their being of the same date as the rest of the porch. The figure of Christ in the head of the doorway has the same convoluted drapery, and the hand is turned back in the same impossible way as those of the apostles. The attempt at greater naturalism speaks of a more advanced stage of art, and is inconsistent with an earlier date than the middle of the 12th century. There are other examples of early sculpture in the façade of Lincoln cathedral, and on slabs that have been found at Chichester, which from their style probably belong to the end of the 11th or to the 12th century, though they have been supposed by some to be earlier. *Sculpture at Malmesbury*

The Prior's door at ELY (Plate CLXIV) is a very beautiful piece of late Norman work. In the tympanum is the same subject as at Rochester, and the arch is enriched with many devices of scrolls and interlacing ornaments, among which small figure subjects are introduced. The flat border of foliage surrounding the arch is reminiscent of Byzantine design. *Sculpture at Ely*

[1] Keyser, *op. cit.* Plate 94.   [2] *v. sup.* vol. I. pp. 41, 114.

Ely, Prior's door

The bases of the jamb shafts rest on what are now decayed projecting blocks of stone, but which seem at first sight to have been little lions like those in the portals of S. Maria Maggiore at Toscanella. With the help however of the 18th century illustration in Bentham's *Ely* they resolve themselves into a group on each side, consisting of a lion placed parallel to the wall, not projecting from it in the Italian fashion, and squatting on his back is a naked human figure with his back outwards, embracing the colonnette with his arms. This quasi-Italian feature is so far as I know unique in England.

Peculiarities of English Romanesque

In conclusion it remains to point out a few peculiarities in English Romanesque, which gradually converted into a distinct national style one originally imported from across the channel.

The square end

It has been already observed that the continental type of church was apsidal, and this was the type the Normans brought with them to this country. Canterbury, Norwich, Peterborough, and Gloucester still have their apses, though the last named conceals it under later work. Ely, Durham, Carlisle, Chester, Chichester, and Worcester, Winchester, Lichfield, Hereford, Exeter, and S. Alban's, though now squarely ended, originally finished in an apse, as is proved by the crypts of some and foundations that have been discovered in others. Rochester seems to have been planned by Gundulph with a square end, we know not why, and S. David's cathedral, Romsey, S. Cross, and S. Frideswide's at Oxford were also so planned, and possibly Southwell. All the rest just named were once apsidal, but when in later times alteration or re-building was called for the continental apse gave way to the square end of the Saxon and the Celt before him.

Plate CLXIV

ELY—The Prior's Door

Plate CLXV

S. LEONARD'S—STAMFORD

CH. XXVIII] ENGLISH ROMANESQUE 253

Originally only the aisles were vaulted. Ely still has its wooden roof over nave and transept, Winchester over the transepts, and Peterborough has the old Norman ceiling with painted decoration. It was left for the succeeding age to accomplish the vaulting of a nave. Aisles only vaulted

One remarkable feature of the English cathedral or abbey church is its great length, which forms a distinctive characteristic of the national style as compared with that of France. It is no doubt less marked in the earlier work than the later, when the choirs of Canterbury and Winchester were lengthened by Prior Ernulf and Bishop de Lucy. But it is not the length of the choirs more than that of the naves that makes our great cathedrals remarkable. Abroad there are no such long drawn naves in proportion to the church as those of S. Alban's, Ely, Norwich, and Winchester. This may be accounted for by the peculiar constitution of our ecclesiastical establishments. In England there was no antagonism between the bishops and the regular clergy such as that we have noticed in France. Here alone the two were united; the bishop was not only the pastor of his diocese but the head or abbot of the convent or college, and the abbey church was his cathedral. The great church of each diocese consequently was shared between the monks and the townsmen; a solid wall pierced by a door in the centre divided it into two parts, and the eastern part was the monks' choir, while the people had the nave for their church with its own altar against the screen. Nowhere can this arrangement be observed better than at Christchurch Priory, but the choir screen remains still in those of our cathedrals which have not suffered from the mischievous craze of throwing everything open to be seen at a glance from end to end.

Marginal notes: Length of English churches; English bishops also abbots; Lay part in the churches

This I take it explains the long drawn naves of our English minsters.

<small>Effect in saving the churches</small>

The connexion of the bishops with the monasteries has no doubt been the means of saving the buildings. At the suppression of the convents in the 16th century those abbey churches which were also cathedrals were of course spared, for episcopacy was not threatened: those which like Peterborough were made the seat of new bishoprics were also preserved for that reason. A few others like Bath, Malvern, and Christchurch were given to the people for parish churches, but with these and similar exceptions most of the old abbeys are now in ruins.

<small>Progress of Norman architecture</small>

In tracing the progress of refinement in English Romanesque from the bald and featureless simplicity of the nave of S. Alban's in 1077 to the elegance of the Galilee at Durham in 1175, and the chapel of S. Mary at Glastonbury ten years later, we shall find that it was most rapid towards the end of the period. For the first eighty or ninety years after the conquest, while the whole face of the land was being covered with buildings in the new style, it changed very little. Between the transepts of Winchester in 1079 and those of Peterborough nearly a century later the difference is much less than might have been looked for. And yet before the nave of Peterborough was finished the Temple church in London was consecrated, a work of pronounced transitional character with pointed arches, and ten years later Bishop Hugh of Avalon built his choir at Lincoln, which bears no trace whatever of Romanesque architecture, or of any French influence. When the change came the old style melted away rapidly enough, but for a long while the Norman style went on with but little sign of further development.

In comparing English cathedral churches with those

of France we find in our own a greater variety, and a greater freedom both in plan and design. If one runs over in memory the general form of our great churches their diversity will seem surprising. Durham, Canterbury, Lincoln, and York have each three towers, but they are not in the least like one another. Wells also has three, but the west front in which two of them are placed is unique. The long low line of Peterborough suits its position in the level fen country, and its great west front has no parallel in Gothic art. The three spires of Lichfield and the two transeptal towers of Exeter are unmistakeable, and so are the central towers of Gloucester, Worcester, and Hereford, and the steeples of Chichester, Salisbury, and Norwich. No other school can show so great and so wide a variety in general mass and outline. Nobody can for a moment mistake one of these buildings for another, whereas at a brief glance one may be forgiven for doubting whether a photograph represents the portals of Amiens, Rheims, or Paris, the cathedrals of Sens or Auxerre, or the façades of Siena or Orvieto. *Variety of English churches*

Generally speaking Romanesque architecture came to an end in England in the last quarter of the 12th century. Bishop Godfrey de Lucy began his presbytery at Winchester in the early English style in 1202, or perhaps a few years sooner. More than 20 years before then William of Sens had re-built the choir at Canterbury, in which the pointed arch was used for the main arcade, though the round arch was retained elsewhere; and English William finished the eastern part in 1184, where the pointed arch finally triumphed. But the round arch made a hard fight for it, and was given up with reluctance, especially by the monastic orders. We find it at Glastonbury in conjunction with foliaged capitals of a Gothic type. *End of English Romanesque*

In S. Leonard's Priory at Stamford (Plate CLXV) we have it—zigzags and all—associated with the slender shafts and capitals of the 13th century, and in the very similar west door of Ketton church, a few miles away, the side arches that are round at S. Leonard's have become pointed, while the central doorway retains its semi-circular head[1]. Many instances of the same kind are to be found throughout the length and breadth of the land, often creating problems as to the date of a building to provoke the antagonism of archaeologists.

Extent of Norman architecture

Never perhaps was there a time when so great a burst of architecture took place as in the period we have been considering. The Norman style has left its mark on the majority of our cathedrals and parish churches to this day. Many of them are almost wholly in that style, and if we except Wells whence all Norman work has disappeared, and Salisbury which was built in post-Norman times, there is perhaps none of our cathedrals in which Norman work does not play an important part, while there are very few village churches without at least a Norman doorway, or a chancel arch, or perhaps only a window slit that dates from Romanesque times. Everywhere do we still see evidences of what William of Malmesbury tells us was going on in his day. "Nearly all," he says, "try to rival one another in sumptuous buildings of the style which Edward the Confessor had first introduced into this country. Everywhere you may see in villages churches, in towns monasteries rising in the new style of building."

[1] Ketton is illustrated in Parker's *Rickman*, ed. 1848, p. 85.

CHAPTER XXIX

CONCLUSION

IN the preceding pages we have traced the rise and development of a new art in eastern and western Europe, based on the style of the old Roman world, but following widely different principles, which led it ever farther and farther from the parent art. Summary

In the Empire of EASTERN ROME the basilican plan of Constantine's time gradually yielded to the influence of the art of the Asiatic provinces. The wooden roof gave way to covering with stone or brick, which after many tentative experiments resulted in the adoption of construction by pendentives, and the mighty dome of S. Sophia at Constantinople. New forms of decoration were invented Sculpture was relegated to subordinate functions and confined to capitals, friezes, and purely architectural features. Painting, and above all mosaic, together with linings of precious marbles gave the walls a loveliness all their own. Byzantine architecture

The decline of native art in ITALY was followed by a gradual revival when Byzantine art passed across the Adriatic: its adoption began at Ravenna with the buildings of Honorius and Galla Placidia; it advanced further under Theodoric and his Gothic kingdom; and it was fully developed after the conquest of Justinian and the establishment of the exarchate, when the dome made its appearance at S. Vitale. Italo-Byzantine architecture

258 BYZANTINE AND ROMANESQUE [CH. XXIX

Venice

Under the Lombards and Franks art declined, and reached its bathos in the 8th century. Venice alone adhered to the Eastern Empire, and kept Byzantine art alive in Italy. When, with the rise of the Communes the country began to enjoy a freer and more prosperous life, art revived also, but took a fresh line and became what we know as Romanesque instead of Byzantine. In the duomo of Pisa, S. Miniato at Florence, the cathedral of Zara in Dalmatia, and the churches of Lucca and Rome the basilican plan reasserts itself, and in S. Ambrogio at Milan we find it combined with vaulting on a grand scale over both nave and aisles, a step which removed the last weakness of basilican architecture. The old ranks of columns had to be superseded by more solid piers, wider arches took the place of narrow intercolumniations, and this paved the way for all future development.

Rise of Romanesque architecture

German Romanesque

From Italy Romanesque architecture passed the Alps into GERMANY, where we find versions of the Lombard tower, and in the churches on the Rhine the galleried apses of Lucca and Como.

Charlemagne's attempt to introduce the Byzantine plan was not successful; his domed church at Aix-la-Chapelle had no following in Gaul or Austrasia, and the German church is basilican.

French Romanesque

In FRANCE, the most classic of all provinces of the Roman Empire, Roman example inspired the rising art of the period that followed the barbarian settlement. But in each province of the disunited kingdom Romanesque art fell into separate schools.

Provence

In Provence it obeyed the influence of the Roman art in which the province abounded; and sculpture, with good models to follow, attained a high degree of excellence.

In Aquitaine, on the line of trade with the Levant, Aquitaine we find the construction influenced by the Byzantine school, which inspired the domed churches of Périgueux, Angoulême, Solignac, and the rest of that group, and reached Le Puy in the Auvergne.

Burgundy was the seat of monasticism, and from the cloistered workshops of Cluny and the Cluniac monasteries not only in France but beyond its borders arose a school of architecture which affected the art far and wide. Burgundy

It was from Burgundy that architecture was carried into Normandy, where a school arose owing less than any other to Roman example, following a line of its own, robust and virile, deficient in sculpture for want of ancient example, and dependent on simple constructional forms and mass for effect. Normandy

From Normandy this art passed with the conquest into England, where it speedily suppressed and almost wiped out the Saxon architecture of the conquered race, which though it had a certain national character possessed little vitality and showed little promise of further progress. English Romanesque

The history of Romanesque architecture was influenced by two opposite principles; on the one hand ancient Roman example held the artists fast-bound, as far as it could, to precedent; on the other the necessities and possibilities of the time drove them into novel experiments, and made an ever widening breach between their work and their models. In Italy, as was natural, Roman tradition was strongest. It was Roman art which Charlemagne's renaissance attempted to revive in Gaul and Austrasia. To build in the manner of the Romans was the ambition of our Saxon forefathers. The Roman round arch gave way to the pointed only Two principles of Romanesque Roman art the model of Romanesque under stress of constructional difficulties, and the builders loved it best, and used it in decorative features even where they had to give it up in the main fabric.

Byzantine superior to Romanesque in originality

It must be confessed that in respect of originality this clinging to the antique places the Romanesque schools below the Byzantine. The eastern school was influenced from another direction, and looked for inspiration to oriental sources rather than to Rome. The Byzantine churches of the 5th century are already far removed from Roman example, of which there can hardly be said to exist any trace whatever in Justinian's buildings at Constantinople and in the Exarchate. The long-drawn basilica from that time disappeared east of the Adriatic, and gave way to the square church, grouped round a central dome; the classic orders were forgotten, and decorative sculpture assumed forms that were quite novel in character.

In the east the breach with the past was deliberate and voluntary; but in the west, the change to which Romanesque art was inevitably committed by the necessities of a new state of society, and the absence of either means or skill to continue the art which it was desired to imitate, was involuntary and possibly at first to some extent unconscious on the part of the artist. The remains of Roman work were still his model. He had no other, and widely as his work differed from the antique it was strongly affected by it from first to last.

Restraint in Romanesque

The surviving influence on Romanesque architecture of its classic origin may be seen in a certain restraint which was lost in the succeeding styles of the 13th and 14th centuries. Roman architecture was eminently a sane and orderly architecture, in which there was no room for daring flights of imagination, or desperate revolts

CH. XXIX] BYZANTINE AND ROMANESQUE 261

from precedent. And the Romanesque style which sprang from it inherited a sobriety and simplicity which distinguishes it from the Gothic art of the following period. The masses of its buildings are plain and solid, with plenty of bare wall-face, and none of that efflorescence into airy pinnacles, niches and canopies, open traceries and tabernacle work, from which, in the fervour of the early Renaissance, Vasari prays heaven to defend us[1]. The contrast is that of Pisa with Milan, Worms with Cologne, Angoulême and Vézelay with Amiens and Rheims, and the nave of Gloucester with its choir. Not that Romanesque could not be splendid enough and indulge in ornament as well as Gothic: the fronts of Angoulême, Notre Dame at Poitiers, and Civray are as richly decorated as those of Paris or Rouen, but the ornament is economised and used with discretion.

Romanesque and Gothic compared

In point of technique and execution no doubt Romanesque sculpture must yield to the later school; in the statuary at Arles and S. Gilles with all its dignity of expression it must be confessed there is something archaic, a trace of barbarism, which prevents its ranking with the figures at Chartres, Rheims, and Paris, some of which are comparable to the antique. But in other respects the comparison is not all in favour of the later work. Viollet-le-Duc[2] indeed, as we have already observed, compares the portal of S. Trophime disadvantageously with that of the Virgin at Paris, which is only

Romanesque sculpture

---

[1] ...facevano una maledizione di tabernacolini l' un sopra l' altro, con tante piramidi e punte e foglie che non ch' elle possano stare, pare impossibile ch' elle si possano reggere. Ed hanno più il modo da parer fatte di carta che di pietre o di marmi......Iddio scampi ogni paesi da venir a tal pensiero ed ordine di lavori...*Proemio dell' Architettura*.

Raffaelle writes to Pope Leo X in the same strain.

[2] *Dict. Rais.* vol. VII. p. 419.

a few years later in date; but as architectural compositions the Romanesque portals are in many respects saner than the more luxuriant portals of the succeeding style. The excellence of the details, especially of the sculpture, in the later school makes one forget some absurdities. For surely there is something absurd in the conventional French portal, where little figures in niches that ought to be upright, standing on pedestals that lean at an angle of 45°, come toppling over one's head in a succession of concentric orders with an admired disregard of the laws of gravity. In the Romanesque doorways the figures stand, as they should, upright, and the arches as a rule are simply moulded. At Angoulême and Civray it is true angels on the wing do circle round the arches, and so do little figures of saints in the doorway at Lincoln, but they are carved in relief on the arch stones, and not housed in tabernacles that tumble overhead; while in the later French portals of this kind, the figures are often actually detached and hung up by metal hooks[1]. This mode of treating the French portal with niches and little figures in them round the arches, once invented, lasted through the middle ages and becomes at last tedious. It gives a brilliancy by affording sharp points of light and shadow, and so produces a picturesque effect, but I think after a candid comparison of the two we must admit that the Romanesque portals are more reasonable, and therefore more in keeping with true artistic principles.

In Italy the contrast is not so observable, for the Gothic style when it did make its way there was more subdued. Milan after all is exceptional,—a product of the *arte Tedesca*, for it was begun under German influence;—the great churches of Assisi, and even those

v. Viollet-le-Duc, *Dict. Rais.* vol. I. p. 53.

CH. XXIX] BYZANTINE AND ROMANESQUE 263

of Siena and Orvieto are comparatively simple in mass and outline, and their splendour is confined to the sculptured and inlaid fronts. One would think that Roman tradition, descending through the Romanesque period, still laid a restraining hand on extravagance of design.

The vitality of classic tradition as expressed by the Romanesque work both in France and Italy is remarkable. In Italy indeed it never really died out, nor in the Italian speaking cities of Dalmatia, but lasted through the Gothic period till it met the returning flood of classic at the Renaissance. The apse of the cathedral of Lucca (*v.* Plate LXIX, vol. I. p. 251), erected after 1320, is purely Romanesque, and but for the foliage of its capitals, might have been built two hundred years earlier; while the upper part of the front of the cathedral at Zara, which was finished in Pisan Romanesque in the 15th century, is coeval with the chapels of Eton and King's College. Classic details appear in Italian architecture all through the middle ages. The fine scrolls on the portal of the Baptistery at Pisa (Plate LXXIV, vol. I. p. 258) might have been cut by a Roman chisel, and on the Gothic pulpit in the same building, made by Nicola Pisano in 1260, the classic egg and dart appears, while the sculptured panels are distinctly based on Roman models. *Classic influence in Italy*

In France abundant examples have been given already of the survival of classic influence, especially in the south, where Roman remains were frequent, and perhaps some Greek traditions lingered. But even in the north it held its own, and the scroll (Fig. 148) on the west portal at Mantes, which dates from the end of the 12th century, is a nearer imitation of the Roman type than that at Lucca (vol. I. p. 255, Fig. 58) while the *Classic influence in France* capitals of the interior are as Corinthian in motive as those of Avallon or Vézelay.

Classic influence weak in English Romanesque

The Romanesque of Normandy and England, for reasons that have been already explained, shows but little trace of classic influence except in its stubborn adherence to the round arch, due mainly to the natural conservatism of the monastic orders. There is a much closer connexion with Roman work in the preceding Saxon style as shown for instance at Bradford-on-Avon (Pl. CXXXVIII, p. 195 *sup.*). And when the pointed arch finally triumphed the English architect could hardly make his arches pointed enough; there is nothing

Fig. 148.

beyond the seas like our sharpest lancet work; and our adoption of the round abacus put an end to all possible imitation of the Corinthian capital, which lasted longer in France where the square abacus was retained.

In constructional skill the Romanesque builders were of course far behind their successors in the 13th, 14th and 15th centuries, when construction had become scientific, no problem of masonry was left unsolved, and the due equilibrium of forces was understood and skilfully employed. The earlier men made up for what they wanted in skill by solidity of mass; but in spite of their enormous piers and thick walls their towers fell, and their barrel vaults pushed their walls out and had to be sustained in later ages by flying buttresses and other devices. But inferior as they are in science, the solidity of Romanesque buildings with their sturdy columns and massive proportions will often satisfy the artist eye better than the more slender and ingenious constructions of a later day, when the architect economised substance almost as closely as the engineer. *Unscientific construction of Romanesque*

In actual execution apart from constructive skill Romanesque work compares favourably with Gothic. Their materials were well selected, as the durability of their work attests, both in England and France. In this respect Viollet-le-Duc considers Romanesque work in France superior to Gothic—of the latter he says that "the architecture is no longer executed with that minute care in the details, with that attention to the choice of materials which strikes us in buildings of the end of the 12th century, when the lay architects were still imbued with monastic traditions. If we set aside some rare edifices like the S. Chapelle at Paris, like the cathedral at Rheims, like certain parts of the cathedral of Paris, we *Excellence of Romanesque building*

Hasty construction of French Gothic

shall find that the monuments of the 13th century are often as careless in their execution as they are cleverly designed in the system of their construction. There was much to be done, done promptly, and done with little money; the builders are in a hurry to enjoy, they neglect foundations; they raise monuments rapidly, using all sorts of materials, good or bad, without taking time to choose. They snatch the stones from the masons' hands half dressed, with unequal joints, and hasty filling in. The constructions are brusquely interrupted, as brusquely begun again with great changes of design. One finds no more that leisurely wisdom of the masters belonging to the regular orders, who did not begin a building till they had collected their materials long before, and chosen them carefully; and had provided money sufficient, and ripened their plans by study[1]."

This contrast between the execution of Romanesque and Gothic building does not I think occur in England. In my own experience I have generally found the early English masonry as good as the Norman, and the mortar much better.

I have dwelt upon one guiding principle of Romanesque architecture, that attachment to precedent which to a certain extent tied the artists down to the imitation, so far as they could manage it, of ancient example. It remains to notice the opposite principle, which is after all the more vital one, which tended to break with the past, and converted what began on mere imitative lines into a new, original, and living art.

It is the same principle which lies at the root of all development of architectural styles; the principle of recognizing change of circumstance, and accommodating

[1] V.-le-Duc, *Dict. Rais.* vol. I. p. 150.

BYZANTINE AND ROMANESQUE

the art of the day to satisfy and express it. In novel requirements, in new and better appliances, the architect finds his happiest sources of inspiration, and the most fertile suggestions for artistic invention. The old Roman architecture had become impossible in the 5th and 6th centuries and indeed sooner than that, and the builders had to do the best they could in other ways. New modes of construction had to be devised, and this necessarily led to new forms of design : for at the root of all radical changes in architecture will be found some reason of construction. *Reason in architecture*

Adopting the arch as the main element of design the masters of the new style carried it much farther than the Romans, from whom they took it. Instead of reducing it to a passive weight-carrying feature they made it an active member of the structure, opposing vault to vault, thrust to thrust, and thus beginning that method of construction by equilibrium of forces which was the motive principle of all succeeding architecture during the middle ages. This new motive pervaded the architecture so as to remodel its outward form. The old Roman use of the orders as an unmeaning surface decoration was forgotten. The column, from being a mere surface decoration as at the Colosseum, was again brought into service, and we see it doing duty as a working member of construction in the arcades of S. Sophia, the colonnades of the basilicas at Salonica and Ravenna, and the churches of Pisa, Lucca, and Genoa. This again gave way to a different form of construction as the art of vaulting wider spaces was gradually acquired, and stronger piers and wider arches replaced the basilican colonnade. Thenceforth the vault was the dominant factor in all the schools of Romanesque art and of the Gothic that followed, *Arch construction* *Roman orders abandoned* *The vault* and from the exigencies of that form of construction arose all the later schools of western Europe.

Classic convention abandoned

Byzantine and Romanesque art was in fact a revulsion from convention to the unaffected expression of natural law and methods of construction. It does not appeal to all minds alike. To those who value consistent obedience to authority and precedent, to strict canons of orthodoxy, correctness, and propriety, according to certain accepted formulas;—in other words in the strict classic purist—both Byzantine and Romanesque art will appear debased and lawless, a violation of all rule, and a rebellion against wholesome tradition. To others not so wedded to authority it will appear the natural and reasonable outcome of an altered state of society, to which the old Roman architecture would be inappropriate had it not been impossible.

Byzantine and Romanesque, styles of transition

Neither Romanesque nor Byzantine architecture can be regarded as perfected styles; they are rather to be viewed as styles in transition. Romanesque, especially in Northern Europe, never shook off the roughness of the barbarous time out of which it came, and of which the thorns and briers clung to it to the last. Byzantine indeed, in its splendid earlier stages almost attained perfection of a kind; but its development was arrested, and it had begun to fall into decay before it was overwhelmed by the Moslem conquests. But Romanesque, struggling upwards through its imperfections, had a stronger life and was more fruitful of consequences; and after an Herculean infancy it developed at last into that Gothic architecture which was the glory of the middle ages.

CHRONOLOGICAL TABLE OF ARCHITECTURAL EXAMPLES

Buildings that no longer exist are in italics

BYZANTINE	ITALIAN AND ITALO-BYZANTINE
	300-305. Spalato. Diocletian's palace. Classic with many irregularities. Some materials second-hand.
	312. Constantine's triumphal arch in regular Roman classic. Debased sculpture. Reliefs partly taken from older monuments.
	313. EDICT OF MILAN. Toleration of Christianity.
324. FOUNDATION OF CONSTANTINOPLE. *Constantine's churches of Irene and the Apostles.* Church at Bethlehem.	330. *St Peter's, Rome. A five-aisled basilica built by Constantine.*
350-360. S. Giorgio, Salonica. A round church, domed, with mosaics.	335. S. Costanza, Rome, built as a tomb-house for the Princess Constantia. S. Lorenzo f. le Mura, Rome, the eastern church by Constantine. Much restored in 588 by Pelagius II.
	353. *Rome. S. Maria Maggiore,* re-built 432.
360. *S. Sophia, Constantinople, dedicated. A basilica built by Emp. Constantius, foundations laid 34 years before.*	380. S. Paolo f. le Mura, Rome, re-built on the present plan. Burnt 1823 and since re-built.
	404. RAVENNA MADE THE CAPITAL. *The Ursian Cathedral. A five-aisled basilica destroyed in* 1734. The Ursian Baptistery.
379-395. Constantinople. Theodosius I's pedestal to the obelisk of Thothmes III, with sculptures in tolerable classic style.	410. SACK OF ROME BY ALARIC.
	425. S. Giov. Evangelista, Ravenna, by Galla Placidia. Since raised. S. Agata Ravenna, do., do.
413. Constantinople. The inner wall, by Theodosius II.	425. S. Sabina, Rome.
425. Eski Djouma, Salonica. Basilica. Columns with pulvino, and mosaic in arches &c.	425-430. Baptistery, Ravenna. Mosaics added by Archbp. Neon.
	432. S. Maria Maggiore, Rome, re-built by Sixtus III.
447. Constantinople. The double wall and Porta Aurea.	432. S. Lorenzo f. le Mura, Rome. The western church, now the nave, by Sixtus III, *v.* 1216.
	450. Death of Galla Placidia. Her mausoleum at Ravenna.

270

Byzantine	Italian	German	French	English
463. Constantinople. The church of S. John Bapt. founded by Studius.	468. Rome. S. Stefano Rotondo, dedicated. Restored 523-30. The cross wall 772. 476. ODOACER. END OF THE WESTERN ROMAN EMPIRE. 493-526. THEODORIC and the Ostrogothic Kingdom. S. Apollinare Nuovo, Ravenna.		*Sidonius Apollinaris* (431-c. 485) *mentions a large church at Lyons built by his friend Bishop Patiens.* 472. *Church of S. Martin in Tours built by Bishop Perpetuus.* *Church at Clermont* 150′ × 60′, *and* 50′ *high.* (Greg. Turon.) 496. CONVERSION OF CLOVIS.	c. 400. Church at Silchester. Foundations exist. 411. DEPARTURE OF THE ROMANS. 449. English invasion.
495. Salonica. S. Sophia, finished. Domed church on square plan. 515. Ezra in Syria. Domed church and stone roof.	526. Death of Theodoric. His mausoleum. 526. S. Vitale, Ravenna, begun.			520. Battle of Mount Badon. Saxon advance checked.
527. JUSTINIAN EMP. Constantinople. SS. Sergius and Bacchus, finished by Justinian, begun in the reign of his uncle Justin. I. 532-7. Constantinople. S. Sophia, built by Justinian after the Nika sedition. S. Irene, re-built by him (but *v.* 740).	534. S. Apollinare in Classe, Ravenna. 535-43. Parenzo. The Euphrasian Basilica. 539. THE EXARCHATE. Ravenna taken by Belisarius. 547. S. Vitale, Ravenna, consecrated.			

271

563. Constantinople. S. Sophia, reconsecrated after fall in 558 and re-building of dome.	549. S. Apollinare in Classe, Ravenna, consecrated.	564. Gildas's History.
c. 585. Salonica. S. Demetrius.	568. THE LOMBARD KINGDOM.	
c. 599. Constantinople. S. Maria Diaconissa founded. ? rebuilt later	571–86. Grado. The basilica by Patriarch Elias.	
	588. S. Lorenzo f. le Mura, Rome, remodelled with gallery by Pelagius II in the eastern part.	
	595. *Monza. Theodelinda's Byzantine cathedral.*	597. LANDING OF AUGUSTINE in Kent. Ancient churches at Canterbury restored and used again.
	625–39. S. Agnes, Rome, re-built by Honorius I, with galleries.	627. *York. King Edwin's church of wood.*
	?625. S. Maria Antica, Rome, with Byzantine paintings.	635. *Winchester cathedral re-built, described by Wolstan in a Latin poem.*
		639. *York. A stone church by King Edwin and Paulinus.*
		652. *Lindisfarne by Finan, timber, thatched with reeds.*
		c. 670. Reculver.
		670. Crosses at Bewcastle and Ruthwell.
		674. Monkwearmouth church by Benedict Bishop, of stone, with glazed windows and paintings.

Byzantine	Italian	German	French	English
				c. 678. *Hexham and Ripon*, by Wilfrid, crypts remain. 680. Brixworth, built by monks from Peterborough. 682. Jarrow, by Biscop. 684. *St Cuthbert's monastery at Lindisfarne, of timber and turf.* 686–700. (Cunibert king of the Lombards marries an English princess.) 705. Bradford-on-Avon, founded by Adhelm.
726. ICONOCLASTIC EDICT of Leo III the Isaurian. 740. Constantinople. S. Irene, restored or rebuilt after an earthquake. 746. Third council of Constantinople. Image worship condemned.	727. RAVENNA TAKEN BY LOMBARDS, end of Exarchate. 739. Toscanella. S. Pietro, the nave and eastern part, west end later. 753. Brescia, S. Salvatore. 762–76. S. Maria in Cividale. 772–95. Rome. S. Maria in Cosmedin, by Hadrian I, triapsal.	774. Lorsch. *The Abbey consecrated in presence of Charlemagne.* Existing gatehouse of doubtful date.	682–96. Temple de S. Jean, Poitiers, built by Bp. Ansoaldus over a Gallo-Roman structure. Altered afterwards, *v.* 1018. ? Beauvais. The Basse Œuvre, but see 990.	740. Cross of Acca bishop of Hexham. 793. *S. Alban's, by King Offa, a church of most beautiful workmanship.* (W. of Malm.)

787. Second council of Nicaea. Image worship restored.	774. CHARLEMAGNE. END OF THE LOMBARD KINGDOM. 789-824. Milan. S. Ambrogio. Apse and monks' tower. 800. Zara. The round church of S. Donato. 817. S. Maria in Domnica, Rome, by Paschal I. 822. Rome. S. Prassede, re-built by Paschal I.	796-804. Aix-la-Chapelle. The Dom by Charlemagne, imitating S. Vitale. 820. S. Gall, Switzerland, MS. plan. 822. Fulda. The rotunda consecrated.	801. Germigny des Prés, Byzantine plan. Mosaics.	c. 800. Deerhurst founded, remodelled in 1056 after damage by Danes.
813. Leo V the Armenian, fresh Iconoclastic Edicts.				
829. Theophilus. Do. do.	827-49. Rome. S. Giorgio in Velabro, re-built by Greg. IV. 835. Milan. S. Ambrogio. The silver pala by Wolvinus. 864. Torcello cathedral. The east end, v. 1001.			
842. Image worship restored finally by Empress Theodora. 867. BASIL I. EMPEROR. 886-911. S. Mary Panachrantos, Constantinople. Μονὴ τοῦ Λιβός. A double church.			? Avignon. Notre Dame des Doms.	
? The Gul-Djami or Rose Mosque (S. Theodosia), Constantinople, probably remodelled later. ? 950. Telkfur Serai, Constantinople.	976. Venice. S. Mark's, injured by fire. Restored by P. Orseolo, with architects from Constantinople. Exclusive of front, v. 1063. 1001-8. Torcello cathedral, nave re-built. 1006. Pisa Duomo begun, but v. 1067. 1013. Florence. S. Miniato al Monte.	960-1050. Gernrode in the Hartz. Lisenen or strips like pilasters, joined at top by arches or straight sided pediments. Apse at both ends of church.	990. BEAUVAIS, foundation of Cathedral by Bishop Hervé. Le Puy en Velay. The eastern part and one side of the cloisters. 1001. Dijon. S. Benigne. The crypt.	950. *Canterbury cathedral restored by Odo.* ? Earl's Barton. Strip work decoration. 999. *Durham first stone church by Bishop Aldhun.* 1013. Greensted. Wooden church.

Byzantine	Italian	German	French	English
		1015–35. Hildesheim. S. Michael. 1016. Worms. Cathedral consecrated, remodelled in next century, v. 1181.		1017. CANUTE, KING. A general re-building of churches followed, e.g. Bosham, Wittering, S. Bene't's Cambridge, Worth, Wootten-Wawen, &c.
			1018. Poitiers. S. Jean restored and enlarged. 1018. Poitiers. S. Hilaire, dedicated 1059. Inner piers and vaults later, 1130. 1019. Montmajeur. Chapel of S. Croix.	
	Milan. S. Ambrogio. Nave and atrium.	1037–49. Mainz re-built, v. 1056. 1039. Speyer. The crypt. 1047. Cologne. S. Maria in Capitolio.	1047. Périgueux. S. Front; the Latin church dedicated. 1047. Périgueux. S. Etienne.	c. 1050. Westminster Abbey, by Edward the Confessor, dedicated 1065. 1056. Deerhurst church re-built. Ditto, Duke Odda's chapel.
1057–1059. Constantinople, S. Thecla. (Van Millingen)	1063. Venice. S. Mark's remodelled to its present form by Doge Contarini. Decoration and facing later. 1067. Pisa. Duomo. Design remodelled with greater splendour after victory over Saracens at Palermo. Busketus, architect. Consecrated 1118. 1071. Venice. Portico of S. Mark's finished.	1056–1106. Mainz, restored after a fire. 1066. Tournai. Nave dedicated.	1066. Caen. Abbaye aux Hommes. Abbaye aux Dames, but remodelled later.	1066. NORMAN CONQUEST. 1070. Canterbury cathedral re-built by Lanfranc, consecrated 1077. 1077–88. S. Alban's, by Abbot Paul. 1079–1103. Winchester, by Bp. Walkelyn.

275

1081. ALEXIUS COMNENUS, Emperor. Constantinople. S. Saviour Panteproptes. 1081-1118. Constantinople. Kahriyeh Djami. Μονὴ τῆς χώρας, Church of the chora. Restored by the Comneni. But v. 1303.	1099-1106. Modena. Duomo by Lanfrancus.	1093. Laach Abbey begun. Eastern part of this date, v. 1112.	1088-1099. Toulouse. S. Sernin finished.	1081. Ely begun by Abbot Simeon, d. 1093.
	1108. Rome. S. Clemente. The upper church by Pascal II.		1089. Cluny. Abbey begun. Consecrated 1131.	1089-1100. Gloucester by Abbot Serlo. Eastern part. Nave probably c. 1130.
	1112-47. S. Frediano, Lucca.	1112. Laach. Building resumed, not consecrated till 1156.	1089-1140. Vézelay nave, with cross vaults	1093. Durham choir by Bp. Carilef.
		1116. Worms. Dedicated. v. 1171.		1096. Norwich cathedral by Bp. Losinga. The eastern part, v. 1121.
	1117. Murano. Cathedral remodelled after an earthquake. v. 1140.		c. 1100. Clermont. Notre Dame du Port.	1096-1110. Canterbury. The glorious choir of Ernulf and Conrad.
	1118. Rome. Tower of S. Maria in Cosmedin.		Issoire and S. Nectaire about coeval.	1099-1128. Durham. Nave by Bp. Flambard. 1099-1128. Christchurch Priory by Bp. Flambard. 1115. Rochester nave.
1118-1143. Constantinople. S. Saviour Pantocrator. A triple church, part perhaps older. (Van Millingen)			1119. Cahors cathedral dedicated. 1120. Périgueux. Re-building of S. Front after a fire on plan of S. Mark's.	1118. Peterborough, eastern part. 1121-45. Norwich. The nave by Bp. Eborard. 1123. Tewkesbury, the nave. 1124. Castor church, Northants.
	1128-44. Milan. S. Ambrogio. Canon's Tower		1130. Angoulême consecrated. Domed nave. c. 1132. S. Denis. Abbot Suger's building, consecrated 1144. 1132. Vézelay. The narthex, pointed arches.	

Byzantine	Italian	German	French	English
? Constantinople. S. Theodore The Tiro.	1138. Verona. S. Zenone. 1140. Murano rebuilt after earthquake of 1117. Outside galleries. 1153. Pisa. Baptistery begun by Diotisalvi. 1173. Pisa. Campanile begun. 1175. Zara. S. Grisogono, apse and south wall. 1183. PEACE OF CONSTANCE. Establishment of Communal independence.	1146. Tournai. Transept in a lighter Romanesque. 1147. Vienna. The Romanesque west front. 1156. Laach, consecrated. 1171. Worms. Cathedral restored by Conrad II, Bp. 1172. Cologne. Great S. Martin finished. 1181. Worms. Cathedral reconsecrated after being remodelled.	1135. Chartres. West portals (pointed arches). 1152. Arles. S. Trophine dedicated. 1163. Paris. N. Dome choir 1163. Paris. S. Germain des Prés. 1168. Sens. Cathedral finished, pointed arcade on coupled columns. 1175-1212. Soissons. South Transept. 1180. Loches. Church finished. 1180. Le Puy. Two western bays with porch below.	1140. Fountains Abbey. Pointed nave arcade. 1150-1180. Oxford. S. Frideswide by Prior Guimond. 1155-93. Peterborough. Transepts and nave. 1174-91. Wells. Eastern part of Nave. 1174-89. Ely. Nave by Bp. Riddell. 1175. Durham. The Galilee by Bp. Pudsey. 1175. Worcester. Western bays of Nave. 1175-78. Canterbury. The choir of William of Sens. 1177-93. Peterborough. Nave and west transept. 1179-84. Canterbury. The eastern part, Trinity Chapel and the Crown, by English William. 1180? S. Peter's, Northampton.

Byzantine / Eastern	Italian	German	French	English
? Salonica. The Apostles.	1193-1211. Rome. Cloister of S. Paolo f. le Mura, by Pietro da Capua. Rome. Cloister of S. Giovanni Laterano, by Vassaletto.	1198. Mainz. Nave vault finished with pointed arches.	1194. Chartres. Re-building begun after a fire. 1198-1206. Vézelay. Choir and transepts. Transitional Gothic.	Mary's chapel consecrated. 1195-1200. Lincoln. Choir and eastern transept by Bp. S. Hugh. English Gothic free from French influence. 1200-22. Peterborough West front. c. 1200. Ely, the Galilee. 1202. Winchester. Bp. de Lucy's building. Thoroughly developed Early English.
1204. LATIN CONQUEST OF CONSTANTINOPLE.	1204. Lucca Duomo. West front by Guidetto.			
	1216. Rome. S. Lorenzo, the two churches thrown together.	1208. Coblentz. S. Castor. Andernach. ,, 1212. Cologne. S. Gereon. The decagon.	1213. Rheims. Re-building by Jean d'Orbais. 1218. Paris. West front. 1220. Amiens begun by Rob. de Luzarches.	1220. Salisbury Cath. begun. Lancet windows. Plate tracery in triforium. Consecrated 1258. 1229-54. Ely. East end.
	1233. Lucca Duomo. Interior of portico with doorways. 1240. Traü. Dalmatia. Romanesque west portal.	1235. Limburg on the Lahn. Transitional Romanesque. 1235-80. Marburg, a "Hall Church." Gothic.		1240. Westminster. Henry III choir and transept. Finished, 1269. Bar tracery windows. 1253. Westminster chapter house.
1261. GREEK EMPIRE RESTORED. THE PALAEOLOGI.	1260. Pisa. Nicola Pisano's pulpit in baptistery. 1290. Orvieto cathedral begun. Consecrated 1309. 1292. Florence. S. Croce begun by Arnolfo.	1270. Cologne. Probable date of the beginning of cathedral.	1255-65. Amiens choir. 1296. Paris. Notre Dame. Chapels begun between buttresses of choir.	1291. Westminster. Henry III tomb, by Torel, finished. 1294. Southwell chapter house.
1303. Constantinople. Kahriyeh Djami; Church of the Chora, restored by Theodore Metochites and decorated with mosaic. c. 1340. Lesnovo. Serbia, Byzantine.	1320. Lucca Duomo. The apse. Romanesque. 1323. Pisa. Capella della Spina. Italian Gothic.	1322. Cologne choir consecrated.		1318-1329. Gloucester. South nave aisle with ball-flowers in window mouldings.

INDEX

Abingdon, Saxon Abbey at, II. 202
Acca, Cross of Bishop, II. 197, 198
Agen, II. 85
Agnellus of Ravenna, I. 149
Aix-la-Chapelle, I. 256; II. 1, 33
Albigenses, Persecution of the, II. 82, 87
Amiens, II. 81
Ancona, I. 257
Andernach, II. 20, 25
Angers, II. 42, 50
Angoulême, I. 241; II. 39, 41, 46, 47, 48, 50, 57, 84
Apse, in Saxon churches, II. 199; in Norman Churches, II. 212, 252; the German double, II. 9, 10; defects of, II. 11; double apse in England, II. 202
Aquitaine, Architecture in, II. 34, 169, 259
Arian art at Ravenna, I. 165
Arbe, I. 268
Arch, its use in earliest time, I. 6; the predominant element in Roman architecture, I. 9
Arles, I. 32; II. 18, 29, 66–68, 72, 80, 103, 162, 261; kingdom of, II. 62–72
Arnolfo del Cambio, I. 134, 249
Atrium, at S. Sophia, I. 93; at S. Irene, I. 109; at Ravenna, I. 155, 177; at Parenzo, I. 183; at Milan, I. 262; in Germany, II. 18; in France, II. 31
Autharis, king of Lombardy, I. 214
Autun, II. 84, 99, 108; S. Jean, II. 112
Auvergne, II. 28, 127; peculiarities of architecture, II. 129, 130, 145, 169, 259
Avallon, II. 105
Avignon, II. 63

Baldacchino, I. 209
Ball-flower ornament, I. 222
Balusters, the Saxon, II. 186, 194, 230
Bangor, II. 184

Barbarian settlements in Italy, I. 145, 161, 228; in France, II. 28, 90, 147
Barfreston, II. 246
Barnack, II. 190, 193
Barrel vaulting, II. 3, 51, 52, 56, 108, 129, 133; prevents a clerestory, II. 100, 130
Barton-on-Humber, II. 190, 191
Basilica, the Roman, I. 16; the model for early Christian churches, I. 23
Basilican plan, its simplicity and its unprogressiveness, I. 18, 24, 205, 206; prevalence in Italy, I. 205; II. 258; in France, II. 33, 63; in Germany, II. 8; in England, II. 199
Bath, Roman Thermae at, II. 178; abbey, II. 208, 254
Bathos of Art in Italy in 8th century, I. 226
Beauvais, the Basse Œuvre, II. 161
Bede, the Venerable, II. 183, 227
Bedford, capital at, II. 245
Bema, I. 46
Benedictine rule, II. 92, 93
Bergamo, I. 251, 271, 272
Bernard, S., II. 96, 98, 164; his attack on luxury and architectural ornament, II. 96, 107, 108, 250
Bethlehem, Constantine's church at, I. 24
Bewcastle, cross at, II. 196
Biscop Benedict, his buildings, II. 181, 183, 197, 202
Bishops, French, their struggles with regulars, II. 171
Bitton, II. 187
Boppart, II. 25, 26
Borgo, S. Donnino, I. 269, 273
Boscherville, S. Georges de, II. 152, 217, 250
Brantôme, II. 141, 142

INDEX

Brioude, II. 127, 135
Britain, Roman, II. 173
Burgundians, the, II. 90
Burgundy, architecture in, II. 94, 123, 259; its influence in France and England, I. 273
Bradford-on-Avon, II. 194, 199, 264
Brixworth, II. 177, 190, 199, 200
Busketus or Boschetto, I. 242, 245
Buttress, development of, II. 162
Byzantine Art, its influence at Rome, I. 204; at Venice, I. 234, 239; in France, I. 241; II. 33, 34, 37, 46, 49, 51, 63, 70, 74, 78, 80, 87, 139, 143, 150; in England, II. 183, 196, 197; its hieratic character, II. 72, 199; its originality, II. 260

Cambridge, S. Bene't's, II. 184, 194, 200
Caen, II. 22, 153, 217, 235, 237
Caerleon-on-Usk, Roman remains, II. 179
Cahors, II. 39, 42, 47, 50, 84
Canterbury, Roman, II. 176; Saxon cathedral, II. 202, 210; Norman cathedral, II. 212 &c., 217, 235, 244, 255; capital at, II. 247, 248; S. Pancras, II. 176, 177, 199, 200
Capitals, Byzantine, I. 52, 57, 62, 233; exported from Constantinople, I. 58
Castle Rising, II. 242
Castor, II. 236, 243
Cattaro, I. 41, 209, 215
Cefalù, I. 41, 274
Cerisy le Forêt, II. 152, 217
Chaqqa, palace at, I. 29
Chamalières, II. 133, 137
Charlemagne, conquest of Lombards, I. 227; II. 1, 5, 65, 258
Chartres, I. 41; II. 81, 142, 250
Chauvigny, II. 45, 52
Chevet, the French, II. 84
Chora, church of the, I. 121; II. 49
Christ, representation of, I. 115, 116, 152, 179; II. 29, 250
Christchurch Priory, II. 217, 234, 253, 254
Christianity established, I. 15, 186; rapid progress in the East, I. 27; slow progress at Rome, I. 146
Cicero, his attitude towards the arts, I. 4
Cimabue, I. 134

Cistercians, II. 92; severity of their architecture, II. 96, 98, 107, 125
Citeaux, Abbey of, II. 92, 96, 98
Cividale, I. 131, 185, 215, 217; II. 242
Civray, II. 47, 52, 57, 239
Clairvaux, Abbey of, II. 96, 98
Clapham, II. 190
Clavigo, Ruy de, his visit, I. 93, 111
Clermont Ferrand, II. 28, 30, 56, 127, 131, 132, 142
Cloisters, II. 18, 72, 78, 88, 104, 139
Cluny, Abbey of, II. 92, 94, 98, 123
Coblentz, II. 20
Cockerell, C. R., his remarks on S. Sophia, I. 100
Cologne, I. 251; II. 9, 18; S. Maria in Capitolio, II. 18; other churches, II. 18, 25, 27; cathedral, II. 25
Comacina Insula, I. 211
Comacini Magistri, I. 211, 212, 213
Communes, rise of Lombard, I. 260; German, II. 8; French, II. 170
Como, I. 211, 239, 250, 269, 272; II. 258
Constance, peace of, I. 260
Constantinople, third Council of, condemns images, I. 118
Constantinople, founded, I. 15; a Greek city, I. 26
  The Apostles church, I. 15, 109, 232
  Church of the Chora, I. 121, 130; II. 49
  S. Irene, I. 15, 76, 106, 115
  S. John Bapt. Studion, I. 67
  S. Maria Diaconissa, I. 124
  S. Maria Pammakaristos, I. 139
  S. Maria Panachrantos, I. 122, 126
  S. Saviour Pantepoptes, I. 128, 130
  S. Saviour Pantocrator, I. 122, 125, 128; II. 34, 84
  S. Sophia, I. 15, 40, 64, 73, 82, and *seq.*, 174, 239; II. 66, 133; construction of buttresses, I. 91; construction of dome, I. 97; II. 36, 50; criticisms on, I. 100; report on present state, I. 102
  S. Thecla, I. 128
  SS. Sergius and Bacchus, I. 68, 78, 111, 173, 174, 239; II. 79
  S. Theodore the Tiro, I. 122, 126, 128, 133; II. 34
  S. Theodosia (Gul Djami), I. 122, 127, 128

Constantinople (*continued*)
  Domestic work, I. 140
    Mosques, I. 143; II. 108
    Tekfur Serai, I. 140; II. 131
    Walls, I. 54; Porta Aurea, I. 55, 138
Contado, Contadini, I. 260
Corbridge, II. 190
Corhampton, I. 218; II. 192, 193, 200
Crypt, I. 219, 246; II. 14, 15, 20, 209, 212, 218
Ctesiphon, palace at, I. 36
Curzola, I. 209, 271
Cushion capital, I. 269, 273; II. 149, 153, 213, 217; improvement of, II. 243
Cuthbert, S., II. 183, 223

Dado, of marble and mosaic, I. 179, 182
Dalmatia, I. 241, 250, 271
Dedication of temples as churches, I. 44
Deerhurst, II. 187, 188, 190, 200
Dijon, S. Benigne, I. 192; II. 119, 152
Diotisalvi, architect, I. 258, 259, 273
Dog-tooth ornament, I. 222
Dome, Eastern origin of, I. 34; various modes of construction in Greece, Rome and the East, I. 35; construction without centering, I. 37; domes on pendentives, I. 39; at S. Sophia, I. 96; at Ravenna, I. 150, 174; at Venice, I. 240; Pisa, I. 244; in Southern Italy, I. 274; in Germany, II. 3, 13, 19; in France, II. 34, 35, 36, 39, 42, 50, 63, 114; the tower dome, I. 128; dome on drum, I. 73, 108; II. 42
Domical plan prevails over Basilican in the East, I. 56, 67; yields to basilican plan in Italy, I. 205, 240
Dosseret *see* Pulvino
Dover Castle, church in, II. 177, 189, 199
Durham, II. 81, 208, 223

Earl's Barton, I. 218; II. 190, 192
Eastern empire, essentially Greek, I. 26; spread of Christianity in, I. 27; strong Asiatic influence on its art, I. 28
Eginhardt, II. 1, 5, 10
Elne, II. 78
Elstow, II. 230

Ely, II. 154, 220, 244; Prior's door at, II. 251
Entablature, returned as impost, I. 23; dispensed with, I. 22
Escomb, II. 199
Eton College Chapel, II. 263
Etruria, its influence on Roman art, I. 5
Etruscan Deities, survival of their worship, I. 147; tombs, I. 217, 225
Exarchate established, I. 172
Exeter, II. 11
Ezra, church at, I. 33, 34, 37, 81; II. 79

Fécamp, II. 122, 151
Fergusson, his view of Roman architecture, I. 1; on early French vaults, II. 65
Fiesole, I. 247
Figure sculpture, absent in Syria, I. 41; and in Byzantine churches, I. 114; barbarous in Italian Romanesque, 215; in early Norman, II. 242
Florence, S. Miniato, I. 243, 246; II. 258; Baptistery, I. 247
Flying buttress, II. 25, 27, 100
Fontevrault, II. 39, 41, 50, 85
Fortified Churches, II. 87, 138
Fountains Abbey, II. 236
France, Gallo-Roman culture, II. 28; its decay, II. 32; Roman remains in, II. 28; effect of barbarian settlements, II. 29, 30; dearth of early Christian buildings, II. 32; its separation into provinces, II. 32; Byzantine influence in, II. 34, 37, 51, 63, 70, 78, 80, 139; decay of, II. 49
Free cities of Germany, II. 8; of Lombardy *see* Communes
Freemasons, I. 213
Frejus, II. 79

Galilee at Durham, II. 227
Galla Placidia, her tomb house, I. 39, 116, 152
Galleries, exterior arcaded, I. 244, 250, 251, 254, 256, 257, 266, 269, 272; II. 9, 13, 24, 258
Genoa, I. 242
German fashions, their popularity, I. 162
German immigration, I. 161, 162; II. 28, 32

INDEX

German Romanesque, its beginning, II. 1; the double apse, II. 9, 11; the gabled spire, II. 20 ; its character, II. 81, 258
Germany, free cities of the Empire, II. 9
Germigny des Près, II. 33
Gernrode, II. 9
Giggleswick, dome at, I. 37
Gildas, II. 174
Giraldus Cambrensis, II. 179-180
Glass, coloured, I. 180 ; its abuse, II. 27 ; in Gaul, II. 31
Glass-making, revived in Britain, II. 182
Glastonbury, II. 177, 185, 235
Gloucester, I. 222 ; II. 27, 208, 216, 231
Gothic, its origin in L'Ile de France, II. 160 ; not adopted in Provence and Auvergne, II. 80, 145
Grado, I. 66, 183, 235 ; S. Maria in, I. 184
Greek artists at Rome, I. 5 ; in Italy, I. 154, 163, 168, 169, 204
Greek church and ritual, I. 44 ; plan of Greek church, I. 46
Greensted church, II. 181
Grotesque, the, II. 49, 57
Guidetto, architect at Lucca, I. 253, 259
Guizot, on Gallo-Roman France, II. 32, 33
Gynaeconitis Matroneum, or women's gallery, I. 47, 56, 84, 95, 177, 197, 204, 205

Hagiology, the Christian, I. 167
Hawksworth, II. 250
Headbourne-Worthy, II. 187
Hereford, II. 233
Hexham, Saxon minster at, II. 201, 209
Hildesheim, II. 21

Iconoclasm, I. 66, 114-120, 227, 228 ; not hostile to art, I. 119
Iconostasis, I. 46
Iffley, II. 242
Insula Comacina, I. 211
Ireland, early churches in, II. 177, 183
Issoire, II. 127, 134, 137, 142, 144
Italian Art in 14th century compared with Byzantine, I. 133

Jàk, I. 268
Jarrow, Monastery at, II. 183
Julian, Emperor, I. 26, 146
Jumièges, II. 153
Justinian, at S. Sophia, I. 85 ; II. 39, 167 ; his reputed skill in construction, I. 85, 86 ; at Ravenna, I. 173, 179 ; his character, I. 111, 112

Kahriyeh Djami, I. 121, 130
Kencott, door-head, II. 249
Ketton, II. 256
King's College Chapel, II. 263

Laach, II. 12, 16, 25
Lanfranc of Pavia, II. 153, 210
Langres, II. 84
Laymen as Architects, I. 253 ; II. 172
Leighton, Lord, on German apses, II. 11
Le Mans, II. 85, 161
Length of English churches, II. 253
Le Puy, II. 39, 43, 51, 138, 142 ; S. Michel de l'Aiguille, II. 131, 143
L'Ile de France, II. 159 ; cradle of Gothic, II. 160 ; scarcity of Romanesque, II. 160
Limoges, I. 241 ; II. 60, 145 ; Venetian colony at, II. 37
Lincoln cathedral, II. 208
Lindisfarne, II. 183, 223
Lions at portals, I. 223, 271 ; II. 252
Loches, II. 46
Lombard architecture, I. 260, 267, 273 ; towers, I. 267 ; II. 258
Lombard invasion, I. 210 ; fall of kingdom, I. 227
Lombardy, cradle of communal liberty, I. 260
London, S. Paul's, II. 208
Long and short work, II. 190
Lorsch, II. 5
Lucca cathedral, I. 245, 250, 251, 257 ; S. Michele, I. 250, 254, 257 ; S. Pietro Somaldi, I. 254 ; other churches, I. 254 ; towers, I. 257, 267 ; façades, I. 273 ; II. 11
Ludlow, capital at, II. 245
Lyons, II. 28, 31, 32, 116, 142

Mainz, I. 251 ; II. 8, 9, 10, 12, 15, 17
Malmesbury, II. 251
Malvern, II. 233, 254
Mantes, II. 263, 264
Marble, use of coloured, I. 10, 48 ;

facing and mosaic, I. 63, 64, 125, 141, 176, 179, 180, 190-191, 238, 244; imported by Charlemagne, II. 2
Mashita, I. 49, 237
Matroneum *see* Gynaeconitis
Milan, Edict of, I. 186
Milan, seat of Empire, I. 14; destroyed, I. 261; head of Lombard league, I. 261; S. Ambrogio, I. 261, 267, 273; II. 155, 258; S. Babila, I. 268, 269; S. Eustorgio, I. 269; S. Satiro, I. 268; S. Sepolcro, I. 268
Mithra, cult of, I. 45, 147, 201
Modena, I. 269, 271, 273
Moissac, II. 87, 88
Monasticism, its origin, II. 91; in Burgundy, II. 91; refuge of the Arts, II. 93, 124
Monkwearmouth, II. 184, 199, 200
Montmajeur, II. 75-78
Mont S. Michel, II. 151
Monza, Theodelinda's church at, I. 214
Mosaic of marble *see* Marble
Mosaic of glass, I. 49, 57, 58, 64, 71, 75, 98, 115, 119, 132, 149, 151, 152, 164, 179, 182, 203, 249; relation of those at the "Chora" to Italian art, I. 133; inconsistency with coloured glass, II. 27; example in France, II. 34
Mosques of Constantinople, I. 143
Mural-painting, inconsistent with coloured glass, II. 27
Murano, I. 235

Narthex, I. 46, 56, 68, 95, 124, 132, 177, 191; II. 176
Neuvy, S. Sepulchre, II. 122, 123
Nevers, Count of, his disputes with Vézelay, II. 170
Nicaea, first council of, I. 26; second council of, restores image worship, I. 118
Nicomedia, church at, I. 17
Nimbus, its use or absence, I. 71, 75, 77, 167, 179
Nîmes, I. 7, 8; II. 28, 29
Norman architecture, its character, II. 149, 158, 169, 208, 259
Normans in Italy, I. 274; II. 149; in France, II. 147, 160; in England, I. 273; II. 149, 205

Northampton, S. Peter's, II. 237, 246
Norwich, II. 81, 154, 208, 221
Nymeguen, II. 8

Odoacer, end of the Western Empire, I. 146, 161, 172
Odon de Deuil, his account of Constantinople, I. 110, 142
Orders, the classic, abandoned in the East, I. 40, 43; Gothic, subordination of, I. 264, 265
Ornament, extravagant use of, by Romans, I. 10
Oxford, S. Michael's, II. 193, 194, 209; S. Peter in the East, II. 209

Padua, S. Antonio, I. 240
Paganism, its duration at Rome, I. 146; its disappearance, I. 147
Painters, Greek in Italy, I. 134, 205
Palermo, I. 242, 245, 274
Papacy, its growth, I. 226; its breach with the East, I. 227; acquires the Exarchate, I. 227
Parenzo, I. 66, 181, 195; II. 224
Paris, Notre Dame, II. 80
Parma, I. 250, 266, 268, 271, 272, 273
Patrons of Art, their place in design, II. 166, 167
Pavements, I. 156, 180, 184, 198, 208, 220; II. 173, 176
Pavia, I. 210, 215, 266, 272, 273
Pendentives, I. 39, 73, 83, 91, 103, 240, *see* Dome
Périgueux, S. Front, I. 241; II. 34, 50, 52; its influence, II. 56; S. Étienne, II. 42, 50
Pershore, II. 85
Perugia, S. Angelo, I. 193
Peterborough, II. 154, 230, 254, 255
Philip II (Augustus) of France, II. 159-160
Pilgrimages, their value, II. 165, 216
Pisa, I. 242; Duomo, I. 242, 273; II. 258; its influence on art, I. 245, 250; campanile, I. 258; baptistery, I. 258, 259, 272; II. 263; Capella della Spina, I. 251
Pisano, Niccola, I. 134, 259; II. 263
Pistoja, I. 245, 272, 273
Pittington church, II. 228
Plutarch, on social status of artists, I. 3
Poitiers, S. Hilaire, II. 42, 44, 52; Notre Dame, II. 45, 46, 52, 56, 239;

INDEX

Montierneuf, II. 52; S. Radegonde, II. 57; Temple de S. Jean, II. 52; cathedral, II. 50
Pola, I. 218
Polignac, II. 45
Polychrome masonry, I. 238-239; II. 102, 130, 139, 237
Pomposa, I. 184
Pontigny, II. 107
Porches, the Lombard, I. 273
Procopius, his account of S. Sophia, I. 82; of other churches by Justinian, I. 109, 110; II. 167; the Historia Arcana, I. 112
Provence, its history, II. 62; Roman remains, II. 28; architecture in, II. 63, 169, 258
Pulpit, at Toscanella, I. 224; at Pisa, I. 259; at Milan, I. 264
Pulvino, its invention, I. 51, 171; at Salonica, I. 57, 62; at Constantinople, I. 99, 108; at Ravenna, I. 149-150, 154, 164, 171, 176; at Rome, I. 191; at Venice, I. 233; at Parenzo, I. 182

Qualb-Louzet, I. 41
Quennaouât, I. 32

Ravenna, I. 145, 148; II. 32.
    S. Apollinare Nuovo, I. 50, 66, 157, 163, 172, 206
    S. Apollinare in Classe, I. 53, 131, 180, 206
    S. Agata, I. 156, 166
    Baptistery, I. 149; II. 54
    Basilica Ursiana, I. 148, 171, 216
    Ivory throne, I. 158
    Galla Placidia's tomb house, I. 39, 116, 152
    S. Giovanni Evangelista, I. 153, 165, 171
    S. Maria in Cosmedin, I. 167, 172
    Ecclesia Petriana, legend of, I. 159
    S. Piero Chrysologo, I. 157
    Rotunda, I. 168
    S. Spirito, I. 157
    S. Vitale, I. 53, 167, 173, 239, 240; II. 3, 257
Ravenna a school of art, I. 169, 170
Reason in architecture, II. 266
Reculver, II. 199, 200
Report on structural condition of S. Sophia, Constantinople, I. 102
Repton, II. 188, 199-209
Riez, II. 78
Ripon, Saxon minster, II. 201, 209
Ritual, growth of Christian, I. 45; in the Greek church, I. 46
Rivoira, on Ravennate art, I. 170
Rochester, II. 152, 235, 250
Rodpertus, architect, I. 213, 217, 219
Roman attitude towards the arts, I. 3, 4; influence on formation of style, I. 5, 6
Roman architecture, the only ancient style of use to us, I. 11; universal use throughout the empire, I. 13; strength of its tradition, II. 180, 259
Rome, contest for the bishopric, I. 187
Rome, Baptistery, the Lateran, I. 189
    Byzantine influence at, I. 204
    S. Agnese fuori le Mura, I. 186, 193, 203
    S. Clemente, I. 186, 198, 209; II. 10
    S. Costanza, I. 52, 80, 119, 158, 189, 192, 205, 249; II. 123, 227
    S. Francesca Romana, I. 207
    S. Giorgio in Velabro, I. 202, 207, 209
    S. Giovanni in Laterano, I. 188
    SS. Giovanni e Paolo, I. 201, 207, 251, 271
    S. Lorenzo fuori le Mura, I. 186, 193, 204, 209
    S. Maria Antica, I. 204; II. 183
    S. Maria in Cosmedin, I. 197, 207, 272; II. 10, 224
    S. Maria in Domnica, I. 201
    S. Maria Maggiore, I. 24, 167, 186, 195
    S. Maria in Trastevere, I. 186
    S. Paolo fuori le Mura, I. 18, 24, 186, 187
    S. Peter's, I. 18 and *seq.*, 24, 96, 186
    S. Prassede, I. 202
    S. Sabina, I. 195, 218
    S. Stefano Rotondo, I. 191, 205
    Campaniles at Rome, I. 207
Romsey, II. 234
Round arch, monastic adherence to, II. 236, 255
Round churches, II. 122
Royal power, extension of, in France, II. 159, 170
Royat, II. 138
Ruthwell, cross at, II. 196

Saintes, II. 57

S. Alban's, II. 81, 208, 229
S. Andrew's, II. 190
S. Aventin, II. 86
S. Bertrand de Comminges, II. 85
S. David's, II. 245
S. Denis, II. 65, 163
S. Evremond, II. 162
S. Gall, II. 10, 18
S. Gilles, I. 272; II. 11, 68, 80, 103, 249, 261
S. Junien, II. 42, 48, 52, 57, 59, 142
S. Just, II. 85
S. Leonard, II. 42, 53, 60, 142
S. Lorenzo in Pasenatico, II. 192, 194
S. Nectaire, II. 127, 135
S. Saturnin, II. 138
S. Savin, II. 52, 59, 114
Sagittarius, II. 248
Salonica, Eski Djouma, I. 46, 56, 65, 69, 71, 171, 206
   Church of the Apostles, I. 128, 137, 233
   Church of S. Demetrius, I. 48, 53, 60, 74, 181, 206, 233; II. 139
   Church of S. Elias, I. 127, 136
   Church of S. George, I. 46, 69
   Church of S. Sophia, I. 53, 73, 115, 171, 181; II. 141
Sarcophagus, patent for, I. 170; christian, I. 109, 216; II. 29
Saulieu, II. 99, 116
Saxon architecture, its characteristics, II. 180 etc., 202, 203, 259; the greater churches, II. 201; its influence on Norman, II. 209
Sculpture, Byzantine, I. 51, 57, 62, 93, 99, 154, 176, 234, 241; Byzantine avoidance of human figure, I. 41, 51, 234; II. 70; in Lombardy, I. 215, 264, 273; in Aquitaine, II. 46; in Germany, II. 16, 25, 26; in Provence, II. 70, 80, 88; at Moissac, II. 88; in Burgundy, II. 103, 106, 110, 112; in Auvergne, II. 133, 144; in Normandy, II. 149, 154; in Saxon England, II. 196; in Norman England, II. 239 etc., 251
Sebenico, I. 32, 271
Sens, II. 84
Sidonius Apollinaris, II. 28, 30, 32, 52, 90, 91, 116, 117
Silchester, II. 173, 175, 199
Sinan, architect, I. 144
Solignac, II. 40, 41, 42, 50
Sompting, II. 21

Souaideh, I. 32
Souillac, II. 39, 49, 50, 84
Southwell, II. 154
Spalato, Diocletian's palace, I. 21, 31, 41, 163; tower, I. 268; II. 56
Speyer, I. 251; II. 9, 12, 14
Spire, in Dalmatia, I. 268; in Germany, II. 20
Square end to church, in France, II. 50; in England, II. 184, 199, 209, 252
Squinch, I. 38
Stamford, S. Leonard's, II. 256
Stow Longa, doorhead, II. 242
Strassburg, II. 21
Strip-work masonry, II. 191
Stucco, ornament in, I. 183, 185; II. 34
Suger, abbot, II. 65, 164
Sul, British deity at Bath, II. 178
Symbolism in sculpture, II. 248-249
Syria, its influence on Byzantine art, I. 28, 42

Taurobolium, rite of, I. 147
Tewkesbury, II. 85, 231
Theodelinda, Queen, I. 214, 215, 247
Theodora, I. 173, 179
Theodoric, king of Italy, I. 161, 173, 226, 228; his care for old buildings, I. 162; tomb, I. 168; palace at Ravenna, I. 163, 165, 166; II. 2
Theodoric II, II. 29
Theodosius the Great, edicts against Paganism, I. 147
Theodosius II, his walls at Constantinople, I. 54
Thoronet, II. 78
Timber, scarcity of, in Syria, I. 29; use in Saxon architecture, II. 180
Torcello, I. 206, 218, 235
Toscanella, S. Pietro, I. 216; II. 11, 193; S. Maria Maggiore, I. 221, 271; Canonica, I. 221; other buildings, I. 225
Toulouse, II. 28, 82
Tourmanin, I. 41
Tournai, II. 21
Tours, II. 30, 56
Towers, at Ravenna, I. 155, 178; at Rome, I. 207; at Lucca, I. 257; in Lombardy, I. 267, 268; II. 190; in Dalmatia, I. 268; in Germany, II. 9, 12, 17; in Saxon England, II. 190

INDEX

Trabeation, its use by the Romans I. 22 ; weakness of, I. 9
Traü, I. 41, 209, 268, 271 ; II. 69
Triforium, I. 269 ; II. 154, 202 ; proportion of, II. 217, 222, 228, 231, 234
Triple chancel arch, II. 200
Tromp, I. 38
Troyes, church of S. Urbain, II. 126

Ursus, bishop of Ravenna, I. 148

Valence, II. 112, 162, 163
Variety of English churches, II. 255
Vasari on Gothic architecture, II. 261
Vaults, mode of building without centering, I. 36 ; German, II. 25 ; French barrel, II. 65, 99, 108 ; Byzantine, II. 66 ; cross vaulting, II. 100, 108 ; its influence on architecture, II. 267
Venetian dentil, I. 238
Venice, attachment to Eastern Empire, I. 229 ; early government, I. 230 ; S. Mark's, I. 50, 53, 230, 240 ; II. 50 ; imitated at Périgueux, II. 36, 51 ; peculiarity of Venetian architecture, I. 229, 238, 239 ; Fondaco dei Turchi, I. 235, 238, 239 ; her commerce, I. 240 ; colony at Limoges, I. 241 ; II. 37
Vercelli, I. 267
Verona, I. 271, 273
Vézelay, II. 98, 131, 169, 170
Vienna, II. 11
Vienne, II. 28, 114
Vignory, II. 84

Viollet-le-Duc, his remarks on Early French architecture, II. 32, 265
Viterbo, I. 225
Volpiano, *see* William of

Waltham, II. 81
Warburton, Eliot, his remarks on S. Sophia, I. 100
Wells, II. 11, 255, 256
Westminster Abbey, I. 208 ; II. 85, 205
Wilfrid, his buildings, II. 181, 183, 197, 201, 202
William of Volpiano, I. 273 ; II. 119, 121, 151–153
Winchester, I. 243 ; II. 27, 81, 154, 208, 213 ; capital from, II. 246, 247
Window slabs, pierced, II. 192
Wittering, II. 190, 199, 200
Women, their place in Greek church, I. 47, *see* Gynaeconitis
Wordwell, door-head, II. 242
Worms, I. 251 ; II. 9, 10, 12, 15 ; the Jews' Synagogue, II. 14
Worth, II. 177, 199, 200
Wykeham, William of, II. 167
Wynford, William, II. 167

York, early churches at, I. 86 ; II. 180, 181

Zara, I. 241, 250, 257, 268 ; II. 258, 263
Zig-zag ornament, I. 222 ; II. 228, 239, 242, 256

Printed in U.S.A. by
NOBLE OFFSET PRINTERS, INC.
NEW YORK, N.Y. 10003

WITHDRAWN